# The Gate

# François Bizot

# The Gate

*Translated from the French by Euan Cameron*

*With a Foreword by John Le Carré*

THE HARVILL PRESS

LONDON

Published by The Harvill Press 2003

2 4 6 8 10 9 7 5 3 1

Originally published in France under the title *Le Portail*

First published in Great Britain in 2003 by
The Harvill Press
Random House, 20 Vauxhall Bridge Road,
London SW1V 2SA

Random House Australia (Pty) Limited
20 Alfred Street, Milsons Point, Sydney,
New South Wales 2061, Australia

Random House New Zealand Limited
18 Poland Road, Glenfield,
Auckland 10, New Zealand

Random House South Africa (Pty) Limited
Endulini, 5A Jubilee Road, Parktown 2193, South Africa

The Random House Group Limited Reg. No. 954009
www.randomhouse.co.uk/harvill

A CIP catalogue record for this book
is available from the British Library

This work has been published with the financial assistance
of the French Ministry of Culture

ISBN 1 84343 001 0 (hbk)
ISBN 1 84343 056 8 (pbk)

Papers used by Random House are natural,
recyclable products made from wood grown in sustainable forests;
the manufacturing processes conform to the environmental
regulations of the country of origin

Printed and bound in Great Britain by
Clays Ltd, St Ives Plc

To Lay and to Son

# Foreword

He was always Bizot. I never knew his first name until ten years ago, when he married a beautiful French woman, who to my bewilderment called him François. To the rest of us, he remains Bizot, scholar, Renaissance man and reluctant hero, with a hero's stride and a poet's head, an unstilled passion for life and a Faustian mission to discover what it contains at its inmost point.

I met him first in Chiang Mai in northern Thailand, at sunset, in the company of a mutual friend, in a beautiful wooden house of his own design, surrounded by enormous trees inhabited by gibbons. One of them, a great king of a fellow, had selected the crown of the tallest tree for his perch, and there he sat, with his back to the sinking sun, ruminatively masturbating in silhouette while we drank our whiskies. The Cambodian war was not over in any meaningful sense, but the Americans had left the region, Pol Pot's awful army was installed in Phnom Penh and Bizot's ordeal was behind him. He spoke of it in glancing, spontaneous references that scaled the wall of his reticence. He was prompted by our mutual friend Yvette Pierpaoli, now dead, who had known Bizot in Phnom Penh, which I had not. When I had visited Phnom Penh two years before, Bizot had been in his village at the centre of the site of Angkor, where his story begins. In Phnom Penh he was merely an absent legend, fostered, tended and adored by Yvette. So I cannot compare the brooding, volatile Bizot I met with the carefree Bizot who apparently existed in the days before the experiences he describes. I can only imagine which of the hairline cracks around the mouth and eyes, which crevices in cheek and brow, which despairing expression of hand or eye were put there by the physical and spiritual agony of his trial by endurance at the hands of his inquisitor, Douch.

Bizot has the authority of pain. It is not our fault if we have not suffered as he has. It is not his fault that he is the authentic version of what the rest of us can only imagine, though he is a big man, and a big destiny becomes him. There is pain that is perceived, and there is pain that is endured, and they are two different worlds, inhabited by creatures of two different races. We cannot choose which one we belong to. In my writing I have sometimes felt an obligation to share the pains I try to report on. Occasionally — in Cambodia or the Middle East — I have obtained some passing sense of absolution by taking risks and saying to myself afterwards, "Wow, that was *really* close" or "That could have been the end of me." But the cure doesn't last. In the end I remained a war tourist, an observer, not a participant, never a victim. I always had a valid passport and a return ticket in my rucksack, and a wad of dollars in my money belt. Even in the worst places — and they were a beginners' course beside Bizot's — I was only visiting. In the scale of human suffering, I did not even qualify for a mention. And there is guilt in that fortunate condition: a mistaken feeling that if you are not being tortured, you are on the torturer's side. I am not immune to it. But neither is Bizot immune to guilt of another kind, and that is the guilt of the survivor: Why was I spared? What or whom did I betray, that I survived and countless others died?

Which is why, as Bizot that evening fed me morsels of his story, I felt an increasing desire for more. I longed to enter his experience, inhabit it and, as a storyteller, give it the shape I mistakenly believed it must receive in order to have an impact on the reader. In doing so — with Bizot's permission and assistance — I took liberties which, after my reading of this book, embarrass me. For a start, I turned Bizot into an introspective Dutchman called Hansen, whereas you can hardly find anyone more French than Bizot. I had him as a lapsed Jesuit and in my mind a Buddhist convert, which isn't so bad, for Bizot is nothing if not a seeker after gods of one kind or another. I gave him the mantle of a spy, whereas Bizot's free spirit and untamed sense of honour would have made him the least manageable spy on earth.

But there are a few parts of my Hansen story, thank Heaven, which do not accuse me quite so loudly. Hansen's courage, his periods of alarming remoteness, his unlikely humility, his aesthetic pride, his despair and his indifference to material gain are all Bizot's. My Hansen might well have proclaimed, as Bizot does in this book, that the worst thing about being chained is the indignity. My memories of Bizot's prowling figure and strained, emphatic voice in the hot dark of Chiang Mai are faithfully given to Hansen, albeit on the outskirts of Bangkok. Sometimes, I felt as I listened, he talks to me as if I, and not Douch, were his interrogator.

But the Bizot I knew those twenty years ago is a mere shadow of the man I have learned to know through my reading of *The Gate*. I sensed — who would not? — that, as he tells us here, he carried monsters around inside him; and that these monsters "stir in him, constantly inciting infernal memories". I have a monster or two of my own, but none, I am sure, as monstrous as his. But it took this book for me to recognise the breadth and depth of his eyewitness, the vividness and accuracy — artistic as well as intellectual — of his powers of reconstructing sight and sound and feeling and human character and the profundity of the passion that nothing can appease.

There are passages in this book that tempt me to mouth the worn-out word "classic". Bizot's account of entering Phnom Penh (thanks to Douch) in time to see the newly arrived Khmer Rouge troops – astonished to find themselves unopposed – standing about, starved and exhausted, in perplexed groups while they wait for orders; his description of the jungle camp where he was held, of the scenes of collective confession by young initiates into the Khmer Rouge; his extraordinary epilogue, in which he returns to his village and rediscovers the very man who captured him; above all, his prolonged and unsparing account of his conversations with Douch his interrogator – this tragic "seeker after certainty" as he calls him – his painstaking documentation of the progress of his own feelings of fondness and respect for his tormentor; his account of life inside the French compound in Phnom Penh during the final weeks; the recitation of his surreal encounters, each in itself a tragedy, with such figures as Prince Sisowath and Mme Long Boret, who appear like accusing ghosts seeking sanctuary in the French Embassy but must be turned away because they have no papers – these scenes seem to me unique in their substance and power, and unmatched by anything comparable done by journalists or historians who have attempted to describe the same events. Bizot, you see, was not an observer, not an analyst, not a silk-shirt expert in an air-conditioned office. He was a player. He was part of the reality. He spoke the language and lived the culture. He possessed a second soul, and it was Khmer.

Now and then you read a book, and, as you put it down, you realise that you envy everybody who hasn't read it, simply because, unlike you, they have the experience before them. This is such a book. It possesses such truth of feeling, such clarity and conviction of narrative, such a wealth of image and adventure and such depths of long-withheld passion that

I do believe it is indeed that rarest thing: an original classic.
So I envy you. And may you be many. Bizot has earned you all.

– John Le Carré
February 2000

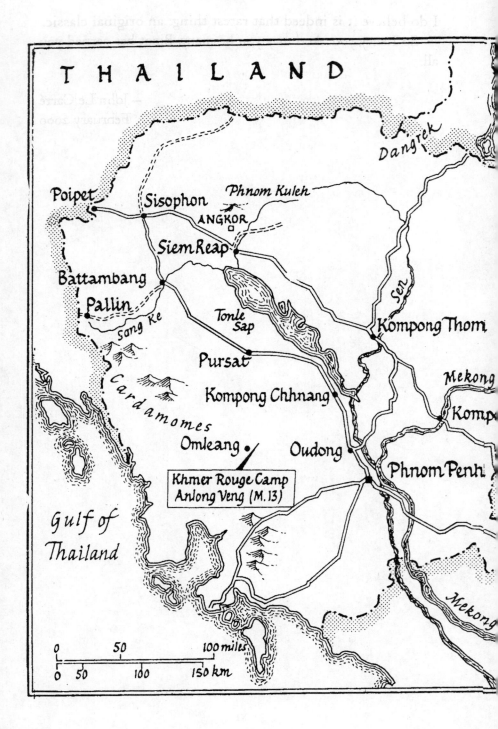

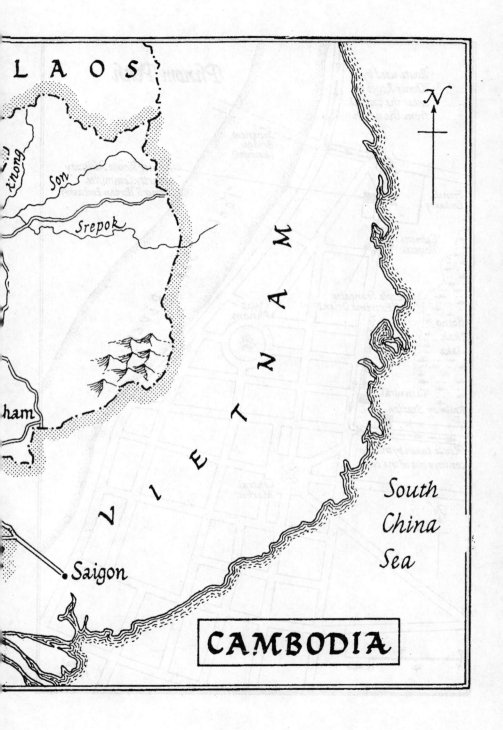

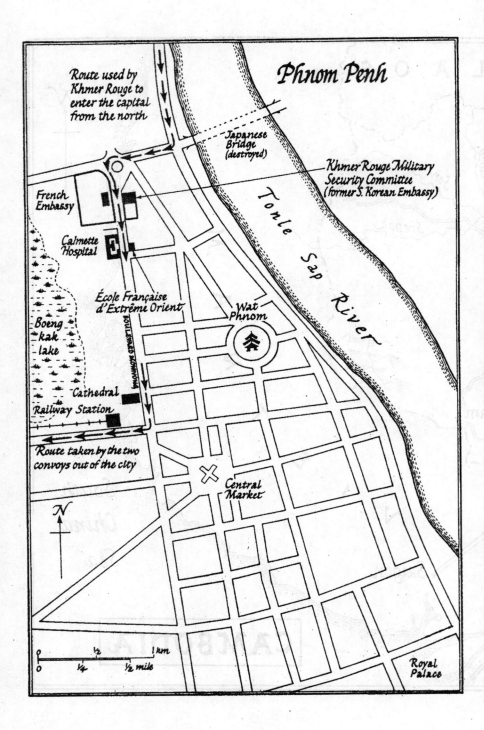

Route used by
Khmer Rouge to
enter the capital
from the north

*Phnom Penh*

Japanese
Bridge
(destroyed)

Khmer Rouge Military
Security Committee
(former S. Korean Embassy)

French
Embassy

Calmette
Hospital

*Tonle Sap River*

École Française
d'Extrême Orient

Wat
Phnom

Boeng
kak
lake

Cathedral

Railway Station

Route taken by the two
convoys out of the city

Central
Market

N

0    ½    1 km
0    ¼    ½ mile

Royal
Palace

# Chronology

1953–4 Cambodian independence declared. Full national sovereignty transferred to the king, Norodom Sihanouk. In Vietnam, the French are defeated at Dien Bien Phu; following the Geneva Agreements, the country is divided into two. The end of French Indochina, a colonial entity comprising Vietnam, Cambodia and Laos.

1965–6 The United States sends in ground troops to protect South Vietnam from Communist invasion. The Khmer Communist movement, founded in 1951, sends a delegation to Peking and becomes known as the Kampuchean Communist Party (KCP).

1968–9 American troops in South Vietnam number 550,000. US air raids launched on Vietcong hideouts in Cambodia.

1969 *Coup d'état* on 18 March, in Phnom Penh. General Lon Nol, who supports US intervention, seizes power and proclaims the Khmer Republic. From Peking, Sihanouk calls for resistance and announces the formation of the Government of the Royal National Union of Kampuchea (GRNUK). American and South Vietnamese troops infiltrate Cambodia. The Vietcong invade the territory and occupy the site of Angkor.

1973 Signing of the Paris Agreements and withdrawal of

American troops. The KCP forces young peasants to enlist in the Revolutionary Army of Liberation.

**1974** Start of the Khmer Rouge offensive against Phnom Penh (December).

**1975** France recognises GRNUK (12 April). On 17 April, the capital falls. Evacuation of the towns and the beginning of the "purification" of all strata of the population. Opening of the Tuol Sleng torture camp at Phnom Penh (S. 21).

**1976** Sihanouk resigns as head of state. Proclamation of Democratic Kampuchea, under the presidency of Khieu Samphan; Pol Pot is prime minister. Attempted putsch at Phnom Penh. Disbanding of the "Pro-Vietnamese network".

**1977** Kampuchea's economy supported entirely by China. Diplomatic relations between Kampuchea and Vietnam broken off.

**1978** Following a series of Khmer incursions into Vietnamese territory, Vietnamese divisions occupy the provinces to the east of the Mekong River.

**1978–80** Major Vietnamese offensive (25 December 1978); Phnom Penh captured on 7 January 1979. Government formed under Vietnamese military protection. Proclamation of the People's Republic of Kampuchea. Famine causes Khmer Rouge fighting units to disband, and their headquarters withdraw to Thailand. The rest of the armed forces retreat to bases in the forest and along the frontier with Thailand. Resumption of guerrilla fighting.

**1985–93** Vietnamese troops capture several Khmer Rouge positions on the frontier with Thailand. Formal withdrawal of Vietnamese expeditionary force (1989). International peace agreement signed in Paris (1991). Numerous defections among Khmer Rouge ranks after elections organised by the United Nations.

**1998** Death of Pol Pot. Collapse of the Khmer Rouge movement.

# The Gate

When I arrived in Cambodia in 1965, the gibbons' exasperated complaint would cut through the muffled hum of the villages every morning. Sunlight hovered on the still pools streaked with green and gold, dispersing the sleepy vapours of the night. I thought this renewal was ineluctable.

The land was rich and beautiful, enamelled with paddy fields, dotted with temples. This was a country of peace and simplicity. Reflections upon the nature of existence were common currency to all its inhabitants. Festivities, divine service, ordinary rituals — nothing was conceived without art, and poetry, and mystery; for always, the spirits of the dead breathed over the turning of the seasons.

No peasant was so poor that he could not offer the finest fruits from his garden to the inmates of the monasteries and hermitages, wherein the sons of each family were called upon to serve. Every male child would take a vow to lead the austere life of a mendicant monk for a few years; there would be sumptuous ceremonies, for which the family would prepare gold, ornaments, fine clothes, lamps and flowers long in advance.

The countryside echoed with the vibration of gongs, and we knew the joyful shouts we heard were to accompany the dead to the place of their rebirth. But most of all I loved to listen to the rasping resonance of the chapay singers, whose crude, harsh blues, floating over the rice fields, expressed all the tonality of the Khmer soul.

At places where narrow pathways intersected the perimeter of the villages — beside a termite mound, in a sacred wood, at the foot of an aged tree — we would

3

find little altars dedicated to divinities of the soil. Sometimes these guardians of the bounds would be ancient sculptures, exhumed by the rains; sometimes they would be crudely carved out of wood; sometimes they were simply a stone. The passing peasants would pay their homage with a handful of fresh leaves.

That is how, in my own way, I remember this country. The past still projects its distant images in me, and these images bring back to life all that bewitched me when I was twenty-five. Something less forgiving than time, however, keeps them at a distance. My melancholy has given way to a definitive and uncompromising sense of revolt. I look on those pre-war years as I would the smile of "a dead loved one resting deep in the earth". *

What oppresses me, more still than the unclosed eyes of the dead who fill the sandy paddy fields, is the way the West applauded the Khmer Rouge, hailing their victory over their brothers in 1975. The ovation was so frenzied as to drown out the protracted wailing of the millions being massacred.

When I arrived in Siem Reap in 1965, Cambodia was dwelling rather peacefully alongside a Vietnam that had been plunged into war; in the hinterland, despite occasional frontier disputes, the villagers seemed to exist outside time. In neighbouring China, the Cultural Revolution was brewing. All Europe was full of encouragement for those who were working to overthrow the old feudal societies and bring about a better world. The intelligentsia of every country denounced American involvement in Vietnam.

I myself was neither for nor against: my thoughts lay elsewhere. I was drawn to the mysteries of the Far East, and fascinated by the gestures and secular rituals of a people that clung to its traditions. My wanderings protected me from the spectres of the anti-Americanism that had taken hold of people everywhere at the time. Although I had never formulated it before, I realised that my only gods were in fact American: Saul Steinberg and Charlie Parker. So when I came to Indochina I had little reason to share the hostility towards the United States shown by most of the French community.

On the contrary, it seemed to me that the peasants around me, whose repetitive existence I was about to share as I established myself in a remote village

*Ernst Jünger, On the Marble Cliffs.

4

*in Angkor, had everything to lose from the arrival of the Communists. In my passion for the religions and customs of the past, which I wanted to see perpetuated, I would have more readily opted for the very opposite of the ideologies then in vogue. Torn in every direction and immediately confronted with the most absurd contradictions, I was reduced to despair. When the Americans arrived in Cambodia, I saw them as allies in my impossible quest. But their irresponsibility, their colossal tactlessness, their inexcusable naivety, even their cynicism, frequently aroused more fury and outrage in me than did the lies of the Communists. Throughout those years of war, as I frantically scoured the hinterland for the old manuscripts that the heads of monasteries had secreted in lacquered chests, I witnessed the Americans' imperviousness to the realities of Cambodia. Yet today I do not know what I reproach them for more, their intervention or their withdrawal.*

*This situation favoured the Khmer Rouge, who knew how to turn its side effects to their own advantage. In the outlying districts, which the central authorities had never bothered to govern, they were a model of order, imposing morality as the basis for revolutionary action, while Lon Nol's soldiers were spreading theft and corruption. Locally, however, one heard of the Khmer Rouge committing some of the vilest deeds of which man is capable (killing children with their bare hands, decapitating people with the sinews of palm leaves, mass murder . . .). But fear of appearing to support the Americans so froze minds that nowhere in Europe were people free enough to voice their indignation and denounce the lies. Popular wisdom had quickly decided that it was on the side of liberty and non-intervention. In 1975, bolstered by international opinion, the revolutionaries defeated an enemy in a state of complete physical and moral collapse.*

*From that moment on, more blood than ever was shed. After the horrors of the Vietnam War had overflowed onto its soil, this unhappy country endured post-revolutionary terror. Once in power, the Khmer Rouge set about destroying the population, systematically eliminating whole classes of society, starting with the peasants. Those who were not moved from their villages and herded into forced labour camps were decimated by hunger, disease and torture.*

*The genocide ended only in 1979, after four long years. With no regard for ideological consistency, Vietnamese troops put an end to it by invading Cambodia* and "liberating" the country a second time, not from American imperialism but from the cruelty and incompetence of their Khmer Rouge "brothers".

When the appalling horrors were at last "discovered", a time of contrition began for many. It makes my blood boil to see that nobody, now, is prepared to uphold the ideology in whose name this evil was methodically accomplished.

Yet there were those witnesses who, many years earlier, had condemned the horror being plotted in the shelter of the forests. A turn of bad luck made me one of them. On 10 October 1971, while conducting research at a monastery in the region of Oudong, thirty kilometres north of Phnom Penh, I was arrested and then chained up in a Khmer Rouge detention camp. For three months, I saw the abomination spread its cloak over the countryside. As soon as I was released, the French Embassy asked me to translate a booklet on the "Political Programme of the United National Front of Kampuchea" that I had brought with me from the bush. Its contents foreshadowed the horror: already there was mention of the evacuation of the towns and the establishment of a state-controlled collectivism based on a reduced population. But these warnings, duly relayed to Paris, had fallen on deaf ears, and France stubbornly maintained its support for the Khmer Rouge.

I returned to Cambodia as soon as the wave of terror had receded. I realised at that point that what had happened was irreparable and that I could never again live in this land. What my eyes were seeing was incompatible with the image in my mind. This constant split vision pulled me apart like some schizophrenic illness.

I have written this book in a bitterness that knows no limit. A sense of hopelessness runs through it. I now believe only in things; the spirit can detect what is eternal beneath their outward appearance. Does not the most enlightened philosophy teach us to mistrust man? The optimal being, the supreme creature, the natural aristocrat of the living world? Man who – when, exceptionally, he becomes his true self – can bring about excellence, yet also bring about the worst. A slayer of monsters, and forever a monster himself . . .

So I ask myself the question: could the religions I study teach us the art of killing the dragon in our flesh? This diabolical presence, buried within us yet constantly surfacing: is this the original sin I was taught about as a child?

*I detest the notion of a new dawn in which* Homo sapiens *would live in harmony. The hope this Utopia engenders has justified the bloodiest exterminations in history.*

*Can we never learn this lesson and recall it in fear every time we stop and look at ourselves? Our tragedy on earth is that life is subject to influences from above, and we can no more revisit the mistakes of yesterday than the sand can avoid being wiped clean as the tide pours in upon it.*

# I

From among my memories there comes up today the image of a gate. It appears before me and I recognise the pathetic hinge which was both a beginning and an end in my life. It is made of two swinging panels, which haunt my dreams, and wire mesh welded on to a tubular frame. It closed off the main entrance to the French Embassy when the Khmer Rouge entered Phnom Penh in April 1975.

I saw it again thirteen years later, when I first returned to Cambodia. That was in 1988, at the onset of the rainy season. This gate seemed much smaller and flimsier. I let my eyes and my hands wander blindly over it, immediately startled by my own temerity, not at all sure what I was looking for and not suspecting what I would find. A lock, slightly askew; evidence of welding; reinforcement plates at each corner: all these scars suddenly seemed to me vitally important. My eyes had always looked past them, never at them. An unexpected blend of confusion and fear overcame me. As the gate became real, and took on an existence of its own, it gave me a sense of pleasure, at the same time as horror welled up inside me.

This was not just the pleasure of the release of tears. It was a new reality, overlaying my memories, which made me think of the workmen who had indifferently welded the metal grille to the

9

framework, and the builders who had pushed the hinges into the cement. Could they ever have imagined that this assemblage would one day be the instrument of such dramatic events? I couldn't understand why an embassy should have such a shoddy gate, or how such fragile mesh could have resisted so many strong hopes or opened itself to so many heavy wrongs. I remembered a far more imposing structure, heavy and impassable, built to restrain and repulse. I saw – almost with embarrassment – the wrought ironwork suddenly exposed before me: its substance, its lesions, its points of distress struck me as laughable.

An unexpected sweetness came into me at the same time as the horror welled up again – a fusion that will forever flow in my veins. It made me totter, but did not dispel my stifling unease. I was overwhelmed by the mockery of time, by the shallow nature of things.

The same feelings affected me inside the former embassy, in the chancellery. Both floors of the building had been taken over by an orphanage for girls. The warden was sitting in the corner of an empty room on the ground floor. He accompanied me to our former offices, now converted into bedrooms. Little girls, as if from some abyss, were there, silent, sitting on mats on the floor. Some of them were doing their hair. They had been born shortly before or after 1975; their parents had been massacred when the Khmer Rouge had seized power. The image of their tranquil faces still moves me deeply. I was immediately overcome by suppressed sobbing and ridiculous bubbles formed at the corners of my mouth. Was it the undisguised hardship, the peaceful masks of these young people who had been spared; or these empty walls, with no doors or shutters – which had framed hours of fear, where my distress had taken refuge, from 17 April to 8 May 1975 – that caused me such bodily pain?

My whole Cambodian past was just waking in me, and now it ran up against an image of a present with no memory. Until then, it had been no more than signs; now the drama of the Khmer country was suddenly and bluntly revealed to me, in this very inconsistency. A drama "without importance",* as it were, unceremoniously pinned up in my imagination; all its tangible traces melting away as things evolved, sealed off beneath the marks left behind, movingly distorted on the surface of time.

Crossing the courtyard to leave the embassy, I examined the asphalt: unchanged, with its old pattern of cracks, and yet, to my eyes, it seemed to be coated with the deposit of events. I looked for places where I had set foot twenty years earlier, and my gaze fell on the very spot where Ung Bun Hor, the last president of the National Assembly, had stood, legs trembling, stubbornly and mechanically undoing his trousers. The two French gendarmes who accompanied him and lent support — for the poor man had collapsed at the sight of the Khmers Rouges waiting for him on the other side of the gate — had hesitated for a long time before realising that he was losing his mind. A jeep and two covered trucks were parked outside. Princess Manivane, Sihanouk's third wife, had already climbed into the back of one of the vehicles, accompanied by her daughter, her son-in-law and her grandchildren, who had merrily come out of their hiding place . . .

I will come back to these moments later on. What is more urgent is to pin down where my thoughts lie; they leap about, pressed upon from all sides. To do this I must think back to the beginning. Back to my father's death, which my thoughts still dwell on. Because the void it carved out left me so alone and so destitute that I had to rebuild my way of thinking, using only basic elements, like a nomad who will not load himself down with anything superfluous. The day my father died, I realised that he had taken with him the masks of protection that I used to put on. To live, to overcome my suffering, I was going to have to erase the slate of the past, just as the revolutionary does, and choose, one by one, whatever gestures promised to be the most

* William Shawcross, *Sideshow* (*Une tragedic sans importance* in French).

immediately effective. It was such a fundamental manoeuvre that even today – and ever since the day of his death – nothing can be decided, and nothing concluded, without referral to this new point of origin.

At the same time, even though my father's passing left an inextinguishable rage in me, it reminds me of a love which I often find happiness in thinking about.

The loss of Cambodia, on the other hand, of the villages hidden among foliage, of the copse-lined paddy fields scattered with tufts of *Borassus* palms, only makes me feel despondent. I spoke so much about this to the same friends during the shameful years after 1975 – remember them – when the "peasants' liberation" shone in the West with the fire of revolution; the words were expelled from my mouth by the ignominy I felt, yet gradually the life force ran out of them. As it is for words, so it is, oddly, for the touches and precise strokes of love: one dares not give the same caress to a woman too often. And so, for years now, I no longer speak about my father or about Cambodia, in order to preserve – as a foundered junk is preserved in peat – the life of the monsters I carry. Moving in me, even if deep inside, their hellish call fuels the memory.

So the gate does not open on to the agonised cries of the tortured in Tuol Sleng prison, but on to absurdity and despair. It is not the events themselves, the brutal facts or their dates that matter. What matters is the weight of the life that gave rise to them, reappearing suddenly out of the silence of things, in the everyday object where those who have borne the events on their flesh can read, thirty years later, the traces of a destiny. This soldier, lying there beneath the stone, is the son or the uncle of someone you know, the lover of the woman you came across, blown to pieces by the side of the road, wearing the new sarong she so carefully chose at the market this morning. Is this not the only reality, this emotion, this link with life and with beings, shut up inside things?

The south panel of the gate is preserved at the far end of the grounds of the French Embassy, which has been rebuilt on the same spot, like a little altar erected to the spirits of the dead. The several million dead. If you hold your breath, you can still hear the heavy footsteps of the exiles as they make their way along the old boulevard with their bundles. The rust that has eaten into the panel has not, in my eyes, affected its radiance. With time, it has taken on a surprising beauty. Like anything beautiful, or accomplished, or enduring – anything finally worthwhile – it has become simple, and the mesh has become regular: like a line in a Matisse drawing. It expresses, in an instant, so many things about the roots of life that you feel all at once like crying, and dying, and living.

I wrote the lines that follow in discomfort, bent forward, with my forehead pressed against that mesh. The Khmer Rouge, some time after 1975, or perhaps the orphan girls who took over the premises in 1980, have treated it to a coat of green cellulose paint; now it is chipped, but beneath it you can, here and there, make out the original grey.

# 2

At the beginning of the war, in 1970, I was in Angkor. The United States had just created the conditions for a successful *coup d'état* against Prince Sihanouk and had set up its own headquarters in Phnom Penh, installing General Lon Nol as the head of a new republic.

Reconnaissance planes loaded with electric machine guns circled overhead, in a sky heavy with rain and golden-brown reflections. Their terrifying sound would clutch at you and make you want to be sick. Surrounded by troops commanded by Hanoi, the little town of Siem Reap, which adjoins the temples of Angkor, could be supplied only through the airport. Soldiers were encamped on the sports field to the north of the Grand Hotel, firing volleys of 105mm shells at the surrounding villages. The targets had been chosen from the map at random by a general staff in contact with Phnom Penh, and each shell ruthlessly achieved its aim: the uncomprehending victims died on the spot. In the morning, the peasants arrived in small groups to buy salt and a few provisions; they were forbidden to buy medical supplies. Upon their return, they were roughly searched, for the military security staff suspected them of being Communist spies. The local authorities focused their full attention on the passing of information.

I knew someone at headquarters whose job it was to sort out the rare pieces of information that came from outside. He was a former peasant who had become a driver at the Auberge des Temples (the old colonial hotel in the site of Angkor) and whose wife came from the village where my house was. He had let me know that very little information was getting through from the occupied zones. Yet one day, towards evening, I observed him taking off his uniform and well-bulled combat boots and putting on baggy shorts and a shirt: his wife had fallen ill, and he was leaving to be with her. Dusk was falling. He was going to pass through the town's defences at night, skirt the mines, cross the enemy lines, avoid the lookouts, keep clear of the roadblocks, bypass any possible military encampments — whose whereabouts he would have to guess — and then walk as far as the village, enter it without being fired at, and finally return the next evening, taking the same risks. He came back without having noted the enemy's positions, which he had walked right by, and without even the slightest sense that he had an obligation to communicate them; his superiors, who knew about his foray, asked him nothing. He served for the money, not for the cause. Despite his profound hatred for the North Vietnamese, who now controlled the site of Angkor, taking the inhabitants (and the temples) hostage and lodging in the very places where he himself had spent his childhood, he made no connection between his own motivations and the army's objectives. He did not see that the military, with whom he could not begin to identify himself, might defend the interests of the peasants. What he was interested in was his own tranquillity, the lost monotony of the days repeating over centuries on the enamel patchwork of the fields. It had nothing to do with the ideals brandished by the city-dwellers of Phnom Penh, who had always been cut off from the countryside. This war was totally foreign to him.

Traditionally, the Khmers have been warriors. At the time of French Indochina, the commando sections were composed entirely of these loyal, upright men, who never waver and are not afraid to die; they have an innate sense of the terrain and an instinct for camouflage and ambush. The Americans, unfortunately were about to transform them into maladjusted soldiers, impossible to bend to the rules of technological warfare or to mobilise against a Vietnamese enemy who, though possibly less naturally talented, was perfectly trained. The Phnom Penh government, at great cost, did its best to ready an army of brave young men disguised as GIs, rigged out in heavy helmets and thick combat boots.

The night of 6 June 1970 had been trying. From the village of Srah Srang, where I lived in the centre of the site of Angkor, thirteen kilometres north-east of Siem Reap, we had heard a number of explosions. Some seemed very close. The muffled ringing of cannon fire reached us from the town's defences, then the shells came straight up above our heads, their shrill whistling fading bit by bit into the depths of the forests. Hélène, my daughter, who slept between her mother and me, was disturbed in her sleep, and kept suckling until morning came. For several days now, the advance of North Vietnamese troops had been commented upon by the villagers, who did not know what to think, and their approach gave rise to the most unbelievable stories: the invader was driving hordes of elephants ahead of his army; he was employing sections of naked female commando troops to attack Khmer positions and unsettle the soldiers . . . the villagers' boundless imagination drew plentifully from their colourful mythology.

Very early in the morning I had taken the "little circuit", as I did every day, to reach the Angkor Conservation Office, where I worked restoring ceramics and bronzes, unaware that Siem Reap was already surrounded. On the way out of the village, an overturned truck, ripped apart by a B-40, blocked the road. Dead passengers lay in every direction around it. I loaded three wounded into the Citroën 2CV van and rushed back to the village. I was met with mute unconcern; no-one wanted to help me, and Hélène's mother – the "little one's mother", as they used to say in Cambodia – categorically refused to have the wounded in our house for fear of eventual reprisals. They were a soldier with a bullet in his stomach and two grown-up boys, sons of soldiers, who had been horribly mutilated, with lacerated abdomens and several open fractures. I improvised a panel out of a cardboard box, painted a red cross on it in Mercurochrome, fixed it on the bonnet of my van, and we set off again for Siem Reap. As I drew near Angkor Vat, at the corner running along the east of the old dyke, two heavily armed soldiers wearing helmets stood in front of us and ordered me to stop. I braked immediately, causing one of my passengers to cry out; I leaped out and dashed towards them, shouting at them in Khmer not to shoot. At that moment, thirty or more men emerged from the bushes bordering the lower side of the road and resumed their march, single file, scarcely giving us a glance. They were all young and tired and wore dismal expressions.

The two Vietnamese soldiers searched me and looked with astonishment at the "magic scarf", printed with diagrams and Buddhist formulae for protection against bullets, which I wore conscientiously crossed over my chest. I had been presented with it at a public ceremony where the men of the village were each tattooed on the tongue and on the top of the skull. Quite clearly, neither of the soldiers spoke Khmer. The van was examined from top to bottom, and the injured, whose wounds were inked with excreta and gave off a strong smell, were prodded and turned over where they lay. The two men clung on as best they could to the front mudguards of the vehicle and led me to understand that I should set off slowly with my human cargo. I turned the ignition key, but – disaster! – the van wouldn't start. The battery was dead.

I cursed Berteloot, the manager of the conservation office's garage, who had handed the vehicle over to me without checking it. The Vietnamese sitting on the bonnet watched me grumbling without reacting. I signalled to them to push as I buttressed myself against the side of the 2CV with one hand on the steering wheel. One of the injured boys was moaning noisily. Mortar shells, fired from Siem Reap, were falling close to us. More soldiers were walking along the road, all equally unperturbed by the danger; I did my best to remain similarly detached. My two warriors began to push, unconcerned about the explosions. The van inched forward with a grating sound. In my rear-view mirror I could see the men, harnessed with weapons and grenades, moving heavily, their arms outstretched against the back of the 2CV, their heads between their shoulders, as they advanced, one slow stride after another.

We drew up beside a shelter that protected one of the electrical transformers serving the Auberge des Temples. There, I was told to sit on the ground and wait. Shells were exploding here and there and no-one was paying much attention. More columns of soldiers were advancing in the distance, towards the town. It was hot. The van had been left on the roadside, and I could imagine how those shut inside would be suffering, deprived of fresh air. Several long hours passed before I was given permission to stand up. Finally a man approached me, walking briskly, accompanied by an interpreter. He was unarmed and wore a simple cap; on his chest, a bag containing maps was held in place by broad straps that crossed at the back. Despite – or because of – his modest attire, I understood that he was a high-ranking officer. His eyes were sharp, his features well delineated, and he spoke with assurance in a clear, precise voice. He asked me via the interpreter to write my name on the ground with my finger and explain what I was doing. I told him that I worked at the Angkor Conservation Office, that I lived in the village to the north of the pond, where the circuit turned at a right angle. Having listened, he instructed me to return to where I had come from and to remain there. I was forbidden to leave my house. He added that we would immediately have been blown to pieces by machine gunners on the town's defence lines had our van not been intercepted by his men.

"They fire in continuous bursts, indiscriminately, on anything that moves or comes near them," he told me in an almost amused tone.

The officer questioned me further about the two wounded boys, the older of whom was apparently already a soldier. Then he took from his front pouch a sheet of paper, folded in four, and hastily scribbled a few words in Vietnamese, addressed to his men, taking care to check the spelling of my name, still visible in the sand.

*Elder Brother Bizot is transporting wounded children, but he has been unable to reach the town. Permission is given for him to return to his village. This statement is brought to the attention of all comrades so that they may allow Elder Brother Bizot to pass freely.*

*Tám*

Ten years later, this high-ranking North Vietnamese officer, who had commanded the attack on Siem Reap, was sent back to the region to conduct further operations. When he reached Angkor, he found the road that led to Srah Srang and, surrounded by bodyguards, entered the village to ask what had become of the Frenchman he had once arrested. He was met only by empty, toothless, starving faces. Hélène's mother, who had just returned to the village, was fetched. She had fled, like thousands of other Khmers, from the camp where she had slaved for three years with virtually nothing to eat. That same evening, he ordered a fifty-kilogram sack of rice to be delivered to her.

I did not venture out again without this pass, which I kept in my pocket as a lucky charm.

The North Vietnamese had seized upon Lon Nol's *coup d'état* as their pretext to cross the frontier from 1970 onwards. The international public was totally unaware of their presence in Cambodia. The French press glossed over it, concentrating instead on Prince Sihanouk, who had been so sickened by his expulsion and forced exile in Peking with his long-standing friend Chou En-lai. Of course, there was no alternative but to save face and drag out some of the slogans of the anti-American left. The Khmer prince's "struggle" against American "imperialism" could not, however, disguise his hereditary hatred of the Vietnamese, much less extend to open solidarity with the historical enemy. He would never have regained his people's trust if they had suspected such an alliance to exist. The "Resistance" movement could only rely on the Khmers!

This Cambodian paradox, which consisted in never being able to admit foreign complicity in the defence of the nation, and this taciturn people's deep-rooted pride, would result, five years later, in the colossal contradiction – an incomprehensible mystery to the outside world – of a nation perpetrating genocide on itself. It would also allow the West to justify, in the name of non-intervention, its failure to lift a finger to prevent the massacre.

Shortly after Siem Reap was surrounded (6 June 1970), I experienced this Western incomprehension at first hand. I had been required to escort a convoy of about fifteen heavy-duty vehicles to Phnom Penh; they had been removed from the construction sites we had abandoned at Angkor and loaded with chests full of statues to be delivered to the National Museum. The moment I reached the capital, Jean Rémy, the manager of the Choup plantation, invited me to dinner at the head office of the Compagnie des Terres-Rouges. Present that evening were several planters, people I had met a few years earlier in their beautiful colonial homes amid the hevea groves. Some of them must have withdrawn with their families to Phnom Penh because of the fighting. Jean Lacouture,* who was passing through Cambodia, was the guest of honour that night. Ten of us were seated around the large dining-room table. Throughout the meal, the conversation was concerned with the latest news from the front, the military situation, and the commando raids that were growing more intense everywhere. The country had fallen into total dependence on American aid.

One of the guests questioned me about working conditions at the Angkor Conservation Office. He asked precise questions about the condition of the road I had taken to come. Not wanting to go into detail, I described how the Viets had attacked a bridge before Battambang.

"You mean the Khmer Rouge," said Jean Lacouture. "I don't think there are many North Vietnamese in Cambodia! Even if this theory may suit Lon Nol . . ."

All eyes looked back to me.

"I saw only Vietnamese, North Vietnamese."

A tight silence gave me to understand that the Parisian journalist took me for a naive victim of anti-Communist propaganda. As a matter of fact, the planter who had put the question was not innocent. Like many observers living in the countryside, he despised the positions Lacouture adopted in his articles.

Indeed, the French intelligentsia, for the most part, still stuck to the stereotypical views of the Vietnam War, and saw these commando raids against the government army as a spontaneous and independent popular rebellion. I was young, and it was not surprising that a man of years whose authority was generally recognised should not pay too much attention to conversation over cocktails. Yet the things I had said should have enabled him

*Jean Lacouture, the well-known French writer and biographer. He was foreign editor of *Le Monde* from 1957 to 1975. [Tr.]

to understand that he was not dealing with some conscript aid worker freshly arrived from the capital.

"Don't be fooled," he stressed with the tone of an expert. "It's very hard to tell them apart, you know. And the ambiguity is widely exploited."

I swallowed my words. In Lacouture's eyes, I had fallen prey to the official discourse. I took out my pass and handed it to him.

"Here's a safe-conduct pass issued to me on the spot, in Angkor. It's written in Vietnamese, and it's also very useful when moving about in other parts of the country!"

The paper was passed around the table. Lacouture, still showing his scepticism, looked at it without saying anything; and he apparently drew no conclusion from it, as demonstrated by the articles that he continued to write, several months afterwards, without changing his views.

After this short interruption, the conversation resumed more vigorously. I got to describing the incredible battle I had witnessed as we had approached Battambang, when our convoy found itself blocked by the attack on the bridge. This violent incident had made a lasting impression: it brought about a real awareness in me. My vague intuition of the events I happened to have been involved in was turned into a clear perception of what was at stake, on the human and the strategic level, in the war that was beginning.

Towards dusk, we had run into a military roadblock, near to where a large monastery, wedged into a paddy field, threw its dark profile up against the sun. The sergeant commanding the section appointed to guard the bridge had come out to meet us.

"You'll have to turn back!" he said loudly, from a distance. "The bridge is going to be attacked. I don't want you getting in my way. Beat it!"

The man who spoke had the black skin of the Khmers, very dark and coppery. He had a hard look, square jaw, short teeth like small, worn blocks; and the three furrows in his neck, stacked horizontally, so characteristic and so elegant in young women that they used to be taken for one of the hieratic attributes of beauty in wall paintings. Beneath his open shirt you could see the ritual tattoos. He wore a mass of necklaces, adorned with Buddhas, tigers' teeth and amulets, which we were to hear clinking together protectively throughout the night.

There was not enough space to turn the trucks around. The sergeant had already run off, shouting orders to his men. We had no choice; with the agreement of the monks, we decided to park at least the lighter vehicles in the courtyard of the monastery. The half-moon, lying on its back, was already visible: a sickle of light against the blue sky.

I walked up to the bridge, which was about five metres wide, and leaned over the edge. Behind the first bushes that cluttered the bottom of the muddy riverbed, I noticed a soldier, bare from the waist up, about twenty years old, hurriedly digging a hole in the ground where the sergeant had told him to do so; I saw others doing the same a little further away. My stomach froze when I realised that he was digging the pit in which he was to conceal himself, below the level of the road, a good twenty metres from the bridge's brickwork supports. His face betrayed a deep fear; I can still feel the grip of my own fear at the mere thought of taking his place. A huge clump of bamboo growing nearby now concealed the setting sun. The sergeant was bustling about giving instructions, getting inside each of the holes to check its sides, and talking very firmly to the young men under his command. All of them obeyed without a word and followed him with their eyes. While he was issuing orders, his hands fixed several pairs of loaded magazines to his chest, held together head to tail by pieces of inner tubing.

Night fell within a few moments, giving the go-ahead to the frogs' disinterested, monotonous croaking. The coppiced bushes around the embankment marked out slow dark ripples under the moon. The landscape lost its colours. Noticing my presence on the bridge, the sergeant sharply urged me to go back. I had scarcely reached the vehicles filling the courtyard when the sputtering of automatic gunfire sounded out, damped by the soundproofing of the surrounding plots. The shadows of the drivers chatting with the monks disappeared beneath the trucks. I ran to shelter behind a low wall, where I remained awake all night.

A brittle silence fell over the bridge. Nothing stirred. The sergeant was lying on his back against the parapet. The moon continued its slow movement across the sky, drowning the relief below with a flat light. The bullfrogs added their prosaic hoot to the night's creaking. It was the start of an interminable wait.

It was not until a few hours before dawn that we could perceive quite clearly, at the edges of the still vibrant serenade, the crumpling of branches: the bushes along the far side of the embankment were moving. My attention was caught on the crawling movements advancing beneath the foliage, when suddenly words were being shouted through a loudhailer:

"Sihanouk! Long live Sihanouk!"

However unusual in the circumstances, this evocation of the prince was no surprise. Citing the destruction by the Americans of their sanctuaries over the border in Cambodia, Hanoi's troops had penetrated to the heart of Khmer country with impunity, with cigarettes as their only viaticum, and Sihanouk's name as their open sesame. At every village, before every peasant they met on their way, the same scenario occurred: from the tired columns along the track, one or two men would split off to meet the inhabitants, a packet of cigarettes in their outstretched hands and this name on their lips: "Sihanouk!"

This is how the invader, presenting himself as "liberator", cut an easy path into hostile territory; and the prince, delivering a daily harangue on Radio Peking, served as backer.

"Comrades," the loudhailer started up again, "we are brothers!

We are fighting for Sihanouk and to liberate the beloved country!"

Crouching in their holes, the Khmers were thrown by this; they scanned the dappled horizon, whose outline was already changing by the growing moon. The man who was speaking had a Phnom Penh accent.

"Comrade! There you are lying in your uncomfortable hole, while Lon Nol sleeps with his wife in a bed."

Suddenly the sergeant stood up – ne was no longer on the bridge, but in a protected spot against the embankment – and fired three or four crisp, short, precise shots; their impetuosity shook my mind from the hypnotic stupor into which it was slipping. After a silence, the same almost mocking voice spoke again.

"Comrade Tuoy! Neither you nor your men have the slightest chance of escaping. There are many of us, and we are well armed. What is the point of firing at your brothers? Give yourselves up! No harm will come to you."

I felt fear take hold of me, and I cursed the misfortune that had led us into this trap.

"Li! Chhè! Akhlok! And all of you," our dangerous distorter went on, "we know you well, you and your families. Don't be fools, you'll all be dead before daybreak . . . Give yourselves up, it's your last chance. Li! Do you really want your son to become an orphan?"

Our assailants uttered the names of some of the new recruits who had been commandeered to defend the bridge; all of them came from neighbouring villages, and the information had been easy to obtain. The subterfuge had proved successful in a number of places, and they did not expect much resistance. But this was overlooking the doggedness of the sergeant. He kept leaping from one hole to another, rallying his men, who were paralysed with fear, climbing back on to the bridge, disappearing into the thicket and reappearing again in the moonlight.

Then we heard the first orders for attack being shouted through the loudhailer:

"Commandos seven and nine: Advance! Commandos one, two and four: Advance!"

Each order was punctuated with blasts of a whistle, and under the branches we could see the rapid movements of the attacking soldiers advancing towards us in a succession of bounds. To communicate their orders amid the noise of an attack, their commanders used whistles. The rather soft sound, produced by three metal tubes set side by side like pan pipes, resembled the simple chord of an electric organ. Combatants would report that in the night this mournful moaning also had the merit of freezing the enemy in a state of cataleptic fright.

These movements had tightened the circle around us in the darkness, the whistles signalling to us the dramatic progression; then the voice sounded out again, with yet more audacity:

"Comrades, look at me! I am your brother! Let us talk together! I stand before you without any weapons. Don't shoot. Look!"

I was about to witness an incredible spectacle: a man stood up, fifty metres away, his right arm outstretched, his left shining the light from a pocket torch on himself . . .

Bewitched by his bravery, nobody dared move.

In the seconds that followed, a violent explosion rent the air. The sergeant had hurled a grenade directly at the phantasmagoric apparition. All around us, violent shooting started crackling in every direction, and didn't stop. A shell from a B-40 damaged the outside of the bridge. A shower of bullets hit one of the tractors.

Day was beginning to break. The landscape recovered the outlines that the moonlight had altered. The first light of the dawn filtered through the undergrowth, putting the attackers to flight, and the firing gradually, almost regretfully, came to a stop. After a while, the sergeant, who had returned to his recumbent position, began to speak in a loud voice, calling out the names of his men. Just then we saw a shadowy shape swaying heavily at the top of the bamboos. The stems were bending under his weight.

Tangled up among the offshoots, or perhaps having climbed up there too late, the daylight had caught him out. The sergeant took aim and fired, and the body fell listlessly through the criss-crossing trunks. Unscathed and very excited, the young men emerged from their holes, yelling out cries of victory and commenting on the fear that still gripped them. The monks and the drivers came running to join them. Then the dislocated bodies were hauled out of the undergrowth and dragged to the bridge.

"So what were they?" asked Rémy. "Khmer or Vietnamese?"

"The one in the bamboos must have been a Khmer," I replied. "But the three others, who were torn to pieces by the grenade, were Vietnamese."

To my great regret, Jean Lacouture, involved in a conversation with his neighbours at the far end of the table, heard virtually nothing of what I had just related.

A year later, however, I was to see for myself how much the Khmer Rouge, still hiding out in the forests, had discreetly grown more powerful. In contrast to the North Vietnamese, whose mission was to fight the republican army, their role was to sow terror, under the cover of the forests, slyly at first, in small doses, so as to paralyse the villagers by destroying their nerve. Then, like a spider spinning its web, they wove a dense network of strands that would eventually subjugate them, removing any resisters at the first tremor. The effectiveness of this hidden organisation, which like a venom was to spread progressively throughout the entire hinterland, depended on a whole apparatus of internal security. The Khmer Rouge cultivated a veritable paranoia, which led them to introduce measures of control and surveillance of the peasantry in the "liberated" territories, aimed at thwarting any hypothetical enemy infiltration.

# 3

It was October 1971. My work had taken me to a monastery in the Oudong region, to the west of Phnom Penh, with two Cambodian colleagues, Lay and Son, who were assisting my research into Buddhist practices associated with the state of trance. We were due to visit an elderly monk who was known for his knowledge of rites. When we arrived, we were ambushed by a group of Khmers Rouges. I recognised their uniforms, imitating the trousers and black shirts of the peasants. They drove us at high speed to a deserted village a few kilometres away.

After a ludicrous interrogation that I endured grumpily (my armpits were examined by a local official, who was convinced he would find a hidden microphone or something), my arms were tied at the elbows behind my back and I was escorted – alone this time – by two adolescents, one of whom had a gun, to another destination, which we did not reach until the middle of the night. The sparse contents of my pockets, the few riels I had on me, my watch, my Vietnamese pass and the keys of my car had all been confiscated. When I was searched, I realised that I had forgotten that morning to wear the little Buddha on a gold chain that the *kru* Yao had placed around my neck for protection two years ago. Usually, I was never without it.

We walked all that day, and the two following days. I was in a state of great agitation. Unable to contain myself or calm down, I walked so quickly that the armed guards accompanying me almost had to run to keep up. At the outset, when someone aimed his gun at me, I exploded with anger. This so disconcerted my assailants that they agreed to leave my van by the edge of the track – when they had actually meant to capture it – and they didn't tie me up right away. Very soon afterwards, my rage gave way to a suffocating pain. The muscles break in your neck, and a terrifying hardness blocks your throat. I held back my tears at every moment.

At first light on the third day, after a short rest in a broken-down *sala*,\* we set off again in the pouring rain, skirting the bumpy track, cutting across slippery, red-tinted pathways full of potholes, and following disused short cuts and low embankments. Before midday we arrived on the outskirts of an inhabited village. In the distance, I could see clumps of areca trees rising into the sky. Dogs barked at us. I was directed towards a staircase leading up to a large wooden house built on stilts. A pool of fairly deep water covered the bottom step. In the upper room I found my two colleagues (who had walked through the night without stopping) lying on their backs, their legs shackled by a wooden *khnoh*, an enormous ankle lock, fifty centimetres above the ground. I read fatigue and despair in the terrible expressions on their pallid faces. A few villagers had come up to lend a hand to the soldiers, who were right behind me. My arms were untied. One of them swiftly knocked out the wedges from the stocks with a sledgehammer, releasing two heavy wooden beams.

The atmosphere was hostile. The eldest, ill at ease, made a short, rather mechanical speech that was not addressed to me but that I was intended to hear. I can still see his teeth, stained red by betel leaf, and his eyes, which avoided my distraught gaze.

\*A sort of shelter for travellers erected by the sides of the roads, found almost everywhere.

"Comrades, we must accomplish our task. We are at war with American imperialism!" (His voice went up a notch and he angrily stamped his heel on the floor as he pronounced the words "American imperialism".) "Do not hesitate to ensure that the Angkar's orders are carried out, in his case and that of the others; they are legitimate. *Neu!*"

I understood immediately. My body grew stiff and I thrashed about, threatening, demanding, begging that they take me to whoever was in charge so I could explain my position. By struggling like that, I hoped above all to measure their reaction to my resistance; yet I was constantly frightened of sparking off an even more disastrous reaction. The fingers that had initially dug into my arms began to relax their pressure; the determination of the guards, who were suddenly intimidated, seemed for a moment to waver beneath my invective. Then, all at once, the one who was holding the hammer hurled himself at me, his lips clenched and trembling, a wild expression on his face, and it was only thanks to the ensuing confusion that I was not hit on the head. My self-confidence immediately drained away; the heavy top beam was slid to one side, and both my legs were simultaneously lifted by several pairs of arms and placed in the semicircular notches carved out of the lower beam.

All resistance had deserted me; I found myself on my back, lying next to my two colleagues, who had modestly turned away so as not to see. A sharp pain suddenly caused me to cry out. The yoke, pressing against my oversized ankles, had crushed my skin and tendons as it was closed. From my right ankle – possibly larger than the left one – a thin trickle of blood started; but I only noticed it later, when I saw drops on the floorboards. The wedges were put back in place. The man who had wanted to strike me was still in a temper and started hitting them with such a frenzy that the others had to stop him. He glared at me with eyes full of hatred. Afterwards, we could hear the pieces of wood that secured the contraption creaking from time to time in their casing.

Whatever the pain I had experienced, I had cried out exaggeratedly, as if to ward off the doom descending on my life at that moment. Don't animals act up their fear, even feigning their own death? Through a sort of primitive instinct, like the pig that squeals just as much when it is caught as when its throat is being slit, I had shouted all the louder to match the extremes of my despair.

We found ourselves on our own. I immediately asked Lay, who was beside me, whether they had any news of Hélène, my three-year-old daughter, who had come with us to Oudong. She had been left with other children in the village where we had stopped before taking the road to the Vat O monastery. At that very moment, I realised that a great part of the appalling pain burning within me was due to this enforced separation from my child. I kept seeing her lovely light brown curls and her sweet little face, holding back sobs in front of people she did not know.

My eyes, wide open, were fixed on the structure of the roof. The pain from my pinched ankles became a constant throbbing: I was finding it hard to keep my knees raised and my shins parallel to the floor, so they wouldn't move in the stocks.

There was a gentle splash in the water at the foot of the ladder; the house moved slightly, and bare feet could be felt brushing the floorboards. By straining my head backwards, I had an upside-down view of a dozen or so young peasant girls approaching in single file. The first to arrive stared at me with genuine curiosity, and I did not know what face to assume. Pretty, just like those from my own village, these were local girls, with that touch of gold in the whites of their eyes that lent their expressions a particular radiance. They had been brought to see the loathsome enemy at close quarters. The youngest ones, who were also the most convinced, walked right up to my head. It was the supreme insult: throughout South-east Asia, the top of the head is taboo, and a woman never places herself above a man. One of them came so close that I was aware of her delicately textured skin, and beneath the worn fabric of her sarong, tight over her full figure, I could sense her smooth, firm body. Their plump, delicately rimmed lips were pressed closed, and their faces grimaced with the repugnance I made them feel, and they all started spitting on me, making short hacking noises to force the saliva to come. I heard my friend Lay let forth a long, disapproving moan as he said in an expressionless tone, his eyelids lowered and his head swaying from side, without looking at anyone, "Oh, girls, what are you doing? What do you know about us?"

I could feel the light, slightly cold impact of the spittle as it fell on my face. This hatred directed at me was so innocent and so sincere that I did not feel the slightest resentment. But once they were gone, my closed eyes grew strained. A long sob seized me, like a child's fit, beginning with a contraction of the stomach, then stifling itself in a silent breathlessness.

When I resumed contact with my two companions, we exchanged a few sad, ironic words about our common predicament. We were crushed with hopelessness. Son, a tall, dark, thin and very gentle boy, recently married, was so upset that he could barely speak. Neither of them entertained any illusions as to our fate — later, they would tell me that before my arrival they had heard some terrible things, but they didn't dare tell me what.

Both of them were heavy smokers, and they had only a few cigarettes left. Because they wanted to make them last, they entrusted me with the rest of their packet to control temptation, instructing me to give them just one each day.

Someone was splashing about in the puddle of water below. Our meal was brought to us: rice, sesame seeds and grilled fish, which we swallowed eagerly and quickly.

Then we heard footsteps in the water again. The three of us propped ourselves up on our elbows, turning towards the door as best we could; I was the one they had come for. The top beam was raised from its base. I gradually got to my feet, slowly stretching my legs as my painful ankles took the strain. The red-and-green nylon cord that I had on my arms to come here was tied on again. I started to go down, balancing unsteadily on the ladder, and one of the guards waiting below put up his arms to help me.

We arrived almost immediately in the village square – which was, in fact, only a few paces away from the house – where about fifty people were gathered in a semicircle. Flanked by two subordinates, who were sitting with their legs crossed, a man sat behind a desk set on a raised platform. Around his neck he wore a *krama*, the piece of checked cotton that Khmer peasants use as both a scarf and a towel, and on his head a Chinese cap, pulled down to his ears. Between him and the audience, a stool had been placed for me next to a low table with a carefully opened packet of cigarettes and a glass of tea. I went and sat down immediately, without being invited, trying to show that I was not frightened.

The officer in charge nodded as he looked at me and gave a big smile that revealed an upper set of teeth crudely covered with copper. He adopted a stern expression when he noticed that I had been tied and, with a sort of forced irritation, asked for the cord to be removed, as if my being presented to him like this showed a totally unacceptable lack of propriety. I was untied and, now satisfied, he inspected me with an air of near complicity, using those assembled as his witnesses. The metal in his mouth affected the way he spoke, but it did not prevent my recognising his accent, that of the Kraum Khmer of South Vietnam. He offered me a cigarette. I declined. Then he turned to the young man seated to his right to ask me, through him, to state my surname, first name and address, and to explain why I had been arrested. The interpreter addressed me in English. Surprised, I pretended not to understand (first lie).

Why this pretence? Such a response might have cost me my life! But the truth was that having lived for years in a Khmer village,

33

having married a Cambodian woman and feeling such a closeness and solidarity with the local inhabitants, I could not bear to be taken for an American. Whenever a Khmer spoke to me in English, it put me in a bad mood straight away. Not because of the dramatic events in Vietnam; for many of the local peasantry, attached to their traditions and resistant to the new ideologies, the Communist revolution was a disruption of their age-old way of life. Rather, it was the Americans' uncouth methods, their crass ignorance of the milieu in which they had intervened, their clumsy demagogy, their misplaced clear conscience, and that easygoing, childlike sincerity that bordered on stupidity. They were total strangers in the area, driven by clichés about Asia worthy of the flimsiest tourist guides, and they behaved accordingly.

They had enlisted as a matter of course, by the hundreds, the best people the country could offer: honest civil servants who wanted to restore order, loyal soldiers, along with a whole network of devoted intermediaries, from chauffeurs to cooks, interpreters, informers, and so on. All these people had hopefully placed themselves in their hands, such was the apparent justice of the fight these new conquerors were leading, defending the Cambodian people against the despised neighbour who wished to submit them to a foreign yoke. The Khmer have always loathed the "Youn"; proud and attached to their liberty, they have ever mistrusted the attempts at annexation that have come from Vietnam. Bound up in their own traditions, they felt a deep hostility towards the social renewal being introduced by their enemy brothers, whose true intentions they suspected.

Unfortunately, the arrival of the Americans did nothing but arouse greed and feed corruption. The new employee heard himself called "brother" and, with a great slap on the back, received a sum of dollars equivalent to what an American in the United States would have earned for the same work, ten to twenty times the salary of a local provincial governor. With wages like this, clerks, labourers and artisans hurriedly gave up their jobs and beat a path to the door of the American Embassy, which was recruiting with all its might. But this paternalism and complacency naturally had their converse effects. Believing sincerely in the brotherhood of man, the employer demanded in return American-style efficiency, which few Khmers could deliver. The relationship of the hierarchy with its employees then deteriorated quickly, creating strain and humiliation and for ever dashing the extraordinary hopes of trust and friendship that everyone had nurtured. These circumstances soon led to duplicity and a total absence of mutual respect at every level, creating a climate of bitterness and irreparable suspicion.

"What is your name?" the interpreter asked again.

"I am a Frenchman, and we are in Cambodia. Speak to me therefore in French or Khmer!" I replied in his own language.

Everybody laughed behind me, and the judge indicated his own pleasure with great nods of the head that caused him to lean forward. The laughter was not that of an amused audience. It started in an orderly and controlled fashion, like applause, and stopped all at the same time. The transparent folder containing the contents of my pockets had been placed in front of him.

"Comrade, you speak Khmer well! Where did you learn it?"

I explained that I had arrived in Cambodia in 1965 to study Buddhist monuments and traditions. I had lived in a village in the Angkor district up until the arrival of the liberation troops in Siem Reap. Then I had moved back to the conservation office, where I was attempting to continue my research in the parts of the country where that was still possible. At the same time, I made regular visits to Phnom Penh for provisions, and to buy spare parts and the tools and materials I needed in order to continue the restoration work (ceramics, bronze, wood) for which I was responsible. He nodded in agreement, then he turned on me sharply.

"I know you well. I've seen you before, many times!"

I looked in astonishment at the little man sitting there, and felt on me the sharpness of his eyes watching for my reaction.

"I don't believe I know you . . . where do you think we met?"

"Yes, yes, I know you well," he insisted again and again, with a laugh addressed to the spectators behind me but adding nothing else, only widening his eyes and lifting his head like someone trying to create suspense and liven up a story. "We've come across one another on numerous occasions in Saigon. Only you, comrade, did not look at me! You don't know me! I've actually been watching you for a long time: you work for the Americans in Vietnam!"

The charade was so crude that I remained seated on my stool, hardly shaken by the accusation. The Kraum Khmer had spoken to me courteously but with unconcealed irony. I could see clearly from his expression that I was nothing but a weak representation of the enemy and that his mind was already made up.

"I've never been to Saigon," I replied calmly (second lie).

I noticed that my comments were being taken down by a clerk seated to the left of the Kraum Khmer.

"The Americans need men like you, who know the country and the local languages well. They send them to the front line to pay the soldiers directly because they do not trust their lackeys, who embezzle the troops' wages whenever they can."

"I work neither for the Americans nor for anyone else," I said as I stood up. "I am a French researcher. If you can prove the contrary, you will have to kill me."

My sincere outburst was applauded once more. The judge allowed a few moments to elapse, stretched out his hands in front of him as if I needed to be calmed down, and, with a big smile, resumed.

"We have a difference of opinion: the Angkar will arbitrate. Kampuchea's* victory over 'American imperialism'" — he struck the rostrum forcefully with his heel — "shall be glorious and resounding! For the time being, comrade, we are at war. We must fight to free our brothers from enemy aggression. As for you, you must be subjected to the regulations concerning prisoners decreed by our revolutionary laws."

His tirade was greeted by further applause; guards led me away.

I found Lay and Son anxiously wondering how I would be dealt with so that they might glean some idea of what awaited them. We communicated in signs or in low voices, convinced that informers were listening to our every word through the gaps in the floorboards. I fell asleep for a moment, drained by fear and exhaustion.

Suddenly, some astonishing words were uttered near the house. Addressing some people we had not realised were there — they had approached noiselessly — a loud and determined voice said, "Strip off his clothes! Undress him and shoot him! What are you waiting for, comrades?"

We had heard that the Khmer Rouge stripped their victims so that their garments could be reused. I have never forgotten the huge shiver that spread through me then, in icy waves, from my head to my ankles. We exchanged a long look; this sparked off an odd sort of nervous, irrepressible laugh. I heard several splashes and my heart stood still. Some men burst in. I saw their hands on me, pushing me around, unshackling me, lifting me up, tying my elbows. I was hurriedly pushed towards the door. The sun was filtering through the leaves of a large gnarled jackfruit tree. Behind, I could glimpse a section of the road I had taken to get here and, on each side, abandoned rice

*Since 1954 this had been the name the Communist Khmers had used for Cambodia.

37

fields, enclosed by crumbling embankments. I can no longer remember the sounds.

There were about ten armed Khmers Rouges waiting at the foot of the steps. The rope that tightly bound my elbows was untied and retied several times, provoking lively discussions about the right way to tie the knot. Someone came up to put a blindfold on me, and I jerked my head back. The young Khmer who was holding the cloth in his hands approached me. With a hint of an embarrassed smile on his face, he took the cigarette out of his mouth. I refused to be blindfolded.

"Where are you taking me? I want to see!"

One of the men surrounding me, older than the rest, was laughing. He took the blindfold calmly, placed his hand on my arm and told me in a reassuring tone, "*At oy té!* It doesn't matter. Don't be frightened, it's the procedure."

I was trembling. I wanted to believe him, but I was unsure. Then, resolutely, I said, "In that case, let me go back upstairs for a second. My companions gave me their cigarettes to look after, and I have to give them back."

My request was so inappropriate that I had to explain myself several times.

"Hand over the cigarettes, we'll give them back ourselves. I'll take care of it myself, you don't need to go up again."

I wouldn't hear of it and refused to budge. It is often when the resignation is the most difficult that we undertake a little bargaining in order to give the lie to our own helplessness.

"No, no! I can't trust you. You'll smoke them. I want to take them back myself."

I had turned around as I spoke, ready to climb the ladder. Hands grasped me, and I struggled; finally, the man who had tried to calm me down before – he must have been an officer – agreed to allow me to go up, in order to ease the tension. One of the guards accompanied me. In the room, which now seemed less spacious, I could see my friends lying motionless in the ankle

38

stocks, beside my empty space. I bent down over Lay, placing the packet from my shirt pocket within his reach, and looking him, then Son, straight in the eyes; I was choked with emotion. I left without daring to speak.

The armed men were waiting below. They put the blindfold on my eyes, and my ears could make out the voice of the commanding officer repeating, "*At oy té!*"

The phrase is common to all the languages of Indochina. I had heard it constantly from the moment I was first arrested, and on each occasion had drawn a little hope from it. Suddenly, I realised that these were not so much words of encouragement as the expression of a fatalistic philosophy, a way of helping to accept the inevitable, of acceding to destiny.

A hand pushed me firmly forward; my legs were set into motion and my feet advanced. The blindfold didn't lie quite flat on my cheeks because of my nose, and I could half see my own footsteps. In the opacity of the material, despite my closed eyes, I could see the whole village, the square we were moving towards, and myself, walking in the middle of armed men. My head swarmed with ideas; nothing reached my consciousness. A cowardice, a numbness of mind, prevented me from thinking or feeling anything.

We went round the square, then cut through a grassy reservation and across another pathway before reaching the turned soil of a bare field. Stiff stems sticking out of the sods wounded my feet. Several hands guided me, forcing brief stops and changes of direction on my body, letting go and taking hold of me according to the terrain. Next to me, the voice of the commanding officer warned me of any obstacles. No-one else spoke, but I could hear the footsteps, the breathing, the rustle of clothing and the clinking of straps and buckles. We stopped. The absence of any words became abnormal. The hands turned my body round to face a certain way, then I was left alone. I stood there, suspended in silence.

Only my heart, flooded with blood, beat loudly in my temples.

The soldiers loaded their guns.

# 4

"**D**o you want to wash?"
        The smile exposed teeth and gums. I paid no attention to the man who had just spoken. Yet I believe my memories of him go back to this first encounter. He had joined the guards encircling me and was watching, his hands behind his back, with a friendly air. His black jacket was too big and his trousers stopped just above the ankle, revealing finely shaped, veined feet. The very light skin and the crowded, uneven teeth betrayed his Chinese origins. He looked young, not yet thirty. Nothing in his unassuming demeanour had indicated to me that he was in charge here. But his authority was total; there were no limits to his power over the detainees. His silences were mightier than words.

No sooner had he turned and walked away than I discovered his name: Ta Douch. The revolutionaries called everyone *mit*, "comrade", or even "young comrade" or "elder comrade", but their leaders were called *ta*, "grandfather", to show distance and respect. I would very quickly realise that the slow comings and goings of his narrow-hipped figure (he was acutely thin and suffered, like everyone else at this time of the year, from recurrent bouts of malaria) were greeted in the camp with a lugubrious silence and a general slowing-down of movements. His face had a surprising capacity to switch abruptly from a happy smile to a solemn, tense regard. Douch had only two faces: frank and open eyes looking out over wide curled lips; and a mute, low gaze with the mouth closed. Like all Communist officials in Asia, he spoke slowly, in a low voice; at moments such as this, he always raised his head a little, looking down so far that his eyelids appeared to be shut.

As soon as I had arrived, emerging from the sparse forest we had crossed, I had noticed two robust lads pounding rice in a mortar in front of the trampled but very green remains of a small palm tree. They were apparently free; they did not dare look up at me, even for a second, which made me aware of my misfortune. Once again I had felt fear. The location and its surroundings were concealed beneath a thick bamboo grove. The smoke from the only open hearth, which was hollowed into a clump of turions beside a huge anthill, seeped out through a makeshift collection of ducts and was dispersed in several places beneath the canopy of leaves. The evening light fell, diffuse and peaceful. The tall, swaying bamboo stalks rustled gently, disgorging the last of the October rains, drop by drop. Apart from the pounding of the pestles, no sound betrayed the secret presence, a few feet from where I stood, of fifty or more prisoners and their nine guards. And, as I looked around, an echo came from the edge of the forest like a distant call, indifferent to my distress: the two-part song of the oriole.

I was led towards one of the long shelters, closed only on one side. Each could contain fifteen or twenty men on laths a metre above the ground. All the men were in a *khnoh*; their ankles held in a sort of collective stock made up of shackles threaded on to a long communal rail. I looked away hurriedly. The slippery ground squelched with water as you walked over it. The soles of your shoes were like suction pads. A terrified hen fled as I approached, followed by her chicks, chirping and running about in every direction. I did not know it yet, but I would later have the possibility of observing for hours this plump, ash-grey fowl, with its serrated comb, rounded wings and a tail that was flecked as if by the brush of a contemporary painter; she was to become my friend.

"Do you want to wash?" Douch asked again.

Exhausted by the three-day march through the mud, I had asked to be allowed to wash as soon as I arrived at the camp, before they tried to put my foot into one of the shackles that were piled up against the partition, beside the urine-filled bamboos. Further down, the clear waters of a river ran over pebbles shored up at a bend skirting the camp.

Eventually I looked up at him, nodding affirmatively without saying anything. I was tired of answering the questions that so many people had put to me since my arrest. At first I had paid eager attention, reckoning on each occasion that my future might depend on my answers. I soon understood that nothing I said would be taken into account, for one simple reason: I was never dealing with the people who could decide my fate.

"Very well, go on then!" he said almost amiably.

He turned around slowly and went away. I did not yet know that I was the only prisoner in the camp allowed such a favour. From that moment on, the young guards – there were five of them, aged between twelve and seventeen, and every second of my existence depended upon them – realised that my foreign nationality made me a special inmate. Without further ado, I set off towards the river. One guard hurriedly seized a Kalashnikov from the shoulder of another and followed close behind me. With a few strides, I reached the bank, which ran down a gentle slope to the deep-sided riverbed, and undressed completely, almost provocatively, to indicate that I wished to be left alone. The young guard was embarrassed and turned away, and I stepped into the stream and walked as far as the bend, out of his sight. The water was scarcely deep enough to cover my knees, but in the hollows formed by the rain-swollen current it reached halfway up my thighs. I plunged in, choking, unable to stifle groans of pleasure. I felt an immediate surge of joy as I immersed myself in the water, stretched out and floated, hanging on to the stones and shaking my head in the flow. The cold water on my body soothed my mind like an anaesthetic.

Once dressed, I was taken back to my shelter. I heaved myself on to the rather springy floor, made up of large split bamboo strips cut from the surrounding clumps. At a sign from the guards, the prisoners closed ranks to make room for me at the end of the stocks. None of them looked at me. Their faces revealed a mixture of shyness, patience and willingness that I found hard to comprehend. I later came to realise what had happened to these captives. They'd come from the liberated areas of the south-west region (under the control of the infamous Ta Mok) and had been brought here without any explanation.

The scenario was always the same. One day the head of a village would receive a notice, scribbled on a scrap of paper folded over several times, with one corner turned in like an envelope. On it would be simply a name, a date and the place of the summons; nothing else. The person concerned could escape; there was still time. But running away is like a confession and entails risks: your family would be anxious, and your belongings would be confiscated. So you have to face facts and start making the rounds of control posts situated all over the bush, beside a track, at a crossroads, or in the *sala* of a destroyed village. There the people in charge make you wait and pretend to forget all about you for hours, sometimes even days on end, enabling you to gather your thoughts and mull over everything that could have constituted an error: boastful remarks, inconsiderate acts, wanton provocation, overt independence, any careless act that might have been brought to the attention of the Angkar. Questions go unanswered; no charge is ever levelled. Then suddenly your arms are bound and you are brought to the camp, where the first few days last a lifetime, and where the voice of revolt, little by little, dies away. You acquire patience and resignation; you learn to stop believing in your own innocence. How can someone be innocent if he's in chains? And so you grow introspective, become aware of your selfishness, your irresponsibility . . . you meditate on your guilt, which you are ultimately prepared to admit, if only those in charge of the camp would be generous enough to devote a little of their precious time, despite the burden of their work, to your own humble situation.

At Srah Srang, I had known one of those proud peasants, a man who was free, always out and about, much loved and respected. He was famous for his talents as an arak singer (his voice was better than anyone's at persuading the spirits of the soil to enter the body of a medium), and one day he became famous for the disastrous way he reacted to a situation.

A group of five men in black suits, wearing krama around their necks — only the eldest was armed — had suddenly arrived and made their way to the sala at the outskirts of the village, on the old banks of the eastern baray, opposite the temple of Prè Rup, which could be seen from afar. They were only there for a few hours, indifferent to the state of the thatch roof, worn away by the rains and pushed in by the accumulation of husks from the old overhanging tamarind tree. Nobody had yet seen any Khmers Rouges, and news of their arrival had spread quickly. They offered cigarettes to the passers-by, whom they called "comrades". After this first contact, they returned a few days later. The local inhabitants, feeling anxious, brought them tea and betel, even suggesting that they might like something to eat; this they refused. They employed a peripheral figure in the village as an intermediary, an embittered man who had difficulty integrating himself and was desperate for change. This man, who had thought it advantageous to bring himself to the attention of the newcomers as soon as they arrived, let it be known that all heads of families were duty-bound to introduce themselves and hear what the revolutionaries had to say. Twenty or so people, almost all women, came, led by the village spokesman. The speeches, riddled with incomprehensible neologisms, began with ideological clichés and ended with a request for help that every family ought to provide the revolution. The village should supply a given number of sacks of rice, with as many carts and zebus as would be required for transporting them. The transports would be returned. During the week, and after a good many discussions, the tribute was collected and the sacks were taken away at night by the Khmers Rouges. But the carts and oxen had been left abandoned, near Phnom Bok, thirty kilometres away. The peasants set off in groups to recover them, and our singer discovered that his cart had been broken. He was so furious that he swore it would never be taken from him again and that from now on the revolution would have to do without him.

Two weeks later, a message with his name on it reached the village. He set off as directed, and never came back.

The padlock at the end of the rail was removed, and the guard handed me a shackle for my ankle. Once again I found myself in the ghastly situation of having to squeeze my joints into such a narrow casing. I tensed my tendon to expand it and pointed out to the guards that it was impossible to apply this system to someone with bones the size of mine. I had, in any case, determined never to allow myself to be shackled again. Tucking my legs beneath me, I prevented any attempt to fetter me. With a bit of force, they could, of course, have managed to get the rod through the metal holes. But by exaggerating the difficulty, I hoped to escape not just the shackles but the frightening forced closeness of the collective stocks.

The second-in-command, a coarse and brutal fellow who was older than Douch, had been watching from where he sat. He sent a guard into the other shelters to enquire about a larger shackle. At this Douch came to the rescue. His solemn face leaned forwards, causing his lower lip to cover his ragged teeth.

"Have you had your bath?" he asked, as he considered a solution.

Then, with that weary manner he often affected, he spoke a few words and returned to his table beneath an awning attached to the guards' billets.

I was helped to my feet and led towards the entrance along the path I had taken when I arrived. Nearby curved the round area where the young guards sat in a circle every evening and conducted their collective confession. A small shelter had been erected here to keep the rain off the four sackloads of paddy rice that the peasants brought every week. One guard arrived with a chain; another squatted down to secure my foot to one of the pillars supporting the shelter.

As daylight faded, it began to rain. I didn't know where to put myself. The smell of the forest rose out of the damp soil. From beneath the carpet of leaves, grass and twigs, the sodden humus gave off the surprising aroma of an old wine. In the half-light, I noticed hens clinging like cats to the bamboo shoots, on their way to roost in the branches. I crouched down, sinking my heels into the wet earth. Jumping over the puddles to amuse himself, a young guard brought me a plate of rice. I had not eaten all day; I swallowed the cold, watery grains and curled up to go to sleep, under the rain.

The hens were the first awake. Well before dawn, they were flapping clumsily among the rain-soaked bamboo stems, some of which sagged to the ground, sending down a shower with every leap. I envied the happiness of the squawking chicks on the ground below, gathered together in families, running back to their attentive mothers and being tenderly corralled. For the cockerel – a cross with a wild cock, whose rust-coloured, sickle-shaped tail culminated in a trail of dark green – with his puffed-up neck feathers, his bright red comb and his spurs raised, it was his hour of glory. His voice resonant despite having just woken up, he set off without further ado, wings beating, feet stamping, on a series of leapfrog courses.

When I arrived, the ménage consisted of a cock, three hens, three pullets and nineteen chicks. Each day, whenever possible, the nine guards boiled a chicken in their collective soup; they ate apart from us. Eating an egg was an anti-revolutionary act – meat alone would assuage a fighter's hunger. The prisoners received only two bowls of rice: the first at about nine in the morning, the other after five in the evening. Was it my permanent hunger or was that mountain rice which they pounded every morning so full of flavour? I don't know, but I have never eaten such good rice.

For three days it rained in torrents. Douch had instructed that the stock of paddy be stored elsewhere and that I be allowed to move under the shelter. But the amount of water falling, which penetrated even the billet where the guards slept in hammocks, made it necessary to build a wooden partition for the sacks; this task dragged on for weeks and was never completed.

From the very first day, I discovered at first hand how destitute our community was: since there was no spare container for me, I was not served the morning meal. One of my fellow prisoners, who provided our sustenance, came towards me but did not give me my ration. In the late afternoon, I was served on the charred lid of one of the two large iron cooking pots. This was, of course, a provisional solution, and the guards let it be known that it was up to me to work something out. I quickly realised that my fate, like that of the other prisoners, depended on their whims and that complaining would be out of the question. And so that afternoon I insisted on being accompanied to the river. The authorisation I had been accorded the previous day had to be renewed in order to establish clearly that I had acquired a right.

As I walked past the first shelter, which I had to skirt to get down to the river, I slowed my pace before the sad, vague smile of my new fellow inmates, who watched me pass from the depths of their solitude. An elderly woman appeared to be sleeping among them, but her yellow face and imperceptible twitching convinced me that she was in fact very ill. On my way back, I stopped to say a few words (without going into the pleasure I had just experienced rolling around in the water), and learned that she was the only woman in the camp. She was suffering from malaria and was no longer feeding herself. The next morning, I found out that she had died during the night. My first reaction was to recall that by her side I had seen a large bowl, carved out of a coconut shell; it had attracted my attention because of its unusual size.

Douch came to see me as dusk was falling. He was carrying a folded sheet of paper and a ballpoint pen. I had to write down my declaration of innocence. I did not know that the document I was about to produce would be compared to the minutes of my public trial, that it would be used as a reference in everything I might say later, or that I would have to write at least a dozen more. I took the opportunity to ask him whether they would kindly give me a bowl, or else let me have the old woman's. Douch had a guard bring it to me the following morning. I accepted the object gratefully. Its rim had been carved with a *phkiek*,* and I could see the dead woman's lips on the chiselled, polished chips in the hard casing; I meditated on the unforeseeable destiny of things. I was later told that my being allocated this bowl had caused quite a commotion; apparently one of the guards had already appropriated the coveted vessel.

*A sort of traditional Khmer machete, made of a fairly short blade fitted into a bamboo handle.

That was the hardest thing: being dependent on the young guards. In particular, you had to obtain their consent, sometimes by begging, simply to relieve yourself. Urinating was not a problem; each shelter contained several fairly large bamboo tubes, which a fellow prisoner would empty each morning downstream. It was much more of an ordeal when one had to ease one's bowels. Faced with this petition, the guards grumbled far more, since they usually had to unshackle the feet of several prisoners just to free the one who had summoned them, and this took time and required the presence of a second armed guard. The man then had to be escorted into the bushes. The trench was outside the camp, towards the forest. I went there only once and recall it as a vision of horror: two small, slippery planks, both covered with squirming white maggots, had been placed across the trench, which was packed with teeming matter, clarified where mud flowed in. It was a vile experience, a sort of unbelievable nightmare beyond all reality; the prisoners constantly mentioned their dread of falling in.

I soon found it preferable to wait for my dip, during which I would find some privacy, a few metres away and a little downriver, in a place that only I used, and where some *Eupatorium* bushes conveniently grew, their fragrant, supple leaves scored with thin veins on one side and covered by a fine down on the other.

These chores soon took on a regular rhythm. And since only one chain had to be unlocked to free me, the irritation of the guards was lessened. Nevertheless, on several occasions I had to squat at the limit of my chain because no-one had deigned to respond to my signals.

Since our diet consisted of only one food, the colour and consistency of our stools were uniform; we could read in any variation the prisoner's state of health. I could discern a modification with the slightest cold spell (it was the beginning of the chilly season) or the smallest change of food. One afternoon, I saw one of the young guards very carefully lifting the dead leaves that covered the undergrowth and gently inserting a stick into the ground: he had spotted a mygale's hole and was popping open the entrance. Throughout the countryside, this fat spider is a delicacy. I was so racked by hunger that my mouth was watering and I stared solidly at him as he returned to toast his catch. He willingly shared the spider, and I was surprised to observe that the piece I ate was enough to alter the colour of my stools.

After three weeks, we had to move. One of the commandant's assistants fell ill in a rather surprising manner, brought down by a tutelary spirit. He was a young man, and I remember well his handsome, dolichocephalic profile, the creamy white of his eyes standing out from his swarthy complexion, the strong red of his mouth spreading out on to his fleshy lips. I witnessed his sudden possession by this supernatural force and his delirious hallucinations right in the middle of the camp as he rolled on the ground convulsively, totally unaware of what he was doing, muttering obscenities with his jaws twisted in a spasm. The poor puppet, animated by the spirit of a dead man, was taken away to his own village and handed over to the medium, who revealed that the god who guarded the river was taking his revenge because his waters had been defiled with urine from the camp. The villagers reported these grim tidings to Douch, who agreed to change the campsite. We were all transported a few kilometres upriver, escorted by armed reinforcements. I shall never forget how I was affected by this move: the loss of bearings filled me with a terrible feeling of distress. I would have given anything not to have to get used to a new piece of ground and adapt to a new stake. My mind dwelt for hours on the mysterious facility of humans to attach themselves to the most derisory objects, even to the instruments of one's own torture, simply because they are there, around us every day, because we have become used to them. This probably holds true throughout our whole lives. Even today, I am amazed at what this truth reveals about the human condition.

I noted that the torments inflicted on me had completely

altered the way I viewed the Khmer peasantry. I had never fully grasped their true personality, despite mixing with them for many years, during which time I had closely studied their beliefs, their way of life, their way of thinking. My relationship with them had always been distorted by my French origins; unwittingly, I was in a prominent position not merely because of my work at the Angkor Conservation Office, but because of what I represented in their eyes, no matter how intimately I came to know them. There was nothing I could do about this historic gulf between us: I was on the other side, a foreigner, and a socially predominant one at that. At the same time, my own idea of the Khmer as I tried to relate to them was stuck in patterns which kept me apart from them. I knew them only in the state of subordination that had been established by tradition, which introduced a permanent discrimination in our relationship. But my sudden captivity was a painful renewal of my apprenticeship, a sharp jolt of reality. I discovered new and unsuspected masks, faces the Khmers had never shown me. I was now deciphering, sometimes in fear, the features I had never been able to see.

Several evenings a week — every evening it didn't rain — the guards gathered for a collective confession. Douch did not take part. I was a privileged witness to these circles, where they would sit on the ground under the direction of an elder. Military homilies alternated with simple, repetitive songs.

"Comrades," began the eldest, "let us appraise the day that has passed, in order to correct our faults. We must cleanse ourselves of the repeated sins that accumulate and slow down our beloved revolution. Do not be surprised at this!"

"I," said the first one, "should have replaced the rattan rod today, the one north of the first shelter, which we use to dry clothes. I have done nothing about it . . . on account of my laziness."

The man presiding over the session nodded with a frown, though not severely, only meaning to show that he knew how hard it was to combat inertia, so natural in man when he is not sustained by solid revolutionary convictions. He passed wordlessly on to the next man, indicating who this should be by pursing his lips in his direction.

"I," this one uttered, "er . . . I fell asleep after my meal, forgetting to make sure that the bamboo urine containers in the shelters had been emptied properly."

When each had spoken in turn, they moved on to the next stage, which the elder introduced as follows: "The beloved Angkar congratulates you, comrades, for these admissions, which are so essential to the progress of each of us. In order to make our actions shine forth for ever, let us now try fearlessly to help our brother better detect his own faults, those he has not confessed because he was unwilling to see them. Who wishes to speak?"

One of the youngest raised a finger. He had a handsome, bright face and deep eyes, and, like the sergeant on the bridge, his gums were marbled with patches of purple, right back to the roof of his mouth. Of all the guards, he was the nicest. In the evenings, after he had chained me up, he would sometimes linger to ask me questions about Phnom Penh and France.

"This afternoon," he began, "I went into the dormitory and surprised Comrade Miet hiding something in his blanket."

"Liar!" cried the accused. "I didn't hide anything, I simply wanted to — "

With a nod the man in charge had already sent someone to search the culprit's hammock; he came running back with an exercise book in his hand. Young Miet was weeping. The leader slipped the exercise book inside his shirt without opening it; he would investigate later. Someone else began to speak.

These "instruction" sessions (the word they used was the Buddhist term, *rien sot*, meaning "religious education") created an atmosphere of suspicion among the guards; they did not hesitate to accuse one another of anything, in the hope only of receiving a compliment from Douch. Denunciation is the first duty of the revolutionary. They quoted the example of some young men who so loved the revolution that they were unafraid to denounce their fathers or their brothers.

In the liberated zones, obligatory indoctrination classes began to be introduced for children from the age of eight or nine. They set off on training courses and often, because of transport difficulties or bombing raids, did not return. They were placed under the authority of an instructor, who imposed a very strict discipline. The master's influence over the minds of these young people was overwhelming.

By the end of the session, the sun was sending out its last rays, down through the tight weave of the bamboo grove's vaulted canopy, landing in patches of light on the ground, as if from a stained-glass window. Comrade Thép came to pay me a visit. He had been a prisoner for almost a year and enjoyed fairly undemanding conditions: exempted from the iron shackles, he could move about as he pleased. Douch had assured him that he would be freed soon, since the cause for his captivity of several months was not very serious. But the weeks passed, and he did not dare demand his release. He had to wait for a sign from on high.

Thép was the only one who came to talk to me, but he never stayed long, and we conversed freely, even though I had to consider the possibility that he might be an informer. I avoided questions that would embarrass him – the names of the neighbouring villages, for example, or of the rivers and mountains – which would have given me an indication of the camp's location. He was a short man, dark, fairly stocky, about fifty years old. News of his father's death had just reached him, and he had come to me to confide, broken-hearted, that he had sworn to be present at his funeral.

To change the subject, I mentioned the betrayal session I had just witnessed. I suggested that indoctrination was all the easier in the case of children, whose innocence could so often be accompanied by cruelty. In reply, he drew near, lowered his voice, and began to tell the following story.

"At the beginning of the year, some Khmers Rouges arrived in my village. They were people who had originally come from South Vietnam, Khmer Kraum. They had come to appoint some local people to administer the district and look after everyday matters in the name of the Angkar. Comrade! Had these men been chosen because they were the stupidest? They thought only of taking advantage of the power they were exercising for the first time, and in their excitement they issued insane orders to one and all. The wretches did not hesitate to condemn to death three heads of families who had refused to allow their only sons to be recruited into a fighting unit along with Vietnamese . . . you must understand, comrade: these people were not plotting anything, but none of them wanted to lose his only child, especially when the boys were still so young! A father whose boy had already had his ordination, or one who had several sons, would probably have reacted differently; but not them. The carrying out of the sentence appalled the village. The outraged inhabitants rebelled and killed the murderers. Then things seemed to return to normal, until a month later, when Vietnamese soldiers surrounded the village, enabling the Khmers Rouges who were with them to gather up the in-habitants to identify the families of the three men at the start of the whole business. Nineteen people were identified, uncles and cousins who were present in the village that day, and five babies. The adults and adolescents were massacred without further ado, in public, by blows to the neck with the back of a spade. And the infants, who had been taken from their mothers and set to one side during the execution, what did they do to them? You must be wondering, eh? Well, their slaughter was entrusted to a youngster who was with them. A boy of fourteen! We all knew his parents, who came from a nearby village. He had begun his ideological instruction only a few months before. Seeing the boy hesitate in front of everyone, one of the leaders – his instructor, probably – came up, put his arms around his shoulders, and urged him on in a low voice. Now, comrade, I saw this with my own eyes: the young boy gathered his courage, moved forward, and one by one, in no sort of a hurry, he took hold of each baby by its foot, and smacked its little body firmly against the trunk of the tree, the old mango tree on the west side of the square . . . Two or three times, each one. He was congratulated for his efforts by the leader, who hailed his example of zeal and composure. That's what the Khmers Rouges are doing to our children! They are transforming them into shameless creatures who can no longer tell good from evil!"

"Comrade Thép!" I addressed him cynically. "Do you not know the cause of this savagery? Don't you realise that the revolution has no money? That anyone who loves the Angkar has to conserve the bullets from his rifle in order to fight American imperialism?"

As I reached the end of my sentence, I stamped my foot on the ground, pretending to be furious. Thép, whose expression reflected the horrific scene he had just described, nodded, his eyes staring into space. He was about to reply when we saw Douch walking towards us. He immediately rose to his feet and left, greeting Douch as he passed.

Thép would die a few days later, struck down by an attack of malaria. We were all prone to it: violent headaches, febrile trembling, tetanic convulsions. In the mountain regions, the disease, in its endemic state, reappeared as soon as the cold season arrived. The local population, though affected, were reasonably resistant; their spleens grew large and hard. The peasants from the valleys, by contrast, unaccustomed to living in a malaria-infested region, often died at the first bout of fever; in three months, fourteen out of little more than forty prisoners had died in the camp. I myself had already contracted the infection in Kulen, north of Angkor, in the villages of the foothills; perhaps that was why I was fortunate enough not to fall ill during my captivity. But my immunity seemed so freakish when compared to the prevalent hysteria that when the guards questioned me about my health I invented a few headaches, so as not to arouse jealousy.

I knew that Thép had become very ill the day before he died and had asked to see me. His condition became so serious that one of the guards came to look for me. When I arrived, he was delirious and scarcely recognised me. I was told that he had talked about his father all night. His chill breath seeped through his teeth, which were clenched so tight they looked as if they would crack. His body arched itself in a last convulsion against the slats he was lying upon. The *krama* that covered him slipped off, uncovering his erect penis. We covered him again, and for a long time his member remained tumescent beneath the fabric.

Douch came to enquire about my declaration of innocence. I had written my statement with difficulty, in a very emotional state of mind. Tears had come to my eyes as I signed it; I had a premonition of the document in the hands of those who would discover it only after my death, the last trace I had managed to leave behind.

As Douch had suggested, I had written a brief résumé outlining the periods of study I had spent outside France, notably in Germany; and pointing out that I had also lived in England for more than a year. I then swore – upon my daughter's head, to give further evidence of my good faith – that my only activities since that time had been related to my research into

Buddhism. Douch carefully read w..... i had written in French. It was then that it occurred to me that we had only ever spoken in Khmer.

I hated the idea of talking to the Khmers in French; the sentences seemed flat and meaningless, for it is not only words that differ from one language to another, but also the ideas they translate, different ways of thinking and speaking. I could not explain in my own tongue what I had to say to my torturer. The bonds gradually forming between us depended entirely on our capacity to understand each other on common ground, and this could be done only in his language.

As he turned around, he tried to jump up and sit on the rice sacks. They were too high for him. He squatted on the ground, slowly lifting his face to me with his eyes cast downwards. "Why were you sent to Cambodia to study Buddhism?"

"Because it's different."

"How is it different?"

"In the countryside, one comes across strange beliefs and customs that are totally inconsistent with the Singhalese texts. Now, all the official Buddhist literature taught in Phnom Penh is taken from the Singhalese canon. It's as if one Buddhism were practised in the capital and another in the villages. So I began to wonder about the origin of these peasant traditions. And to begin with, I had to draw up a detailed list of the most unusual customs. So that's what I do."

"At Kompong Khleang," he said, "the village where I spent all my childhood, beside the Great Lake – "

"I know Kompong Khleang," I interrupted. "It's a magnificent lakeside town, swarming with mosquitoes, but – "

"I lived there with my grandmother," he continued. "At the monastery, the monks are also mediums, and the fishermen consult them. The spirits of the dead speak through their mouths. Others are called *lok angkouy* because their bodies remain 'seated' while they take leave of them to inspect the surroundings of the village and discover the cause of the misfortunes of those who consult them. Half the time, I might add, the problems stem from a local spirit who has become enraged because someone has inadvertently urinated over him. Is that the sort of eccentric tradition you're talking about?".

"Yes, in part, at least. In this case, it could be to do with pre-Buddhist cults that have persisted by attaching themselves to shamanistic practices and to healing rituals used within the monastery. Actually, overall, I think . . ."

Sceptical and fastidious, Douch listened and contradicted me. He wanted to test me. In order to explain my presence in Cambodia, I had to justify my groundwork. Moreover, I had to define the objectives of my research, perhaps more fully than I had ever done before. It appeared to be the only way to convince him of my innocence. I asked him to buy me a pencil and a notebook with the money that had been confiscated from me. And I suggested that he also bring me back some soap and a tin of condensed milk.

Sweetened condensed milk was supposed to contain so many nutrients that it was considered the ideal tonic throughout the Cambodian hinterland. Everywhere, one came across tins produced under Australian supervision with the name "Golden Sparrow" (*chap meas*). The label, printed in three languages (Khmer, Chinese and French), read like some mysterious prescription or recipe: "To obtain one litre of sweetened milk at 171 grams per litre, containing 2,800 units of vitamin A, 392 units of vitamin D and 1.96mg of vitamin B1, just add 810 grams of boiled water to the contents of this tin."

Douch was about to reply when thirty or more soldiers from Lon Nol's army burst upon the scene, their arms firmly tied behind their backs. It was already getting dark. The new prisoners were wearing their camouflage gear, dyed in patches of green, black and brown, and were hard to make out in the partial darkness. They bore fresh traces of the battle they had just lost.

They all looked distressed. They were barefoot; some wore only a vest, and a few were wounded. Five or six Khmers Rouges, armed with American M16s, kept them in their sights. One of them reported directly to the guards' billets, where he spent a long time negotiating with Douch, who had gone straight to see him: their arrival came at an inconvenient time and presented security problems. The prisoners were ordered to lie down and were quickly shackled together along the length of two bars, which were too short to accommodate all of them; the others were strung together with chains and ropes. They remained where they had been put, not moving or making a sound. It was almost November; at night, the forest grew damp and cold. For the sake of my health, Douch arranged to have a large glowing log brought to me; while I slept, on my side, I drew close to it, alternately exposing my back and my chest to the warmth of the embers. The smoke that wafted from the log and stung my eyes still pervades my nostrils. I fell asleep imagining their distress.

When I awoke from a sleep interrupted continually by gloomy thoughts that prevented me from resting, the log had gone out and my muscles were paralysed with cold. The soldiers had all got to their feet during the night, unable to endure the saturated icyness of the ground. They were standing up but not moving. Their worn faces were frightening. They were all looking at me, teeth chattering, frozen stiff.

"Where are you from?" I asked quietly, after a while.

Those who were nearest heard me without responding and looked away. One had a scarf decorated with diagrams and letters tied round his stomach.

"Where did you get it?" I asked, looking him full in the eyes while making a quick gesture around my waist with both hands.

Glancing around at his companions in astonishment, he replied abruptly, "Kompong Cham."

His throat, numb with cold, had emitted the two words with a painfully husky sound.

"Is it one of the *achar* Loch's designs?" I asked.

I was very familiar with the diagrams used for protection, which the war had made fashionable again. Every enlisted man – except the Khmers Rouges – wore one of these, in the form of a shirt, a scarf or a turban, given by his father or by a spiritual teacher. They were sacred items, and the principle of their protective properties was based upon the powers Buddhism ascribes to letters: wrapped in the immortal words of the doctrine the warrior is invulnerable. Certain designs were very ancient and signed by a great master. With a little practice, it was easy to identify the styles.

"Yes, it's by my master, the *achar* Loch, and done with his own hand," he replied proudly.

The camp was stirring, and the armed escort had regrouped around them. Our young guards helped them undo the shackles and chains. The "Lon Nols" obediently fell into line, biting their lips and trying to conceal the pain in their frozen limbs. Then the column set off on its final march. When he drew level with me, the man with the magic scarf broke rank. One of the guards immediately called out to him, but by then he had almost reached me.

"I want to give my scarf to the Frenchman!" he said, turning to the Khmer Rouge who had come charging up.

"Take it!" he added, looking at me. He moved forward slightly, eyes wide open, and stood over me so I could untie the material.

The armed guard, who was being questioned by someone further away, looked puzzled but did not interfere. He shrugged and then shoved him lightly with the end of his rifle so that he would rejoin his group quickly.

"What's going on here?" he demanded, staring at me before he strode away. "The revolution does not approve of this!"

One of the young guards who had witnessed the scene immediately came up and took the scarf to inspect it.

"Grandfather,* have you never seen magic diagrams in your own village?" I asked him.

"No, I've only seen them in Omleang, where I went for my training. The instructors used to make underpants out of them. They would take them from the prisoners who were bound for the Angkar Leu, before the material could get bloodstained."

Unwittingly, the boy had revealed, in spite of all instructions to keep silent, not just the name of the principal town of the region where we found ourselves, but had also explained the grim meaning of the expression "Angkar Leu", the "top organisation", which I had not realised signified death.

As for the scarcely credible anecdote about underpants, it showed just how far the Khmer Rouge revolution was willing to go to debase a traditional system of values. To place letters of Buddhist doctrine in contact with regions of the body considered to be "impure" was an absolute sacrilege, one no peasant would risk committing. Only town-dwellers would be capable of such iconoclastic radicalism. The majority were poorly integrated Sino-Khmers, the sons of shopkeepers or frustrated employees. Having replaced the traditional village structures with the fraternal solidarity of the resistance, motivated by a sincere idealism, and appalled by the gap between rich and poor, they had shared an existence outside of the rural world, which they knew nothing about. None of them had ever tended rice fields. The way they roamed through the countryside proved they had no respect for crops, gardens, trees or pathways. Neither did they show any deference to sacred images or to anything Buddhism held dear, regarding it all as peasant superstition, cultivated from Angkor by every monarch, to subdue the people.

Paradoxically, these city folk, who loathed the plough, the soil, the palm groves and domestic animals, who disliked the open,

*Through a rather comical shift due to the major role of the young guards in our daily life, it was the custom to call them *ta*, "grandfather", an expression of respect that took no account of their age.

rustic life of the villagers, had an idealised concept of the Khmer peasant as agent of the perpetual revolution, a model of simplicity, endurance and patriotism, the standard against which the new man would be measured, liberated from religious taboos. In this contradictory scenario, Buddhism was replaced by objectives dear to the Angkar, in order to ensure the triumph of equality and justice. The Khmer theorists had substituted the Angkar for Dhamma, the personification of Teaching, the Primordial Being at the beginning of the world, whose body, composed of the letters of the alphabet, gave birth to the first man and woman.

The new camp, like the first, had been constructed in a vast bamboo grove, where the tall, pliant stalks rose and fell like luminous trails of fireworks. Well before we arrived, we could see from afar their multiple crowns, clusters of pale plumes rising above the purple layers of forest. On top of everything else we had struggled to get used to, this transfer coincided with new directives announced by Douch himself: we had to produce for ourselves what we needed. To begin with, those prisoners who had permission to work would be split into two specialist groups, one whose duty was to prepare traditional medicines, the other to work with rattan and bamboo, manufacturing everyday objects such as baskets and wickerwork. Those who were permanently shackled were to assist in the collective effort from where they were.

The Angkar supplied pharmaceutical formulae, a large basin and various basic ingredients that were hard to acquire. For whole days, we were mobilised into producing multi-purpose tablets for treating (among other things) malaria: shoots, bark, roots, kernels, pulps, sapwoods and cores were whipped, beaten, crushed, ground and dried. I was intoxicated by the wonderful, fresh aroma the stripped green wood exuded in the heat. Then we patiently transformed the powder obtained into extracts, decoctions, infusions . . . all blended with molasses and heated until completely reduced. We obtained a bitter-tasting paste not unlike quinine. We all had to take it, and the guards proudly repeated that the self-sufficiency policy of the liberated Cambodia was about to achieve its objectives in the field of health care. Besides manufacturing medicines, we had a weekly visit from an official acupuncturist. These "doctors" were peasants whom the Angkar had put through a three-day initiation course, under the supervision of a Chinese physician, in acupuncture points and the therapeutic application of needles, which was completely unknown in Cambodia. They were to care for all the fighters and to go around the villages. Very soon, their numerous blunders betrayed their inexperience. I saw an acute ear infection treated by pushing a needle several centimetres inside a prisoner's ear. Anyone who was ill was nevertheless bound to consult them, as evidence of his unshakeable trust in the revolution.

Our community did not possess the range of trades necessary to develop a village. We had no-one with expertise in basketry, and everyone went about it in his own way, following his own methods, keeping his own counsel. The initial stage, splitting the bamboo shoots and fining them down into thin strips for weaving, posed fewer problems than shaping the receptacles. This part involved pressing the woven part into a hollow in the ground with your foot and then plaiting the strands together with rattan. These cavities, which were of different sizes, had been dug in the middle of the open space just in front of me, so I had a ringside view of our makeshift artisans endeavouring unsuccessfully to force their baskets into moulds with their heel: the rigid curves became twisted and the misshapen edges came undone every time . . .

This difficulty made me stop and think. We tapered the ends of the shoots slightly so they would have room to fit tightly together, forming the shape of the wall. I even measured the length over which the bamboo strips had to be thinned, according to the depths of the holes, and recut some of them as models. The first attempt was encouraging, and with the benefit of experience we managed to produce some acceptable baskets.

"*Veuy*," exclaimed one of the basket makers. "It had to be the Frenchman who showed us what to do."

"Well," replied another, "if he knows how to build aeroplanes, he can easily make baskets!"

# 5

Every morning, just before dawn, Poulette would jump down heavily from her perch. This would make Cocotte fly off, but she couldn't land, and invariably ended up crashing into the bushes. The rustling and clucking and flapping alerted the chicks in their hiding place, and set them off cheeping shrilly and fluffing out their feathers.

"Prrrrrou, cheep, cheep, cheep!" I would call, gently proffering my hand to Poulette. "Come on then, my lovely, cheep, cheep! Come on . . ."

She would venture forwards, strutting and clucking, and fluffing herself up, then was off again, making a sudden show of attentiveness towards her chicks, turning this way and that . . . all the while coming gradually closer to me, managing to present the light iridescent feathers of her collar first. They ruffled with every shake of her head, the humble grey taking on reflections of opal. I would gently push them up with the tips of my fingers, waiting for her to rub against my hand of her own accord before picking her up. Then I would lift her to eye level and tap my nose against her worn beak. The sweet, dusty bird kept still and let me enter the stable field of her onyx eyes, washed over by the blue of her grainy eyelids, like a windscreen wiper. Poulette let herself be kissed.

Our circus act was the result of a lengthy endeavour that had never been entirely disinterested. In allowing me to court her, she was paying me a toll. In return for this compliance, I would let her peck holes in the rice sacks. But I never succeeded in obtaining the favours of Cocotte, a fine cochin hen, lively and timorous, endowed with dark bronze plumage and a comb that was so little serrated that it might have been a cock's. Even if she occasionally deigned to nibble from my hand, she always refused to go any further. This did not mean that she would forgo the hard-won privileges of her neighbour. I found myself applying the same distinctions to chickens as the old boys from the Protectorate* liked to make between the supple Cambodian women and the gracious ladies of Saigon.

When I thought of it, I would listen, at the break of day – not before, because it likes light – for the mocking call of the oriole. *Touuuuuu . . . thiou!* the children of Srah Srang would sing out in high-pitched voices, imitating its call. But its shrill and timid song can so seldom be heard above the rustle of foliage that you only think of listening for it at the moment when your ear has already detected it. There are so many things in the world we notice only once we already know about them.

Once a week, Douch would leave before dawn and not return until night-time. I could see him returning from afar, along a curve in the track visible through a gap between the trees. The surface was so pitted at that point that he had to get off his bicycle. His silhouette stood out in white against the moonlight, his arms leaning on the ends of the handlebars. He would disappear for several minutes and then emerge in front of me, his back to the light, in the shade of the canopy of trees. He would

*The Protectorate comprised the three countries of French Indo-China: Vietnam, Cambodia and Laos. [Tr.]

pass by with an unreadable face, not seeing me. When he was worn down by fatigue, he was transformed into an irascible character, and it was as if all his inner strength could feed only a suppressed anger. His lips opened loosely over tightly clenched teeth. I would turn over or pretend to sleep. He was coming back to eat, in silence, the leftovers that had been kept for him next to the fire, which had gone out.

Entrusted with security in the scrublands of the Cardamomes, to which the Communist attackers had retreated in order to conceal their movements and start raising troops, Douch went to a weekly meeting of the party committee. Brutal force was already being employed, unopposed, and ultimate authority was in the hands of the torturer. The names of some of his superiors would soon enjoy a grim reputation: Ta Mok, Saloth Sar, Von Veth . . . He had to provide them with a report on each of the prisoners he had been sent: those destined to spend long months in chains awaiting any decision, as well as those whose fate had been sealed before their arrival. For the latter, the camp was merely a place of transit; unlike the others, who came mainly from the area, they were unable to give the name of anyone local to vouch for them.

Douch merely carried out the decisions of the Angkar. The condemned man would be taken into the forest, never having been told of the sentence. If, instinctively, he surmised the imminent danger, the soldiers were to respond with soothing words. The place of execution was not very far off, but we never heard anything: Thép confirmed that the weapon used was either a spade or a large stick.

As a rule, the truth was suppressed, but in this case there was a moral objective: to avoid the distressing spectacle of panic for as long as possible. The executioners made it a point of honour to postpone until the last moment of shame when the prisoner, overcome with uncontrollable terror, dissolved into pitiful sobbing and pathetic twitching. They denied the obvious even while making the poor wretches dig their own graves. They also knew-that once these awful moments had passed, during the seconds preceding the final blow, the victim would become still and docile. At mass executions, when the prisoners, side by side, on their knees, await their turn, their fate is already sealed. The body droops, the mind grows blurred and the hearing goes. Then the orders are shouted out; it is now only a matter of practical instructions: "Stay still! Heads forward! Do not tuck your neck in between your shoulders!"

The Khmers Rouges instinctively knew the age-old law without trying to understand it: a man is killed more easily than an animal. Is it a tragic result of his intellectual development? How many crimes might have been brought to an abrupt halt if he had been able to bite to the very end, as cats or pigs do!

"Psst!"

There was a movement in the thicket behind me. The wrinkled face of an old man appeared beneath the branches.

"Psst! Psst!" he said again, as if I had not already turned to face him.

He continued to wave, trying to show that this sign was a gesture of friendship.

Glancing left and right several times, he emerged into the open, advancing on all fours towards me. I could smell the diverse odours that he emitted: damp clothing, betel, smoke from a cooking fire. Quickly getting up into a crouching position with his legs crossed beneath him, he lifted his eyebrows, opened his mouth wide like a conjuror about to produce a dove, and removed a packet from his haversack. He laid his gnarled hand on my forearm. From the depths of his moist, red eyes, he studied me suspiciously, with that insistent look old men have.

"You mustn't escape!" he panted. "During the war against the Japanese, I saw many prisoners like you. *Pouttho!* Those who tried to escape were caught and killed. Every last one! You've got no chance of getting away!"

"Do they keep watch over the forest?" I asked, waving my hand instinctively in that direction.

"You'd be spotted right away! Don't try to escape, *lok euy!* Don't escape, eh! Here, take this: a kilo of white sugar. Eat, it's good! You must eat!"

I took the package gratefully; I was so hungry. He left immediately and disappeared into the bushes, though not before directing a few more knowing waves at me.

At the time, I was shaken by the temerity of his visit, but today I wonder what motivated it. What could have prompted the old man to risk talking to me? Where did he come from? Was it an operation deliberately contrived to suppress any desire I may have had to escape? I think, in fact, that at that time Douch had begun to believe in my innocence; or else he was uncertain, and needed time for the strong suspicions that hung over me to dissipate. If that were the case, any reckless act, any attempt at escape would have ruined his efforts. He knew my impulsive reactions and was wary of them.

A few days earlier, feeling impetuous, I had rushed up to him under the puzzled gaze of my fellow detainees, some of whom had never seen "the Frenchman". The previous day, the guards had forgotten to chain me up. It was not the first time: the kids who were supposed to watch over us fluctuated constantly between perverse obsession and a childish insouciance. These moments of freedom set me alight. The difference between being chained and not being chained had become overwhelming. I wavered now between the urge to escape and the desire to live better.

And sometimes, out of the blue, like shafts of light in so much suffering, moments of euphoria swept over me. Bathing in the river, I stumbled as I stood up, trying to find a foothold on the uneven pebbles, my body suddenly heavy, the water now only around my feet. I kept my eyes closed and cupped my dripping face with my hands. Between those river banks, cleanly cut in the rich soil, my spirit soared. The elation that overwhelmed me ran on in slow motion. I peered intently into the undergrowth now crowned with a halo of light. The clear water gurgled and pushed my feet onwards. The hairs on my body stood up as the soft breeze ran on my skin.

These exhilarating sensations were abruptly followed by total destitution. The best moments of emotion are gifts of chance. Monks, in their quest for a frugal and severe existence, aspire to such flashes of radiance. And yet, this short awakening of my senses took me away from my sufferings. And deep down, I was distressed to feel them lessen. As I lay next to my log at night, this paradoxical anguish gave rise to strange lines of poetry. I turned them over and over in my mind, unable to find sleep, unable to make them express my pain, unwilling to let it go:

> *Man spills from the furnace, glowing still.*
> *Stirred now by a breeze, his senses wake;*
> *Emboldened thus, his ardour springs to life —*
> *The fire crackles, and the embers take.*
>
> *Caught by his fervour, so the flames increase;*
> *Around his hearth the fire grows and takes hold.*
> *But suddenly the soul is torn away;*
> *The embers turn to ash, the ground grows cold.*
>
> *All passion dies in one who is withheld.*
> *The blackened cinder chokes. But if a breath*
> *Should come and make him burn without his own?*
> *If not with them, he'd rather welcome death.*
>
> *Then comes the gentle shiver of a wind,*
> *Touching the cracked and greying, smoking wood;*

*The wound of memory, beating at his flanks,*
*Soon calms, then heals, then disappears for good.*

*He howls to see his own pain disappear.*
*For as it fades, so vanish, veiled from view,*
*The images of loved ones, now to burn*
*Within the fire that seizes him anew.*

Striding hurriedly across the square, in the brilliant light of a sun beating vertically down, I caught sight of Lay and Son, chained separately in their stocks; they appeared to be sleeping. I could no longer endure being shackled! The constant jangling of chains, the bruised bones, the impossibility of movement were nothing: worst of all was the shame. At the beginning of the week, when the villagers came to bring us supplies, I would lean back against the post with my legs crossed to conceal my chains. The humiliation was unbearable.

I could not understand how such feelings had come about. Perhaps it was the fixed stares of the girls lingering in the cart to watch me before helping unload the sacks. I was used to the mischievous looks of the peasant girls from my village, and I could not forget their meaningful expressions. Under closing almond lids, half hidden by the *krama* around their heads, their pupils would sometimes light up with a flickering flame . . .

"I know exactly where we are!" I said in a loud voice as I came up to Douch. "Phnom Penh is over there! Oudong, that way! Last night the B-52s dropped bombs to the south of Oudong. Have these shackles taken off me! I swear to you that I will not escape."

I had stressed the words "I swear to you", as one might when making a deal. Douch was speaking to his assistant. My importuning had interrupted him. He immediately lowered his gaze and stopped speaking, not enquiring how I had managed to leave my post. The warm air grew heavy. The other man got up from the table he had been leaning on, hesitated, then, distracted yet concerned, went to sit in one of the hammocks strung up at the back. His presence made me uncomfortable. I had not foreseen that Douch might not be alone.

"I beseech you," I persisted. "Unchain me!"

The confusion that overtook him brought swiftly home to me the extent of my tactlessness. Such passionate pleading from a man condemned to death was so misplaced that Douch could see it only as an act of madness, a suicidal nonchalance: could I have forgotten that it was quite simply my life that was at stake, and that, by coming to speak to him in this way, I was putting it very much at risk? I was lucky that, beneath the blackmail, he detected an artlessness that did not fit the clichés about CIA agents. This uncalculated frankness didn't make sense: it was too far removed from his own experience. It had already made him feel awkward on more than one occasion during our interrogation. He remained silent, turning over in his mind a reply that would not come . . .

"What you ask is impossible!" he said at last, in a calm, but barely audible voice.

"Why?"

His face expressionless, Douch said solemnly, "I would be afraid that you might strangle me during the night."

In fact, I thought of nothing but breaking free. Not allowing myself to dwell on the distressing need to find Hélène again, I concentrated on my escape, for which the meticulous preparations blotted out every other thought. It had become my sole reason for living. I dreamed of it. I gave myself a hundred days.

The moment I had arrived at the camp, I had asked for something to shave with. They had brought me an unusable blade, "made in India". Every morning, I used it to make a notch in the spectacles case I had been allowed to keep. It struck me that a sense of time would be essential to my survival. I was the only one who knew how many days we had spent there. A prisoner loses track so quickly, depriving himself thereby of one of his principal anchors in reality. I had also insisted that they buy me a *krama*. All day long I was naked, with just the *krama* around my loins, and put on my clothes at night only because of the relative cold, peculiar to the forested foothills where we were. Before dawn, the high humidity froze your blood and paralysed your limbs, even at fifty degrees Fahrenheit.

Similarly, I had decided not to wear my flip-flops any longer; they had already been through enough to get there. The precious rubber soles were one of the keys to my freedom. Fortunately, they had been practically new when I had been arrested.

On the far bank of the river, I had also concealed a fairly large stone with a sharp edge. I planned to use it as a weapon during my flight. This requirement frightened me. From the moment I decided to escape, I could not imagine encountering anyone – even a child – without killing him, or else running the risk of letting him get away to sound the alarm. The acute pain this prospect instilled in me made me doubt my capacity for such an adventure. It was not so much the idea of taking a life as the immense difficulty of the action itself: raising my arm and hitting someone, over and over again. The scenes conjured in my imagination were steeped in horror-movie gore, blood rivering down innocent faces. In my dreams, I always saw the same beautiful teenage girl, running out in front of me, turning and staring at me in astonishment. I would run to catch up with her; the dull sound of the blows on her paling body would wake me in tears.

When I started up like this and my bewildered eyes opened on to the silence – I could no longer hear the familiar sound of the hens in the branches, or the clicking sound of the geckoes – my misfortune struck me as yet more fearful. The thick cover of the trees seemed drawn down by the darkness. Furry rings, little branches, seeds and drops of water would fall one by one, as the dampness hanging in the air settled over the ground. The absence of sky always frightened me. My only refuge was the log close to my body. One chilly night, I awoke with an erection. Could that life of which I was deprived still stir in me? With my penis I tried to find the vitality – the one link to primal mystery – that I thought had been lost. I wrapped my hand around it, letting the taut tip emerge, when a shock, cold and neutral, shook through my muscles and left me alone beneath a sky whose stars I could never see.

I had calculated that I would slip away at dusk. I would travel only at night and lie low until the evening. This would enable me to walk quickly for the first half-hour and thereafter take advantage of the darkness, once the alarm had been given. As I was always racked with hunger, I did not contemplate leaving on an empty stomach, especially since I would not have anything to eat thereafter.

One day, there was a great commotion among the guards, who had set off at the double in various directions, all of them with their rifles. Confused and bemusing rumours of an escaped prisoner had just broken out in the camp. It was one of the tough young men who had been grinding rice when I arrived. A prisoner for more than a year, he had been given to the job of hulling and cooking the rice. My eyes would often linger on his bulging muscles, as clearly defined as if an anatomist had stripped them bare, which stood in stark contrast to the emaciated bodies of the other prisoners. We never spoke to each other. Sometimes he would bring me a piece of *bay kdang*, the crust of rice that had been hardened and burnt during cooking. The first time, I had made him smile shyly – we seldom laughed in the camp because our lungs felt constricted within their cage – by mechanically reciting an adage well known in country areas: *Bay kdang, reug kda.**

*Crust of rice, stiff penis.

The guards returned from their hunt at about one in the morning. The following day, Douch's assistants announced that they had caught him. His corpse had been left lying on the small dyke where he had fallen. No-one believed a word of it. I spent a long time imagining his return home.

Towards midday, a new prisoner arrived, accompanied by a nine-year-old girl. I was indignant that a child had been brought to this place of adults and death. Douch was sitting beneath the awning. The father wore a dark suit. He bowed as he placed his forearms at his sides to suggest the traditional *sompieh*, which his bound elbows prevented him from fully executing. His ignorance of the customs of the Khmer Rouge, who had introduced the Chinese style of shaking hands to replace the despised gesture of joining palms at chest level, said a great deal about him and his fate. Douch responded with a movement of his head, keeping his eyes lowered while reaching out to take the file the guard was holding. He flicked through it the wrong way, quickly turning over the pages with his left hand, then began again at the beginning.

The little girl bowed her head. Occasionally she would glance around, her restless eyes taking everything in. After slowly closing the file, Douch said something. I could see the man give a hint of a smile, bow once more, hesitate as he turned to his daughter, and then leave with just a brief word to her, as if he were about to come back. He passed in front of me again, accompanied by his guard, walking fairly quickly, his mind deep in a clutter of thoughts. Meanwhile, the child had been led away to one of the communal dormitories and then almost immediately transferred to the place left vacant by the old woman who had died, in the first shelter. Three other prisoners had died in the meantime, and Douch had put all the sick prisoners there. She lay curled up in a corner.

I was distraught; I could see Hélène.

The time for my bath was approaching, and I asked to be

untied quickly so that I could stop in front of the little girl lying huddled on the wooden slats. Those beside her told me that she was crying and refused to speak.

"Young lady," I ventured nonetheless, "what is your name?"

Her foot stopped moving for barely a second. It was wriggling nervously, like a cat's tail. Urged on by the guard, I went on my way, moved to tears.

She wouldn't eat, either. I spent the night thinking about her, devising ways to approach her. The very next day, I got them to give me a little hot water in my bowl and opened the tin of milk Douch had brought me. I added a little sugar, and had the sophisticated brew sent to her. At about midday, the prisoner now in the place of the tough young man who had run off signalled to me that she had not touched it.

Douch came to see me in the early afternoon to ask me further questions relating to my successive statements. I was busy writing in the hundred-page notebook with the blue ballpoint, both of which he had brought back for me. The cover of the notebook bore an eagle and advertised Eagle brand batteries, made in Vietnam. Straight away I told him how disgraceful I thought it was that a little girl should be kept here.

"But she's free," he said. "You can see that I haven't taken her prisoner."

"That's true," I said, suddenly realising that he could also have had her taken away with her father. "But all the same, she'll end up dying if she carries on not eating anything! This is no place for her, where there are only men."

"I can't help that. But she'll be much better in a few days! Children soon get used to things . . . and besides, she's found a protector here who sends her milk and sugar!"

As he said this, his face became still and expressionless. After a few moments, as if he could contain himself no longer, he snorted loudly and began to laugh. His bright eyes shone on me good-humouredly. Calmly, he continued, "You worry too much about her! In your situation, I'd be more concerned for myself. Now tell me why you don't speak English, when you spent more than a year in England?"

His change of tone caught me totally off guard. I could feel myself blushing. His about-face had surprised me at a moment when all my feelings were directed towards the child and my defences were down.

The evening before, he had returned from one of his meetings, at which my case had been discussed. Seeing my annoyed embarrassment when confronted by his question, he explained that this inconsistency in my dossier was a very serious matter and bothered him a great deal. What had occurred in England that I wished to cover up, even to the point of asserting that I did not know the language?

"But I've got nothing to hide! I know what you're referring to. If I said then that I didn't speak English, it's because we're in Cambodia! And because it's the language of the Americans! And because I'm French! I also wanted to convince the Khmer Kraum comrade that his persistence in suspecting me of being a CIA agent was all the more unfounded since I did not speak English!"

" 'Convince'? So you're guilty of lying and you admit it! Did you take these people for fools? I find your manner very offhand. What were you doing in England? Who was paying you?"

"I was a potter. I learned pottery at the same time as I learned the language. One day my sister telephoned to inform me that my father was ill, and I returned home immediately to be with him when he breathed his last. Do you know that a potter is like a god? He uses water, clay, fire; and during the firing he opens the kiln to allow air in . . . I tell you this because in the Khmer texts those four elements are described as the basis of the Creation at the beginning of the world. Definitions like this are part of the originality of the religion of Buddha in Cambodia. Last time, you wanted examples . . . well, in England, I was already mulling over ideas such as these! As for the CIA . . . now, if it's proof you're after, I'm doomed! I'll never be able to supply you with any."

My replies confused him. Although they didn't satisfy him, I delivered them in such a way that he did not doubt their frankness. The peculiarities of my character, my way of thinking and my reactions made him aware that there was another way of living and existing, one very different from his own, which seemed to appeal to him. I was aware that I rarely provided him with arguments he could make use of, but I nevertheless placed my fate squarely in his hands. I made my being freed depend directly upon him, and I told him so: "If you don't believe me . . . who will?"

In fact, Douch was the only card I had to play, and somehow I trusted him. Of course he would have me killed without hesitation if the order came, inventing any pretext (which I would have believed) to lure me to the place of horror, but only after genuinely trying to save my life. This terrible man was not duplicitous; all he had were principles and convictions. And if that hypothesis were true, then I had an ally.

As was usual at that season, evening fell quickly and early; the setting sun tinted the clouds and I was bathed in golden light as its fire descended. Occasionally, a blinding ray would slip through the vaulted canopy, then disappear, or reappear, as it moved.

I was going to the river a little earlier, for the water was getting cold. The little girl had sat up, still refusing to eat or drink. She looked at me, but there was not a flicker on her face when I stopped to say a few words to her. She was looking through me, so I moved my body left and right, attempting without success to catch her eye. But I raised a grudging smile, which she quickly wiped away, rubbing her nose on the back of her hand and turning her back on me.

The long weeks I had already spent in the camp had introduced a certain familiarity into my relationship with the young guards, whom I now referred to as "young comrades". This often moved them to be less attentive to my demands, but also to their supervision of me. When the occasion presented itself, this laxness encouraged me to explore the grounds and sometimes venture further than I should. The only instruction that the guards had been given was to keep me from entering the central area, where the four shelters were situated, three of which contained the fifty or more prisoners. I would cast a glance at them as I went to the river, but I never went near them. Above all, I was forbidden to communicate with my two companions.

We were not, in any case, allowed to speak. This rule was not entirely respected. It did, however, limit our exchanges to a few words, spoken hurriedly, in a low voice, and without showing it. So I knew practically nothing about what went on in the camp itself. My world was restricted to the entrance gate, marked out by a clump of licuala; to the area around the fire and those who tended it all day long; to the first of the shelters, which I could partially see, and which I walked past when I went for a bath; and to what I could see of the other shelters and the guards' lodgings when I returned from the river. From my post, my view of the guards was blocked, except when Douch moved his table forward, by two enormous clusters of tangled tubes of bamboo, the summit of which was lost among the canopy of branches. Between the bamboos, where they pushed up the soil, rose the great trunk of a *chhlik* (*Terminalia alata*), its top disappearing from my view above the vault of the foliage. Thép had been my only "informer", and thanks to him I had been able to exchange bits of news with Lay and Son, who were still chained up and kept apart. Since his death, I had had virtually no contact with anyone. I spoke only to Douch, the hens and to myself.

Having reached the river, I crossed over to see whether there was any way to get to the undergrowth which, when the day came, would allow me to disappear without groping around dangerously.

Venturing eastwards, I passed the foul-smelling place where those who looked after the shelter emptied their tubes of urine, and came to a hut in good repair, with a thatched roof covered in leaves. The floor inside had been carefully swept. Though quite clearly it was used, it was now empty. I noticed a solid bamboo beam which divided the room six feet above the floor. It was threaded with strong rattan straps that could slide along its length. I quickly retraced my steps, not understanding what this hut could be used for.

Once I had bathed, I rejoined my guard and walked back past the child, stopping once again.

"Young lady," I asked, somewhat playfully, "what's your name? I've put aside some warm milk for you. Would you like some? Now? How about it, eh? Come on, I'll make a bowl for you!"

She kept her head down and said nothing, but I knew that silence, especially in children, can indicate assent. Without hesitating, I jumped at this possible opportunity to see her spirits revive a little.

Her touching face sank back into the sadness of her eyes. She had beautiful, almost blue lips, with a furrow in the middle that made the corners of her mouth stand out and accentuated its rim. The dark skin of her neck was dotted with sore patches. Not knowing her name, I continued to call her *neang*, "young lady", refusing to use the word *neari*, the one the Khmer Rouge wanted to introduce.

With the assistance of the young guard who was absent-mindedly observing my activity, I obtained some hot water, and the precious concoction was taken to her. When the empty bowl was returned to me, I experienced a satisfaction that went far beyond the comfort of knowing that the little girl had agreed to take sustenance: my efforts had had something to do with her revival.

"Well, well, comrade!" said the prisoner who had brought back the bowl to me. "You succeeded. She drank it all! *Pouttho*, you'll earn a lot of credit for that!"

That same evening, Douch came and mused sarcastically on my new role of "adoptive father" and on this resurrection for which I had striven so hard, as if my own survival were at stake. But he did agree, without a word being spoken, to bring me another can of milk on his next excursion. All night I felt impatient to see the girl again, and as soon as morning came I arranged for another bowl to be handed to her, which she once more accepted. During the day, I even obtained some leftover rice, which I sprinkled with sugar for her. She ate it all.

The child gradually grew bolder, but she would not speak. I watched her from a distance as she jumped about, then stopped, landing smoothly on her heels, or drawing on the ground, without daring to leave her shelter. In the evening I took her the milk myself. When I spoke to her, she looked away, but she didn't withdraw. One fine day, she made her way over in my direction, gradually and hesitantly, stopping every few feet. I pretended not to take any notice of her, so that she wouldn't run away. She was standing beside me, turning around; eventually she sat down. Gradually, she began to look at what I was doing. I carried on writing, not letting her see that her presence occupied all my attention. Bending over the notebook, she watched the marks my hand was forming on the paper, then sat up straight whenever I stopped. When I felt her beside me like this, I was filled with renewed vitality, as if the flame of life that now burned in her little body once again had dispersed new daylight across the esplanade that lay between us, over the camp and the forest all around me. She drank her milk and sometimes came to eat her meal beside me. Even Poulette, who ordinarily fled like a mad creature whenever anyone approached, seemed not to be frightened of her. When I was unchained at the end of the day, she followed me as far as the river before returning to her shelter to sleep. In the morning, very early, she was back again. The sight of this child under my protection filled me with immense courage.

After a few days, she was invited to participate in maintenance jobs, working under one of the leaders, a reserved young man about twenty years old whom we saw very seldom. She took part in the self-reproach sessions, which began with singing. Speechless as ever and looking lonely, she joined in without thinking, clapping her hands along with the others. The small community of young peasants in charge of us was opening up to her.

The soft noises of the camp floated on the evening air as my guard mechanically locked the chain that gripped my foot. I changed legs each time, making sure that my heel bulged so that the ring should have some play. My little protégée arrived, as she sometimes liked to do, at dusk. I saw her approaching, floating along like a butterfly, her *krama* billowing in the light of a bright patch of sky. She squatted down, and her hand sought my drawn-up leg. Her delicate forefinger – I can still remember its transparent, fragile nail – slipped easily beneath the iron links, which she solemnly lifted to gauge the tightness. The touch of this finger on my bruised skin did me good. Moved by her concern, I quickly did my best to minimise the pain caused by the irons around my ankles by nodding my head in a gesture of denial and smiling reassurance.

She skipped away and returned with a bunch of keys in her hand. I looked at her in astonishment. She undid the padlock and, with some difficulty, carefully retightened the chain.

# 6

Douch had left the camp early in the morning. The sky was already bright. I had been awake for a long time in an indescribable state of excitement. The previous day, he had warned me that today's meeting would be important. I kept turning his words over in my mind. I had immediately detected an unusual gravity in his voice, a certain strain, mingled with a trace of insistence, as if he were trying to tell me something. The following day, however, I no longer knew how to interpret this inflection; I even wondered whether it was a product of my imagination.

As the weeks went by, Douch's regular departures had instilled such expectations in me that, without fully realising it, I began to yearn passionately for the moment when a verdict – even a death sentence – would finally be delivered. A mixture of doubt and impatience made me fear that I could not hold out much longer without attempting to break free. In any case, Christmas was coming and I had determined to escape in January, the moment an opportunity arose. Douch must have dreaded some outburst on my part, and perhaps this is why he had somewhat dramatised his leaving on this occasion, only to keep me on tenterhooks a little longer. I didn't know whether he was really convinced of my innocence; but, for the sake of all the revolutionary principles in which he invested so much trust, he had to prove his genuine belief in justice. My running away, in these circumstances, would expose my guilt and wreck all his efforts. My accusers would not fail to take him to task for his error of judgement. I suddenly realised what a huge risk he had taken by gambling on my innocence. But far more than his affection for me, what betrayed his resolve was his passionate pursuit of moral rectitude, something rather like a quest for the absolute. Douch was one of those pure, fervent idealists who yearned above all for truth. In the course of our conversations, he had told me about his past as an intellectual.

As a pupil at the Sisowath *lycée*, he had, in 1959, come second in the *baccalauréat* in mathematics, a subject in which he excelled and which he had taught afterwards for several years at Kompong Thom – the best years of his life, he recalled – before being appointed to the Phnom Penh Pedagogical Institute in 1964. After that, he had been transferred to the Kompong Cham *lycée*, where he had stayed until his brutal arrest – Sihanouk's police beat him about the head – for engaging in Communist activities. The amnesty of 1970, which Lon Nol had granted to all political prisoners, enabled him to make his way to the cover of the Cardamomes.

I brooded over these recollections throughout the morning, sometimes doubting that my fate could really be settled that same day, and at other times convinced that an outcome was near. The confidence with which Douch had addressed me could mean that he was at last persuaded of my innocence and had reasonable hopes for a favourable verdict. But it could just as well denote the solemnity of the day on which my sentence would be delivered.

The more the hours went by, the more unbearable my anguish became. The intense, clammy heat beneath the bamboo, which you could see glistening as if under a glass dome, made my chest heave and pant. None of my usual strategies for calming myself – standing back to reflect on my misfortune, comparing my own situation to that of the other prisoners, making light of my own weaknesses – were of any use. I felt crushed by the gravity of what was at stake. I was suffocating; I had to hold back cries of fear. The tenseness grew so strong that I had to bend my body backwards, wincing with the effort, to wring out the terror that was knotting my entrails.

Their commander's continual absences had instilled a rather offhand manner among the guards – the younger ones especially – that I could have exploited to make my escape. One of them would sometimes slip away secretly, which made me think that his home was not far and that there might be a sort of scattered forest settlement – not quite a village – nearby, which I should take account of in my planning.

The sun was already high in the sky; a grid of rays fell on the ground in myriad petals of light that spread the heat. Like an obsession, Hélène's face kept recurring in my mind. I decided to take advantage of the general slackness to have myself untethered a bit earlier than usual and to proceed to the first phase of my escape.

The guard I summoned refused my request. He walked away, ignoring me. I began shouting. One of the younger supervisors, the one who had taken the "adopted child" under his wing, practically ran towards me, followed by the disgruntled guard, who was coming back to justify himself. The hens scuttled off as they arrived. Once again I expressed my wish to go to the river; seeing him hesitate, I became more threatening. At last he agreed to unchain me, but in the presence of two guards, one of whom was armed with a Kalashnikov. Not wanting to arouse suspicions by walking across the camp wearing my flip-flops, I had concealed them in my shirt, which was rolled up in a ball ready to be washed, and carried the bundle with me. When I got there, I hid them in a bush. That way they were within my reach if, on Douch's return, I did decide to escape.

As I came out of the water, I noticed one of the prisoners, a man I had passed before without ever exchanging looks, sitting against the corner pillar of the second shelter. My guards were resting in the shade, so I went over to him. He was carefully carving a length of rattan.

"Who's this stick for?" I asked on my way past. "Who are you going to beat with it?"

"Comrade!" he said, nodding and closing his eyes to refute the accusation. "Do you think I'm the one who does the beating?"

My question, asked in jest, out of the blue, had been totally innocent. But I understood from his reaction that I had struck a nerve; this was something I did not suspect existed, something one could not joke about. In my embarrassment, I tried to clarify his allusion by questioning him again, this time seriously: "Who does do the beating, if it's not you?"

He gently applied the knife to the stick, slicing off very fine slivers that coiled like hairs as they fell on to him. The tool, which had a long, curved handle tucked under his arm, stopped moving when he encountered a knot; with his left hand he drew the stick across the blade. Above his head, I had a view of twenty motion- less feet in a row. At closer range, you could hear the sounds of coughing, throats being cleared and constant creaking from behind the partition. Without replying he let me leave.

Back at my spot, I looked straight ahead, not allowing my gaze to alight on anything, and spent the rest of the day watching for Douch's return. Poulette and Cocotte came to keep me silent company.

The one who did the beating must have been his principal assistant, that sullen, uncouth man I disliked. Yet the possibility of corporal punishment, something that evidently dangled over our heads, was never mentioned. Once again, nothing was seen, nothing was heard. No prisoner dared refer to it. Just as this sinister secret was beginning to arouse my curiosity, I remembered the empty cabin I had visited on the far side of the river. I immediately understood the purpose of those straps on the beam: the victims' wrists were attached to them. The interrogations must therefore take place in the hut. As I had heard, the accused were beaten on their sides with a rattan stick. All traces could then be easily covered up by shirts.

I saw Douch coming along the path. He normally never returned so early, and this variation in the routine put me off straight away. I stood up on trembling legs. The asymmetric features that characterised his flat, noseless Chinese face had merged frighteningly into his haggard complexion. Was it still his extreme fatigue? He walked slowly; the bicycle creaked beside him. Instead of continuing along the bend that skirted my post, as he would do when he didn't wish to speak, he changed course to pass only a few metres from me. I vainly tried to catch his eye. The blood throbbed powerfully all through my body; I could feel the rhythm accelerating to the tips of my fingers.

Douch laid down his bicycle on the rhizomes which had come up with the rains; some of them had already managed to forge a path skywards through the tangle of stems. Twilight, coming from the open space above the shelters, lit up the bamboo canopy. Douch stayed with the guards for a long time, then came out again, carrying his empty plate. I watched him move with assurance, his gestures like those of an actor who performs without heeding the audience's gaze. His ration of soup had been left in the saucepan over an extinguished flame. Standing in front of the fire, he turned around and his eyes caught mine. He walked steadily towards me without lowering his eyes. Then I heard his voice, enunciating every syllable, suddenly cutting like steel: "You have been exposed! Your calculations have been totally thwarted!"

For a moment, I remained clinging to the end of his sentence, not immediately noticing that he had spoken in French. My legs gave way. I sank to my knees.

Seeing my reaction, Douch was taken aback and rushed over, grabbing me by the shoulders. The muscles in my body had relaxed; at the same time my spirit had slumped and I was unable to react. The expression on his face had entirely changed. He now wore a look between surprise and embarrassment. His mouth broke into a laugh, and he gazed at me. "But of course not . . . did you believe me? Come on, it was a joke! You're going to be set free."

He helped me to my feet, but I fell again, trembling all over. Nervous twitches forced my eyes shut and I could neither give vent to my tears nor control the rise of convulsive gasps. I was exhausted. I freed myself from his grasp and turned my back to him so that I could compose myself.

"That's it, you're free," he repeated behind me. "It has not been easy! You'll be home for Christmas."

Moving slowly, I got to my feet. I was incredulous. "If it's true, prove it! Have me unchained!" I exclaimed as I turned round.

His little game had so vexed me that I could neither express my delight nor show him my gratitude. Still shocked, I persisted in a sort of temperamental mistrust as a riposte to the humiliation I had endured. Douch hastily called for a guard to open the padlock. I insisted that he take the chain away.

"I also want the belongings that were taken from me," I said resolutely.

"I'll give them to you," he said. "We have them."

"If I am free, it's because the Angkar has acknowledged my innocence. In that case, Lay and Son should also be released!"

He frowned and did not reply immediately.

"It's all three of us or none!" I added without pausing.

He looked up at me. He folded his arms behind his back, then turned around, walked away, did an about-face and began to speak. Momentarily disconcerted by his own awkwardness, he managed to pull himself together.

"They will be set free on site. They're lucky to be in the free zone. It would make no sense to send them back to the enemy. The revolution needs them here."

"But all they did was follow me!" I replied, deliberately not understanding. "It's because of me that they're separated from their families. And now you're expecting me to go back by myself? Lay is not merely a colleague. He's my friend. I can't abandon him. Or Son, either! After shackling me, do you now want to shame me? How could you — "

Douch interrupted me, almost angrily. I realised that I had gone too far.

"They're Khmers! This is their country. You're a foreigner. So it's normal that they remain and you leave! Your obstinacy is blinding you, and you think only of yourself. Don't forget that we're at war. There's nothing more to be said."

Douch walked away. Even though it was obviously not up to me to stay or go, I would have preferred him to have displayed still greater resolve, even to have made some threats. For my confusion was getting the better of me, and at the same time, deep down, I could feel my confident protests weakening. I did not know how to take responsibility for my two companions, and wished I could be exonerated from the burden by force.

Dispirited and drained of all pride, I caught up with Douch and asked him in a soft, almost cowardly tone for permission to go and talk with them, adding, with the little courage left to me, "Give the order for them to be unshackled too; it's the least you can do."

Douch agreed but continued on his way. He ordered the guards accompanying him to go and remove their shackles. With a few strides, I was in the middle of the central pathway. A sudden chill filled the evening air. Darkness fell over the shelters, concealing the camp beneath a sombre vault. Above me, the stars, which I could see for the first time, twinkled in the clear night air. Freed from my chains, I moved among the cabins with an awkward, almost heavy gait. The noises of the forest impinged on my consciousness with a new vividness. The grating of the cicadas would build up to a violent, orgasmic peak, then stop completely, resulting in an arresting silence. In the place where I thought I had seen them a few days earlier, I searched for my companions among the sleeping bodies. One of the guards approached. Several prisoners raised themselves up on their elbows. I saw Lay and Son sitting in front of me.

"If what Douch has just told me is true, I will soon be free to go home. Both of you, too, will also be set free! But he says that you cannot leave with me, that you must stay here. Free, but here – " I said without pausing, wanting to be rid of this oppressive burden and to lay all my cards on the table.

Standing beside me, the guard was watching them and listening to me. I had not yet finished speaking when Douch arrived, casting a weak beam of light before him. He was trying out a new pocket torch, which he had brought back from his meeting. In the shifting light, I could see a bat silently fluttering about. The guard following him hoisted himself up on to the slats to remove the padlock from the long rail; the prisoners slid it along until my companions' shackles were released. Douch addressed Son in a very solemn tone: "Bizot has asked that Comrade Lay should leave with him and that you, on the other hand, should remain a prisoner here. What do you think of that?"

Astounded, I turned and looked at Douch. Realising that he was joking, I began to smile in order to defuse the awkwardness. His little game was all the more vicious since it hinted at the levels of relationship I had with each of them, which Douch had understood to be different. I had recruited Son only a few months before, whereas my friendship for Lay was deep and went back more than five years. The Khmer Rouge leader continued his enquiries, still speaking with the same seriousness but this time addressing Lay: "What do you think? Comrade Lay, tell me: are you prepared to leave your colleague?"

Lay, embarrassed but having sensed the treachery beneath the intended mockery, smiled shyly and shook his head, then respectfully confessed that he did not believe that this proposal had come from me.

"And you, Comrade Son," asked Douch, "do you not believe it either?"

Son was massaging his calves nervously. In the darkness I could see the enamel of his teeth and his big eyes. His hesitant reply pained me cruelly.

"Yes," he declared, "I think it's possible."

"Ah!" Douch went on, turning towards me. "At least there's one who believes me."

Then he went away laughing silently.

Having reached his billet, where several candles were flickering, causing the faces of the guards settled in their hammocks to stand out in the darkness, I could see him turn in my direction. One of them came back to find me. I left Lay and Son behind, though not before having tried to explain his bad joke by arguing that he had a morbid sense of humour.

"Here," he said to me, "here are your things."

He handed me a transparent plastic bag containing the various possessions that I had had on me at the moment of my arrest: my Vietnamese safe conduct pass; my keys; an entry card to Potchentong airport; and a few riels, which represented a considerable sum of money here.

"And my watch?"

In remote parts of the country, a watch with a strap, especially one of the Orient brand, is probably the rarest and most prized of objects. Mine, which was waterproof and made in Switzerland, was also considered a very valuable item. Douch claimed it had not been put into the bag when I arrived and that he'd never had it. But as he answered me, he did not attempt to conceal his embarrassment. Seeing that this was not just a minor detail for him and that he must know something, I did not hesitate to insist that the memento of my father be returned to me.

"I want the watch!" I said, staring into his eyes.

He said nothing, shaking his head, ostensibly to exonerate himself, evidently embarrassed again, yet not wishing to name anyone.

"I don't know," he replied. "I'll see about it tomorrow."

As long as a single thing was missing, I refused to take the bag. In my position, such intransigence was somewhat ridiculous and inopportune. Nevertheless, I felt it was in keeping with the reaction Douch expected of me. Theft was an anti-revolutionary act par excellence. More than anything else in the world, he yearned to give a pure, upright image of the Khmer resistance. Above all, he dreaded the idea that his patriotic comrades could be mistaken for common gangsters. We were beginning to know each other well, and because of this growing understanding I knew what his embarrassment signified: in it I saw, once again, the mark of a man of principle – even if his face did not at all fit with the deviousness he had shown in the previous incident.

I returned to my spot in the darkness. The hens were already roosting. The log that had been brought in my absence was still burning; I extinguished the flames with the aid of a charred stick, causing sparks to fly up and fall on to the cold ground. Released from the chains, I squatted down, feeling my chain-free ankles beneath me, and remained there, motionless, for a long time, baffled and anxious. If I did escape from this ordeal, I would never be the same. It seemed to me that I had gone to the deepest part of my pain, as one taking refuge hides himself away. I saw life from another viewpoint, the perspective of a man emerging from a cave where he has been huddled for months. Existence would henceforward amount to little, and I found this limiting of my concerns extremely soothing. When I thought of the commotion of my previous existence, it only reminded me of its futility and discomfort. I felt that I was refocusing on the essential, and that the new life waiting for me would be simple and easy, now that I was armed against all its artifice. I had only three plans, and just thinking about them made me bristle with impatience: to live peacefully at Hélène's mother's side; to ride my motorbike down quiet tracks; to resume my research into Khmer Buddhism.

I shivered as I put on my clothes and wrapped my head in my *krama*. I folded the soldier's magic scarf over my stomach to ward off the cold. Lying beside the embers, I could feel my tight muscles exposed to the forest air transmitting a tiresome pain all down my back. I amused myself by letting my jaws tremble; suddenly, they froze as the hoot of a barn owl rang through the night. For an instant, its grating cries blotted out the rippling sound of the bamboo trees, then merged into the distant, intermittent thrum of insects. Then the deafening noise of cicadas announced that morning had come: dawn was already tinting the horizon a shade of purple; I must have fallen into a light and restless sleep.

Douch had left very early. I went to find Lay and Son, who were standing in front of their shelter, dazed by the sun, which bathed them in its gentle heat. Its rays, now quite high, hit in two places the uneven tops of the greenery surrounding the camp to the north. The *irvingia* lit its new-grown purple tufts in the day's first heat, and thousands of drumming insects came alive in each of them. A multitude of shrill sounds shook the cold air that had gathered in the night. Vast and luminous, the sky opened out above the heads of my two companions.

Chained to their bars, the prisoners were stirring on the slats. They were getting ready for the first job of the day: the mass urination. Everybody got to his feet, and the bamboo tubes were passed along and quickly filled. In the mornings, five or six were needed for each shelter. Those in charge would then empty and rinse them in the river.

The first part of the prisoners you could see was their feet: large, with toes as slender as fingers. The soles were yellow and shiny and slightly thickened, like leather that has been worked by a saddler. Next, you noticed their eyes, hollowed out of the depths of their faces and immersed in incurable grief. Then the emaciated bodies, dressed in the clothes they had worn since their first day: black pyjamas mostly, grey from wear and torn at the knees and elbows.

None of the inmates crammed into the three shelters before us appeared to be in pain, despite their emaciation; their skin held tight to their ribs. At the first sign of ill health, they were transferred to the sick bay, opposite the guards' quarters, where most died unattended. With the appearance of the first symptoms, the wretched creatures, already in a state of depression, would refuse sustenance. Their bodies, exhausted by the cold nights, would quickly be destroyed, whereas a healthy, well-fed man would scarcely have suffered. Stretched out alongside the others, they would assume the mask of illness, devoid of any hope of being cured.

However, I remember the death of one particular prisoner, which was drawn out over several months. He was a large man, massively built, who already appeared to be totally exhausted when I arrived. Thép told me that he still drank a little but would take nothing else. His resistance to death became impressive, particularly since he spent all his time lying on his back, still as a statue, with his rigid fingers crossed over his chest, already blue with black nails which went on growing. The spectre always replied in a firm voice whenever a question was put to him. His countenance, which was gaunt but had softened and lost its virility, had earned him a fruitless celebrity in the camp, as well as the nickname "grandmother". A game was regularly played: checking whether he was dead. Every morning, his neighbours or the guards would call out to him. He was careful not to say a word, leaving them wondering for a while, before opening his scrawny mouth and raising the glimmer of a smile. The bets remained open until just before Christmas, and I myself saw his body, which the passage of death had not altered in any way.

Douch returned shortly after the meal, which I had the

transient pleasure of sharing with my companions. We had gone to eat our rice at the end of the pathway, seated against the long horizontal beam of the pounder which was built on the reservation enclosing the western edge of the camp. To operate it, several men had to push down on the beam with their legs to create a counterbalance to the pestle, which was attached to the opposite end. They would then release it simultaneously into the bottom of the mortar, which was filled to half its depth with paddy.

As soon as he arrived, he looked for me and walked towards us; then, with a wave of his hand, he invited me to follow him. Clearly impatient to please me, he took my watch out of his pocket and held it by the strap for a few moments, tapping it with his fingertip, making as if to give it to me before jerking it away.

"Ah, ah!" he said with a laugh. "Ta Mok is not pleased! I think he wanted you dead just so he could keep your watch. He's been wearing it ever since your arrest and didn't want to give it back."

When I heard this name, I recalled the taciturn officer into whose hands I had been delivered the day after my public trial. The guard, a peasant with whom I had exchanged a few words and who did not often have the opportunity to talk to a Frenchman, had rather timorously disclosed the name given to the master of the villages in that region. It was he who had given instructions to keep me chained all day long to the central pillar of a large, tall wooden house in a village along the road leading to the camp.

Douch finally slipped the precious object into the bag containing my belongings and, with a satisfied expression, handed everything back to me.

"Thank you," I said politely. "Now what is the next step? When do I leave?"

"Tomorrow. You'll leave the camp tomorrow. In the morning, I'll go and make the final preparations for your departure."

I returned to my position and gazed thoughtfully at the post to which I had been chained for so long. The constant friction of the metal rings had left a few marks on the wooden cylinder. The components were basic, the construction crude, the pieces of wooden partitioning poorly cut, and the whole thing void of any interest. The thick fabric of the sacks, which were still there, gave off an acrid smell of jute. Staring at it, I could suddenly feel the extent of the strange links that bound me to this spot, where my suffering had found shelter. And I realised that this attachment was meaningful only to me, because I was the only one to have given it life, and that as far as others were concerned there was no visible basis for it.

The same is true of the temples of Angkor, where every stone has a story to tell that only the spirits can hear; and of the beds at Tuol Sleng, which I would one day see as a tourist passing through Phnom Penh: they no longer showed any trace of the pieces of lacerated flesh which had stuck grimly to the metal.

And while I was stooping over the bleached bamboo, there came the piercing cry of an oriole from out of the distant undergrowth.

I took the watch and put it on my wrist, imagining the Khmer Rouge leader who had worn it all this time. What ghastly scenes had it witnessed? What invisible stories did it conceal?

I walked over to the river, feeling the extraordinary presence of the piece of jewellery on my arm. The guards taunted me about the fine object gleaming on my wrist, as beautiful, they asserted, as a rich Chinese businessman's. When I emerged from the water, I discreetly recovered my flip-flops from the bush where I had hidden them. I retraced my steps and went to find Lay and Son. They had not washed since arriving three months before, except at the very beginning, when it was still raining and they had used the rainwater gathered in the bamboo tubes from the shelters. I encouraged them to bathe in the river and, seeing them hesitate, went myself to find a guard to give them permission.

I walked up the path as far as the reservation that immediately abutted the forest: the well-spaced trees, searching for light as if from the bottom of a well, rose out of the thick undergrowth; here and there, the emerald plumes of an arborescent cycad shone through. Now and again, the lonely buzz of an insect hidden in an enormous clump of pandanus produced a slow, deep sound that seemed to emerge from a reed pipe. Everywhere, the air was echoing with sounds, and the rhythmic flow that reached my consciousness was so scrambled that I could no longer distinguish individual notes: the *croa-croa* of furious soloists, the screech of a string ensemble, the one-note song of a choir in unison, the strange, dull twang of a jew's harp, the dominant chords of duettists puffing out their white goitres, the symphonic croaking of an orchestra further away. Deafened by these dissonant harmonies, I leaned on the massive arm of the foot-operated pestle. The camp purred in the evening light. I stretched my aching body along the whole length of the long beam, with one hand beneath the nape of my neck and my feet crossed; by positioning my hips and shifting my shoulder blades, I was able to balance myself. The recumbent crescent moon emerged from behind a cloud . . . I dozed off.

The colours of the setting sun hovered over Angkor, and Hélène's hair was flying about in the wind. Clinging to the motorbike's handlebars and wedged between my arms, she sat astride the petrol tank. The continuous humming of the insects blotted out the noise of the engine. Flitting softly and hurriedly, bats were feasting on the abundance of dragonflies in the mild evening air. We were passing through the Gate of the Elephants. To reach our village more quickly, I took a short cut, which ran between some enormous, hundred-year-old dipterocarps. The motorbike plunged noiselessly into the warm steaminess of the undergrowth. Rippling gusts of air beat at my ears and puffed out the back of my shirt. We were passing alongside the small tobacco and banana plantation tended by the family of a keeper at the Bayon temple. As we did every evening, we set out from the

Gate of the Dead and made our way to the "small circuit", just before the stone bridge. Here a group of macaques lingered by the roadside, frolicking among the trees at the forest's edge. To bar the way to their females, who were on heat, the large male monkeys snarled and bared their teeth, pretending to follow us. Hélène's silvery laugh rang out. She proffered her hand as we passed, stroking the little creatures clinging to their mothers . . . My chest heaved with unalloyed happiness. We knew we were almost there: from the dark dome of the great silk-cotton trees (*tetrameles*) clinging on to the stones of Ta Prohm with their aerial roots, we could hear the same shrill whistle of the Mandarin mynah birds that could be heard from the village. Hélène joined in with little bird noises and rocked backwards and forwards, as though to hasten our progress.

Short, sharp calls, spoken in a loud voice, registered on my consciousness. Without stirring from the perch my body had settled into, I let my mind, still engulfed in sleep, grow gradually more vigilant. When I opened my eyes, guards were rushing about in every direction. Three of them, rifles in hand, were running towards the river. Douch was at the far end of the camp; I could see him crossing a patch of sunlight, hurrying back, followed closely by his adjutant. Emerging from behind the shelters, one of the sentries excitedly shouted at the officers who were approaching him, "No! He's not there either!"

Douch disappeared into the guards' quarters.

Intoxicated by the scent of Hélène's hair and the blonde curls I could still feel on my face, I kept my eyes half closed, observing the tumult — with no particular curiousity — until I realised that it was me they were searching for. Not seeing me anywhere, the Khmers Rouges thought that I had taken the opportunity of my newly gained freedom to escape. I could picture Douch kicking himself for not having been more suspicious. Delighted and taking full advantage of this misjudgement — the situation was all the more comical for being plausible — I decided to play a trick and remain completely still upon my beam, which had become an excellent hiding place, while pretending to be in a deep sleep. Detached from the commotion in the camp and the confused noises I could hear, I began to laugh quietly to myself.

All the armed men in the camp had set off in pursuit of me. Returning empty-handed, one of them was getting ready to dash off into the forest again when he came to a sudden halt near the pounder: he had discovered me. I heard his breath stop, then the sound of his rubber soles on the ground. He gazed at me for a few moments and then retreated without saying a word. Through my half-closed eyes, I could now see Douch arriving. He slowed his pace as he drew near and stopped short. Hesitating, he turned around; then he finally came over and, standing on tiptoe, leaned with his elbows on one of the props supporting the arm on which I was lying. His voice broke the silence: "Comrade, was it the dusk that caused you to fall asleep?"

I opened my eyes wide, feigning astonishment. "What's going on?" I asked. "I thought I heard someone calling."

With an air of surprise, Douch covered up smoothly. "No," he said. "Could it have been the noise of the bullfrogs?"

I raised myself and sat on the beam, my legs dangling above the ground. I glanced at the Khmer Rouge, who was looking at me with an uninvolved air. It had just been my turn to manipulate him and cause him to lie.

I drew keen satisfaction from this little game. And with this enjoyment, it occurred to me that in his place, I, too, would have had what it takes to be a good torturer.

# 7

It had been a bad night. I had been very cold. In my dreams, the promise of freedom that I had been given was a decoy to lead me more easily to my death. The removal of my companions' shackles was not definitive; it was all part of an act. At the moment of my departure, I had seen Lay in tears; the prisoners, sitting up on their slats, all had sinister expressions on their faces, making me realise that my last moment had come. I awoke with a jolt, horribly upset.

As the sun was rising, I walked towards the main pathway, wrapped in my *krama*, to soak up the warmth of its early rays. I entered this part of the camp reluctantly, for the proximity of the prone bodies of the prisoners filled me with an anxiety I preferred to avoid. Douch was at his desk.

"Comrade," I asked in surprise, "weren't you meant to be setting off this morning?"

"I don't have a bicycle!" he replied, pretty cross. "I've detailed someone to look for it."

I continued on my way without answering, constructing various hypotheses about the disappearance of the bicycle, thereby serving only to increase my suspicion. At the place where the principal paths crossed, I encountered the little girl, who no longer came to see me. It was as if she did not dare to look at me any more. The child seemed to hate me now, as if I were an enemy.

I noticed that Lay and Son were with the prisoner who had not wanted to speak to me the other day, when I had seen him carving a stick. I went up to them and asked if they had heard anything about the bicycle. It was rumoured that one of the guards had borrowed it the night before – without permission – to visit his home and that he had not yet returned. Unable to verify whether I was being manipulated or whether I should believe this unlikely story, which was postponing my liberation and which – who knows – could put everything into jeopardy, I felt myself growing anxious and my mind falling apart with nervous exhaustion. Dejected, I went and sat down by myself beside the fast-flowing river, covered still in a veil of mist.

In the early afternoon Douch came to join me; this set the hens, nearby beneath the bamboo trees, squawking. At that hour, I liked to stretch out on the ground and half doze, listening to the harsh music of the cicadas.

"No-one can find the bike," he said. "It's too late now, in any case. We'll have to wait until tomorrow."

"Are you sure you'll have it in time, at least?" I asked, in a tone full of bitterness.

He glared at my sallow face. Tense and strained, the muscles in my forehead pulled my eyebrows into such a painful frown that the Khmer Rouge looked on in amused sadness. The way he gazed at me froze my face into a brazen expression which shamed me. Tears welled up in my eyes. I was so confused that I felt as though I were being tossed around like some shipwrecked sailor.

"*At oy té!*" he said in a tone that was meant to sound protective. "If not, we'll spend Christmas together. Ah! I mustn't forget to give you back your notebook. I finished reading it yesterday evening. You can take it with you."

I wish I had asked him questions to find out what he had made of it. His precise questions about Buddhism, with which he had plagued me for months, had forced me to clarify my ideas, so much so that the answers I had managed to extract from myself, which I had begun to put down in writing, would change the direction of my future research. But this was not the time to discuss it.

Deep in thought, I walked a little way with him, then continued on my own. I decided to leave the money I had on me to Lay and Son. But they were worried that my gesture might be misinterpreted to their disadvantage by the Khmer Rouge. Lay suggested that it might be better to give it to the Angkar. In any case, he assured me, the only thing he wished to buy did not exist here: pork fat. He wanted to eat the red pork that only the Chinese from Phnom Penh know how to prepare: sliced on a block with great, rhythmical sweeps of a cleaver held at arm's length, with morsels that contain, between the lean part of the meat and the crackling rind, a large strip of opal-coloured fat of the kind he dreamed about. This gave me an idea: before I left, I would pay for a farewell meal. I immediately went to see Douch to make the request.

"Comrade, I would like to make a gesture to the community before I leave. With my remaining money, could I buy a meal for all the prisoners: chicken, papaya, aubergines, tea?"

Douch lowered his eyes and said nothing; then he stood up, in his usual way, and paced about. "I don't know if it's possible," he said. "We'll see about it tomorrow."

"Tomorrow?" I repeated. "But I have to leave tomorrow! Everything has to be bought straight away! Comrade, do me this favour. I came here as an enemy; don't let me leave like a thief. Besides, it's Christmas . . ."

The face of the man in charge of the camp froze. I realised that every one of my demands put obstacles in his path. He eventually turned to the soldiers standing near us and questioned them collectively about the possibilities of finding what was required in time. His gaze fell upon young Miet.

"Comrade Miet," he called out to him, "would your mother have enough chickens? We would need – "

"Thirteen," I interjected confidently. "I've counted: forty-three prisoners and eight grandfathers, that makes fifty-one; if we have one chicken between four, that makes thirteen."

Without appearing in any way disconcerted by my ready answer, Douch addressed young Miet again: "Comrade, go and ask your mother if she can manage this."

"May I accompany him?" I asked. "Somebody will have to pay, and I'm the one with the money."

I did not want to miss this unexpected opportunity to leave the camp. To my surprise, and without any prevarication, Douch nodded his assent. I immediately set off behind the young guard.

As we left, we forded the river. Miet took the very same footpath that I had planned to follow for my escape. We crossed the thickly forested area that, as I already knew, surrounded the bamboo groves and the shelters, and emerged into what my friend Jean Boulbet had explained was a "mixed forest", with overlapping varieties of plants that grew under the natural cover. In front of us stretched a sort of savannah covered unevenly with shrubs, with a thick carpet of leaves that gave forth musty odours. Beyond the diffuse clumps of younger growth, clusters of large trees were scattered among the forest that disappeared into the distance.

Miet had no rifle and walked briskly in front of me. Within a few minutes, his prison warder's expression had vanished. Looking back over his shoulder to make sure I was following him, he now resembled a normal village boy. I followed, but I was getting hot. Not a leaf stirred around us. The vegetation was swathed in a stifling humidity. I was deafened by the loud screeching of insects. This trek through the woods required an effort to which I was no longer accustomed. I was perspiring. After a good hour, we arrived at the family's patch of land. The house had an insubstantial roof and was built on thin, twisted stilts. Its being here in the forest may have had something to do with the presence of the camp. But it could also have been part of a much larger pioneer settlement, for I had noticed some other flimsy buildings in the distance.

Young, smiling and self-conscious, a-Miet's mother (a child's name is traditionally prefixed with the conjunction "a") came to meet us. She knew nothing about her eldest son's work; as far as she was concerned, he was no more a jailer than I was a prisoner. The father was not there. In this woman's simple, weary face I could see at once how much this war had left wives and mothers on their own. She drew the *krama* she had thrown on over her round, swollen breasts as we approached. Her newborn baby was sleeping beneath the house in a hammock that was still swaying.

"He wants to buy some chickens," said the boy, hoisting himself up the ladder and on to the platform.

"A dozen or so," I added.

The young woman gave an eager smile. She had heard what we had said without really listening. A pile of vegetable waste, heaped on a hearth from which a wisp of smoke rose, was smouldering. A large area of the cabin floor had been swept carefully. All around, among the grass and the leaves covering the ground, among the tufts of *caryota* palms mutilated by bush fires, scores of robust-looking chickens were scratching at the damp ground. Two other guards who had been trailing us arrived just in time to lend a hand. In less than two hours we had thirteen plump chickens plucked and gutted.

On our return, we passed through a landscape bathed in the last rays of the evening sun. We arrived at night, experiencing a comical concert of piccolos, car horns and trombones. Douch was waiting for me. He had had a fire lit. I hurried to gulp down my rice and join him. He was wearing a cap on his head and a *krama* around his neck. Layers of cool air descended on us. The night echoed with sounds.

"Come, comrade," he announced with conviction, "we're going to sing!"

Douch scarcely knew the revolutionary songs better than I did, but he summoned one of his young trebles to our rescue. The boy was ready, having been forewarned. He sat down shyly opposite us, wearing an oversized Chinese cap. The dancing flames made the outlines of his face waver. The trunks of the large trees gleamed like red columns in the glare of the fire. The sound came effortlessly out of his half-open mouth, drawn like ink across a page, light and fragile, trembling and delicate. Is there any emotion more poignant than that inspired by words of love and hatred, sung by a child? There was such purity in his silvery voice, weaving between the stars, that every syllable was wreathed in eternal beauty. Even today, I shudder at the memory of those simple, unaccented tunes drawn from Chinese revolutionary music. It leaves me with a sensation so bitter that I almost want to retch.

I drew near the fire. Several of us were now squatting around it, our outstretched elbows resting on our knees, our palms facing the fire, our fingers involuntarily outlining strange shapes in the air.

"We got the bike back," Douch told me. "The young comrade who had taken it was ill and could not bring it back."

"Everybody's ill here! If I can, I'll arrange for a stock of quinine to be delivered. For you and the guards, but for the prisoners too, not forgetting Lay and Son ... which reminds me," I continued after a silence, "what did you mean, comrade, when you stated that Lay and Son will be 'set free on site'?"

" 'Set free on site' means that from now on they are soldiers of the army of liberation, taking part in the struggle against the American imperialists and their lackeys, fighting for the liberty of the Khmer people, and launching fresh offensives to construct a new, independent and sovereign society." There was excitement in Douch's voice.

"I'm cold," I said, standing up and hunching my shoulders.

Was he holding forth just because the guards were there? I turned and walked a few paces in the darkness. Realising that but for the guard's indiscipline I might have spent Christmas with Hélène, a throb of indignation welled up inside me. Holding his face back from the fire, Douch was turning over a log with outstretched arms, causing sparks to leap up above the blaze. It was late. Eventually one of the guards left. Then the others followed, one by one. I drew closer to the fire.

"Comrade, I don't understand," I said to him. I had, for a while, been contemplating the new flames bursting from the clefts in the log, licking its sides with blue reflections. "Cambodia has been independent since 1954, and its independence was acquired without spilling a drop of blood. Why don't you try to negotiate with the Phnom Penh government to preserve your sovereignty, rather than plunging your country into war again? Otherwise, whose country's interests are you defending?"

"Do you really think we had a choice?" he replied with a smile. "Lon Nol's bureaucrats have betrayed the people; they have sold them to the Americans in order to usurp power. They think of nothing but making a profit on the backs of the peasants by fleecing and exploiting them. While our Communist brothers fight to protect my fellow countrymen, who have been harassed for months by American planes along the border, and while hundreds of defenceless men and women die every day, these lackeys of imperialism grow outrageously rich, work openly to undermine our economy, make ever more arbitrary arrests and murder our patriots. I know them," he said, breaking off his sentence. "They are lazy, gutless, have no pride, and are exploiting our country's misfortune and the war on our doorstep to amass dollars. They have imposed a fascist and racist dictatorship on the people, whom they keep in ignorance. Because of them, Cambodia has not been able to preserve the peace and neutrality that had protected us from humiliation ever since our victory over French colonialism."

His quavering voice made me aware of the strength and authenticity of his dedication. But he spoke clearly and eloquently, never raising his voice, his eyes lowered and his mind concentrated.

"We could not sit and do nothing," he continued. "We are the glorious descendants of Angkor. Ever since then, we have never ceased our struggle against occupying forces of every kind, accepting supreme sacrifices to protect our dignity and safeguard our country's independence."

Listening to his declamation, I could not help thinking of the cynical, self-styled "Khmer kings" who, at several points in their history, had turned to Vietnam or to Siam, ready to do anything in order to retain power. All too often, Cambodian history has amounted to this: an all-powerful monarch who "makes the world's wheel go round" but who is either dependent on yesterday's enemy for the sake of survival, or ends up being murdered by a son, a son-in-law, or some other usurper. Look back in history as far as you will – in the modern period, at least – the kings have rarely represented the land of the Khmers. Neither have they bothered to administer it, being too concerned with their own wealth. Not even under Sihanouk's reign did civil servants venture into the countryside. Until recently, the language spoken at the court in Phnom Penh was Siamese. The French were probably the only people who respected and tried to understand the behaviour and customs of the "hinterland" – that is to say, the kingdom as a whole beyond the capital and the main towns. There have been so many interruptions in the history of this poor country that one can no longer find any trace of conscious memory. Even if Angkor was probably never abandoned, Khmers with a Western-style education have only recently become aware of their legendary patrimony and thought of it as belonging to them. The thousands of temples scattered throughout the country had no other history besides that of the earth spirits that have haunted them for centuries; their divinities were not worshipped there, unless you count the veneration the inhabitants of all the monsoon countries of Asia still pay to old stones.

At the same time, confronted with the rigid vigilance of this Communist leader, I thought of the colossal negligence of Lon Nol's soldiers; of the arrogance of the officers at Siem Reap who cared nothing about the peasants and treated me as a Marxist; of the wretchedness of the foot soldiers recruited en masse – "twenty-four-hour soldiers" – and thrown, without any strategic planning, into battles they could never win against highly organised Vietnamese troops. In short, I could sense the unbridgeable gulf between the two sides, and I was simultaneously dismayed and intrigued by the commitment of this Khmer Rouge, whose flawless speech accorded so well with what the West wanted to hear.

"Lay and Son should be proud of joining the Angkar," he added. "Instead of remaining puppets of the colonisers and their corrupt lackeys, they will be able to become heroes and hold their heads high. It's the best thing that could have happened to them. You should tell them!"

"But you're separating them from their wives and children!" I protested. "You're tearing them away from what is dearest to them!"

"Their families can go with them, if they want to," he interjected. "We must fight unceasingly to establish a new society. Those who wish to join us are welcome. The Angkar will greet them as its children and will look after them. But those who wish to remain slaves and serve the imperialists are lost. It's too late for them. They are already infected. They're the ones we should pity for no longer having any family."

I interrupted him in order to quote – imitating a bonze reciting litany, with quavering trills on the final vowels – a passage of doctrinal text that I knew well:

*A mother should not boast*
*Saying: this is my child;*
*For he is the child of Dhamma!*

Douch burst out laughing, looking about him as if for a witness to whom he could exclaim: "How about that! This Frenchman does amuse me."

"Comrade," I continued in a suddenly embarrassed tone, heavy with unexpressed meaning. "I would like to ask you a question. May I? I really want you to give me a sincere answer."

Douch looked up at me. He hesitated slightly, not wishing to refuse outright. Clearly, he had no idea of what I was leading up to. "It depends," he replied in a voice both cautious and curious. "There are probably some things I cannot speak to you about."

I was in fact employing an old trick used by Boulbet, who would sometimes envelop his questions in so much mystery that the other person, expecting the worst, would give his answer quite freely, almost with relief.

"Comrade!" I began. "You speak about the Angkar in the way that monks speak about Dhamma. So I want to ask you this: Is there some ideologist among you, constructing a revolutionary theory based upon the myths and rules of the Buddhist religion?"

Douch was taken aback.

"Because, after all," I went on, "are you not defending a new religion? I've followed your educational sessions. They're not unlike courses in Buddhist doctrine: renouncing material possessions; giving up family ties, which weaken us and prevent us from devoting ourselves entirely to the Angkar; leaving our parents and our children in order to serve the revolution. Submitting to discipline and confessing our faults – "

"That has nothing to do with it!" Douch cut in.

"There are ten 'moral commandments' that you call *sila*," I persisted, "that have the same name as the ten Buddhist 'abstentions' (*sila*). The revolutionary must accept the rules of a *vinaya*, exactly as the monk observes a religious 'discipline' (*vinaya*). At the start of his instruction, a young soldier is given a pack containing six articles (trousers, shirt, cap, *krama*, sandals, bag), just as the novice monk receives a regulation kit of seven items – "

"These are intellectual ravings!" he broke in.

"That's not all! Wait, comrade," I said, raising my hand. "Look at the facts! In everything you tell me, and in what I have heard myself, one finds religious themes from the past: taking on a new name, for example; enduring hardships, rather like ritual mortification; even the soothing, enticing words of Radio Peking announcing the advent of a regenerated people, born of the revolution. In a word, the Communist leaders to whom you are accountable want to impose an initiatory death on the nation."

My long speech was answered by a stubborn silence.

"Comrade Douch!" I continued, raising my voice before he could start speaking again. "The resoluteness of the teachers who speak in the name of the Angkar is unconditional! Sometimes it is even devoid of hatred and is purely objective, as if the human aspect of the question did not come into consideration, as if it were an intellectual concept. They mechanically carry out the impersonal, absolute directives of the Angkar, even going to extreme lengths. As to the peasants who come under your control, they are subjected, purely and simply, to a sort of purification rite: new 'teaching' (*rien sutr*), new mythology and an amended vocabulary that no-one initially understands. Then the Angkar is adopted as family, while true kin are rejected. And after that the population is divided into 'initiates' and 'novices'. The first constitute the true people, that is to say, those who have been won over; the others are those who have not completed the period of preparation and training; only after that can they be admitted into the former group and acquire the superior status of accomplished citizen. Need I go on?"

"That has nothing to do with it!" Douch repeated. "Buddhism benumbs the peasants, whereas the Angkar seeks to glorify them and build the prosperity of the beloved homeland on them! You attribute scholarly ravings to bogus ideologues when they belong only to yourself. Buddhism is the opium of the people. And I don't see why we should draw our inspiration from a capitalist past, which is the very thing we want to abolish! When we have rid our country of the vermin that infect people's minds," he went on, "when we have liberated it from this army of cowards and traitors who debase the people, then we will rebuild a Cambodia of solidarity, united by genuine bonds of fraternity and equality. First, we must construct our democracy on healthy foundations that have nothing to do with Buddhism. Corruption has seeped in everywhere, even among families. How can you trust your brother when he accepts the imperialists' wages and employs their arms against you? Believe me, Comrade Bizot, our people need to rediscover moral values that correspond to their deeper aspirations. The revolution wishes nothing for them besides simple happiness: that of the peasant who feeds himself from the fruits of his labours, with no need for the Western products that have made him a dependent consumer. We can manage and organise ourselves on our own to bring radiant happiness to our beloved country."

"Consumer?" I asked, opening my eyes wide. "I don't remember the fishermen from Kompong Khleang using many imported products. I don't know who you're talking about, unless perhaps it's yourself, comrade. Did your grandmother pamper you as much as all that?" I whispered mischievously. "You are the ones who are totally dependent! You fell into a trap by taking up the cause of the North Vietnamese. They are using your men to advance on the battle front of a war that is not yours. You are armed by the Soviets, your speeches are written in Peking, your songs and your music – which nowadays are accompanied by the tambourine, violin and accordion – no longer have anything Khmer about them! Is that what you call 'national integrity' and the 'sovereignty' of the people? I see nothing of traditional Cambodia in your plans for society. To me everything seems imported. When the North Vietnamese have made use of you and, thanks to your sacrifices, gained their victory against the 'imperialists'," I said, stamping my foot and with a note of hatred in my voice, "they'll take control of your country and subject you to an even harsher yoke."

"Don't concern yourself about us, comrade," he said, banishing the smile in his eyes brought about by my imitation. "There's no chance of the North Vietnamese seizing power in Cambodia. We have already taken steps," he said mysteriously.* Our alliance with them is part of our plans. For the time being, we must deal with what is most urgent: driving out the invader with the support of our brothers, who have been good enough to stand by us in our struggle. Sihanouk sent out an appeal from Peking for us to fight in any way possible, from wherever we are, against the dictatorship of the traitor Lon Nol. Does that make him a foreigner?"

"Frankly, comrade, you astonish me! Instead of rejecting Sihanouk and all that he represents, both as a man and in his role, you refer back to his radio appeals as if they were anything other than political tomfoolery designed solely to ensure his own survival."

"It's true. Sihanouk is just a symbol for us. That's why we use him. We Khmers, we can always find ways to defend our dignity. It's not the first time in our history that we have accepted help from a neighbouring state to recover the reins of our destiny. Our elder brothers have fought as we have done against feudalism and imperialism, and we should take them as models in preparing for our freedom."

"In a word," I persisted, "you prefer to extend your hand to the Chinese and stir up hatred against your brother, rather than unite with him to find peace."

*Douch was clearly well informed about what had been said a few months earlier, in September 1971, when the PCK had held its Third Party Congress in the Cardamomes maquis, at which he may have been present: a secret resolution referred to Vietnam as dangerous and presaged a gradual departure of the Vietnamese and a purging of pro-Vietnamese elements in the party. When I told Douch of my fear that Vietnam might take control of Cambodia, I was thus, without knowing it, in line with the party's new policy.

"You don't understand," he told me calmly, sounding like a schoolmaster about to explain his point again patiently. "He who has betrayed is no longer my brother. He is merely a lackey of imperialism, and it is he who has turned against me."

This reversal of the situation – which suddenly transformed the aggressor into the aggressed – and perhaps also the light that flashed in his eyes, made me think of the empty cabin I had discovered on the far bank of the river.

"Comrade," I murmured, looking straight at him, "there's a question on the tip of my tongue . . ."

He and I were making the same gestures. Each of us held a stick for poking the fire, burning our fingers in the process, our eyes lost in the flickering flames. A chill wind blew from the bamboo groves, making the embers glow and driving the smoke towards Douch, forcing him to turn to breathe. He grimaced and closed his eyes, but his expression was calm and he seemed at ease. Our discussion may have incensed him at times, but it was as compelling to him as it was to me. And I was reassured by the contentment I could see in his features.

"I thought I overheard something about prisoners in our camp being tied up and beaten . . ."

"Most of the people who arrive here," he explained after a short silence, "have been caught in the act of spying. It's my responsibility to interrogate them, to find out who their contacts are, what type of information they're looking for, and who's paying them. Just one of these traitors could jeopardise our whole struggle. Do you think they're going to reveal what they know of their own free will?"

"But who does the beating? It – "

"Ah!" he cut in. "I can't stand their duplicity! The only way is to terrorise them, isolate them and starve them. It's very tough. I have to force myself. You cannot imagine how much their lying infuriates me! When I cross-examine them and they resort to every ruse to avoid talking, denying our senior officers potentially vital information, then I beat them! I beat until I'm out of breath."

The fire began to flicker. A sinister shadow split his face in two. I was frightened. I would never have believed that this mathematics teacher, this committed Communist and conscientious leader, could also be a henchman.

Later, I often thought about this conversation; a dark revelation beneath a star of foreboding. That Christmas night, a huge part of my naivety crumbled. Up until then, I had been convinced by the reassuring image of a brutal executioner. Now the man of faith, staring ahead of himself with an expression combining gloom and bitterness, suddenly emerged in his immense solitude. Just as he revealed such cruelty, I surprised myself by feeling affectionate towards him.

There was still generosity in him; perhaps the presence of a constant suffering as visible in his posture as in his face was what held me. As I looked at him, tears came to my eyes, as if I were dealing with a dangerous predator I could not bring myself to hate. But wasn't the danger simply the man within him? I was looking not at a monster from the abyss but at a human being, taken by nature and conditioned for killing. His intelligence had been honed as the tooth of the wolf or the shark, but his human psychology had been carefully preserved. Thus prepared, his masters employed him as a cog in a vast timepiece beyond his comprehension.

I began to see clearly just how deeply technical specialisation had affected his sense of morality. His work had imprisoned him inside a large machine from which he could no longer escape. And so he, like everyone, from his fellow leaders to the humblest conscripts, was ruled by fear, a fear that was evident in their clandestine dealings, in their overplayed secret discussions, in the precautions they took in the forests out of simple mistrust.

At the time, Douch had yet to take his place in the museum of horrors. He was not even thirty years old. But in deciding his fate, life had given free rein to his spontaneous inclinations, which are for everyone a mixture of the clear and the less clear. For the good of the cause, he had resolutely set off into the labyrinthine quagmire of ideology, to try and reach the flowers of deceit growing in the shadows, no longer able to look up to the sky. From then on, his lot was to obey the rule of terror, but in conditions of such darkness and silence that I wonder whether he had ever been aware of the appalling power he had been granted.

"Comrade," he said, making me jump, "one day I, too, will have children, and being deprived of them will make me cry like you. But for the time being my only values are those that will lead to the liberation of our compatriots. My duty is to lead each of them back to a life of simple pleasures; what more can anyone want from life than a bicycle, a watch and a transistor radio?"

The reflection of the embers bathed his features in a scarlet glow, giving his still-youthful face the gentle expression of a cherub. I began thinking that you could probably find the same childlike characteristics in the faces of all revolutionaries.

"Look at how I live here," he continued. "I try to give an example: work, austerity, sacrifice . . . utter destitution surrounds me. And I see all about me the poverty that affects everyone."

"Forgive me, comrade," I interrupted with conviction, "but in the territories outside the Angkar's control, where free movement, commerce, life and a certain degree of liberty are still possible, most people do now possess a watch, a bicycle and a radio, if that's what you want. In any case, the poverty that does exist only affects a part of the population."

"Well, that's worse!" he retorted, suddenly beside himself.

I sensed that my remark had stirred a thought previously discarded and that this was something that could not be discussed. He seemed particularly irritated by his response, since it sounded like a confession. Had he not naively exclaimed that man suffers more from the happiness of others than from his own misfortunes?

"Tok tok tok tok tok tok . . . To-ké! To-ké! To-ké!"

"Five!" I said, holding up five fingers.

"Eight!" replied Douch, with a show of cheeriness.

"To-ké!"

Clinging to the bamboo shoots, a gecko, whose vibrant call rang out into the night, stopped its strokes at four.

"Comrade," I said sadly, "we have both lost. I hope it's not a premonition. Admit, at least, that these ideas are not your own. You learned them when you studied with the French. They were imposed on you by the Western education you received. Yet now you not only want to apply them to a society that has nothing in common with the administration you're fighting against, but use them to justify the deaths we see around us."

"Exploitation of man by man is the same everywhere!" he said, flaring up again. "It's as old as the world and extends beyond our frontiers. For a Frenchman, I find you very timid. Did you yourselves not have a revolution and execute hundreds and hundreds of people? Would you care to tell me when the memory of these victims prevented you from glorifying in your history books the men who founded a new nation that day? It's the same with the monuments at Angkor, whose architecture and majesty everyone admires . . . who now thinks about the price, about the countless individuals who died from the endless labour over the centuries? The extent of the sacrifice matters little; what counts is the greatness of the goal you choose for yourself."

The Khmer Rouge officer was deeply immersed in our duel. A few days earlier, when he had been questioning me about my work, I had replied that the history I studied – meticulously recorded over the course of centuries – usually struck me as panegyrics meant to legitimise new leaders in the eyes of future generations without a care for the horror they had inflicted on their elders. I had also suggested, with vexation and cynicism, that the gods were always on the side of the strongest, that there was no difference in this world between beauty and cruelty, and that, when all was said and done, no traces would survive of even the most tragic destruction. He was now turning my ambiguous remarks to his own advantage. These reflections perplexed me and left me staring for a while, my eyes drawn to the whiteness of the curling flames like two moths.

"Indeed," I replied at last, nodding my head in a resigned way. "Man is made that way; he seems to accept anything and to forget everything. The fact that he has created works like those at Angkor will always be to his credit, however much inhumanity may have been involved in their construction. You see, comrade, for me the great question in life is the suffering we cause to others. We have no rights – nobody does – over each other. That's why I reject, from the very core of my being, the idea that spilling blood is a bloodletting needed to strengthen the patient. How can we let some people decide their own salvation by enforcing the sacrifice of others? Where does this apportioning come from? Does the land of the Khmer now follow the law that requires one fish to devour the other?"

"But that's what class warfare is!" he went on enthusiastically. "It's to do away with this injustice! Don't you see that the Khmer peasant is like a slave, labouring unceasingly to feed a band of corrupt layabouts? If the revolution demands an even more strenuous effort from him, he will at least be respected for his work. Doing his utmost for production and struggling for the development of his country will be to his advantage. He will harvest rice twice a year. He'll be the one to benefit, and in this way he will become the sole master of his happiness and his destiny."

"Two harvests a year?" I asked, amazed. "But with just one harvest and the current yield of eight hundred kilograms in the countryside, the nation not only eats its fill, it still manages to export some of the best-quality rice in the world. Forgive me, comrade, but it would be more sensible to rotate the crops to renew the soil and to plant, for example, peanuts and beans, or – even better, on flooded land – manioc and maize, which sell for much higher prices. As for the peasants, I can assure you that those I knew in my village would not have wanted anything to change. They were carrying on traditions that had scarcely altered in centuries, methods that the French had seen fit to preserve. But perhaps that is what you reproach us for . . . Isn't preserving village culture and your ancient customs a better way of serving national integrity than all your speeches? If you destroy these structures of peasant society, if you impose a new rational model, don't you risk humiliating them even more than your enemies do? Won't they be completely confused? What will their reference points be?"

"Quite the reverse!" he erupted. "It's because we respect their customs, because we know that the peasants are the source of true knowledge, that we want to free them from oppression and abuse. They're not like the lazy monks who don't know how to grow rice. They know how to take control of their destiny. We hope to build our future on their intelligence and their strength. This society will retain the best of itself and will get rid of all the con-taminated remains of the current period of decline Lon Nol's traitors are responsible for. Comrade," he added peremptorily, "it's better to have a sparsely populated Cambodia than a country full of incompetents!"

I was riveted by the unbending stringency of his contradictory remarks.

"Your ideas are pure and generous, comrade, but they are frightening. As I told you, I fear that your revolution may pave the way for your worst enemies. You are dreaming of a system intended to make man happy in spite of himself. When will we stop allowing men to die in the name of man? This notion of Man, with a capital M, lies at the root of so much suffering. The individual is always alone beneath the heavens; it's pointless to try to make him master of the world. Do the people you're speaking about have a say in any of this? Have you ever questioned them about what they want?"

"But the people have been manipulated," he asserted. "They no longer know what's good for them."

"How do you know? My impression is that whatever happens to them, they are merely victims of history. Their future hinges on events completely beyond their control. What sorts of things do you think the peasant has on his mind? I'll tell you what he wants: he wants to go to the forest to choose the *krakoh* trees to build the pillars for his house; to harness fine red-and-white oxen to a *phcek* wood cart, with independent poles and a long raised shaft decorated with a pompom; to maintain his seedbeds and to plant them like the rest of the village; to lay hoop nets to trap the silvery *trai changvar* in the water of the paddy fields; to adorn his daughter with gold earrings for her wedding and a yellow silk *sampot chorapap* with gold patterns; to lead his son to the pagoda at the head of the procession, bearing the begging bowl upon his own shoulder. And above all, comrade, he wants a respectable funeral, with a well-known *yogi* to lead the mourning and his grandchildren to receive their ordination in front of his pyre. The peasant to whom you and your leaders constantly refer, comrade, has no connection with the events on the front pages of the international newspapers; he is the hero whom no-one could care less about in a war that has nothing to do with him."

"That's what I'm telling you!" he exclaimed. "Lies are heaped on him, and he is treated like an animal."

"Do you think that by recruiting him into the North Vietnamese army you're making him more responsible for his fate?"

"What are you talking about? Can't you see that you're surrounded by Khmers? You're also a victim of the American propaganda that sees Vietnamese everywhere. As far as we're concerned, you can be sure that we have our own programme that we shall put into operation without the help of the Vietnamese. Our own leaders have developed it, and it will lead us to democracy and bring us the respect of the Khmer nation. That's the revolution I support!"

"I would like to believe you," I said with a weary sigh. "But to be frank, as far as I'm concerned, it frightens me; it goes too far towards reducing society to the means of production and man to his digestive tube. It leaves no room for dreaming."

"Dreaming? I thought I was the dreamer. Come on, now! You can take this message to the West. They must know what we are preparing our people for. We want peace and prosperity. It's not for the Americans to tell us what to do. Their intervention is hypocritical and calculating. Besides, they know nothing about us or our traditions. They're bullies who have never had the slightest consideration for our customs and have never respected our feelings."

Night had slowly closed in on us. I can remember everything. The immense dark sky touching our heads; our truncated profiles. I shall always remember the silences, too: Douch would gravely lower his eyes like an exhausted fighter drawing strength from sleep. We confronted each other with the closeness of two friends out to change the world, neglecting sleep, hearts full of excitement and sadness. But in his case, behind all the propaganda, there was a terrifying reality that was his to activate. He had invested his entire being in it but was no better prepared than I was.

When he opened his eyes again at the end of his sentence, his misty, dilated pupils were transformed by a frayed silkiness that sapped the steady expression of his eyes. During the course of the night, I watched this man so set in his certainties, through veils that broke up his rigour, and saw him softened in a way I had never thought possible.

Beneath the blood-red foliage, the first ripples of dawn mingled with the crackling of the flames dancing over the logs. As the sky grew paler, the cock crowed.

# 8

I immediately invited my lady friends to come down from their roosts, and I encouraged them to gobble up as much as they could. Stimulated by my encouragement, they clucked frantically, their excitement spreading to their chicks around them. In my reverie, I could visualise the moment (as soon as I was not there to protect them) when their throats would be slit, and for a second I pondered my mind's strange inability to contemplate my own execution. I stroked them for the last time, my eyes filled with sadness. Lay and Son came and sat morosely beside me. Together, we tied up the strands of sacking that had been pecked apart by the hens' beaks.

There was an unusual hubbub all around us. Those prisoners permitted to work had all been instructed to prepare for the banquet. Two had set off to search for river snails. Douch had given his consent for one of our guards, who had a talent for gathering food from the forest, to lead a team of prisoners to search for the fresh shoots that, now that the season was changing, were sprouting in the undergrowth. We saw them returning, their *krama* filled with specialities known only to the foothills gourmet: acidic leaves, crisp and very bitter shoots from shrubs, crosiers of ferns, bittersweet clusters of flowers, bamboo shoots, palm hearts . . . Chopped into pieces, the chickens, including their necks and feet, had already been tossed into the cooking water. Douch had also agreed that two fires could be made. Lay told me with a laugh that the prisoners were so starving that the mere mention of chicken soup was enough to cause stomach cramps.

When everything was ready, I helped serve the meal, trying to make sure it was fairly apportioned. I was as careful as if I were performing a ritual. The prisoners took their share in silence, as if receiving an offering, and as the aroma rose from the bowls, awakening buried memories, their eyes grew misty. Moved myself and unable to speak, I examined one by one the faces of these men, whom I had never looked at closely before.

One of them signalled to me with his eyes. He had just arrived, and I had arranged for him to be given a container. There was still some rebellion in him: his audacity in approaching me under the nose of the jailers showed that he had not fully realised what had befallen him. Leaning over the slats, he whispered in my ear, "I live in Phnom Penh, near the power station, just by the road junction. My house is the second on the left, along the road that leads to the water tower. Please, tell my wife that I am alive and that I will come back."

The guards were amusing themselves. The prisoners, looking very composed, were noisily slurping their soup, careful, in their uncomfortable positions, not to spill anything from the bowls or plates, holding them in both hands. In the absence of spoons (we used to eat rice with our fingers), they tore at chunks of meat or papaya with their teeth and then chewed them for a long time, turning the chicken over and over in their mouths until only the bone remained. The food struck them as so tasty that they nodded their heads pensively as they ate, finding it pitiful that such fulfilment should come from a soup which, at home, would have seemed quite ordinary.

Light shone on to the area with such intensity that it hurt my eyes. I decided to go and wash. I went over to Lay and asked him to find out the new arrival's name and exact address, and to tell him that I would visit his wife. In Lay's anguished face I could still see a cruel uncertainty preventing him from breathing properly, just as it had done to us when we were first arrested. He could not trust anything the Khmer Rouge told us. He saw the whole set-up as an enormous hoax. There were terrifying rumours about my fate going around the camp; he did not dare report them to me. He even doubted the meaning the Khmer Rouge gave to the words "set free". At the same time, I felt deep guilt about my two companions, suddenly aware that I should also reassure their own families and support them.

The burning midday sun shone straight down on the river. I spent less time than normal in the water, then sat in the sun to dry myself, perched on a large stone jutting out of the water, the level of which had gone down. Douch had told one of the guards, who came running up to me, to let me know that we had to leave. I hurried to say goodbye to Lay and Son, leaving to them the bowl, the *krama* and what remained of the soap. We shook hands awkwardly, not managing to make this revolutionary greeting demonstrate much more than an empty and affected warmth. I walked through the barracks, expressing my good wishes as I passed.

Three armed guards were waiting for me with Douch, who turned to me with an affable expression on his face. "We're going to miss the Frenchman!" he said enthusiastically, his eyes wide open.

The vibrant rasping of the cicadas drowned his voice.

"We must leave," he said in a louder voice. "We have to go!"

But beneath his jolly mood I could sense some embarrassment; my body, ever alert, stiffened. The soldiers were winking at one another in the sunlight. I saw one of them fiddling with a length of nylon cord. They were going to tie me up, and Douch was bracing himself for my protests, unable to disguise his fear of having to cope with me in front of the guards. Fully determined not to let myself be treated like this, I swung round on my heels and set off theatrically to the sheltering shade of the bamboo grove. Just as an animal at bay can spot the slightest hesitation in its adversary, Douch's embarrassment had immediately encouraged me in my resolve not to allow myself to be tied up.

"Yesterday you removed my chains; today you put them on again!" I shouted as I walked back towards him. "Is this freedom you're leading me to so awful that you have to bind my arms?"

Unlike Lay, I actually believed in his sincerity, and the notion that this might all be a trap seemed scarcely credible. But his discomfort indicated a weakness that I instinctively wanted to exploit.

"What are you going on about?" he asked in a tone that betrayed impatience. "It's just a simple formality, the normal procedure, that's all."

"You're the one who makes the rules here!" I persisted. "Comrade, binding my arms today makes no sense."

Douch looked annoyed and silently walked a few paces. "It's not in my power to give way on matters of security," he eventually replied. "The instructions are very strict and all the more necessary since you're returning to enemy territory. You can leave only on these terms, comrade: we must bind and blindfold you."

Douch saw me turn pale but was unable to tell whether I was reacting out of fear or anger. Nevertheless, he walked resolutely towards me and tied a blindfold around my head. Taken aback, I was speechless and unable to move.

My first thought was to turn the other way, to keep Lay from seeing what was happening. My arms were tied loosely behind my back. The guards started walking, rattling their weapons. My thoughts became jumbled, unable to force their way through to my consciousness. My blood seemed to set in my veins.

The pressure of the blindfold on my nose brought back memories of the cool, grassy earth I had felt beneath my feet three months earlier. I felt myself caught again in the steel sights of those rifles . . . Will I ever know what it was, that day, that stopped the firing pins from clicking forward on to the cartridges?


In the middle of the field, my shoulders drooped and my body sagged, riddled with nervous spasms. I felt infinitesimal muscular contractions inside my head. I was steadying myself for the shock. Just as I had waited at boarding school for the impact of Père Hochard's open hand on my face, I stood tense and nervous. I don't know how long this lasted. But then someone suddenly pushed me – forcefully, almost brutally – across the field to a slippery slope beside an earth road, which I climbed only with the greatest difficulty. Tears leaked from my eyes. I attempted to utter a few words and started coughing softly, unable to clear my throat. Then I was dumped on the road. I stood there, unsteady, alone, defeated and crushed. Around me, people were talking, taking no notice of me. From beneath the blindfold I could glimpse their feet. I understood that we were about to leave. There was a long moment of indecision. I took the opportunity to ask to urinate; several people laboriously undid my bonds. I walked a few paces without knowing where to turn. Unable to see, I asked them, "Where are you taking me? What's going to happen to me?"

After a moment's silence, the loud voice of an adolescent beside me replied, "*At oy té!*" in the tone one might use to say "Shut up!" It had started to rain. I shivered as the first cold drops ran down my back and trickled down my legs. Then they moved me forward. A coarse, sweaty hand, whose touch I found unpleasant, gripped me unremittingly by the elbow; as the kilometres passed, the contact grew more gentle, until it became a subtle, silent bond between me and the man I relied on to steady me along these steep tracks.

During the afternoon, the squad stopped unexpectedly.

Violent gusts of warm wind drove the rain into the undergrowth that surrounded us. Standing motionless in the puddles, my senses alert and my gaze turned inward like a fakir's, I heard my guards whispering and could make out the slosh of footsteps – not theirs – along the muddy clay of the track. The muffled rumbling made me shudder; there was an enormous quiver of life all around us, above our heads, near, far, everywhere. Mingled with the squalls of wind that summoned wild odours from the earth and the woods, I got a strong smell of oil and engine. Then we continued on our way, surrounded by masses of soldiers who had spent the night in the open and moved noiselessly. On either side of the track, I furtively caught glimpses of units of a motorised North Vietnamese division; the men, dressed in green uniforms, were silent as we passed; only the occasional sound, immediately stifled, slipped out: the knock of a monkey wrench on the metal of a chassis, the clank of a rifle butt knocking against a water bottle. The blindfold covering my eyes saved my life that day.

Such a concentration of armed forces concealed in a back-woods area was a feat of logistics and showed just how far the Vietnamese were determined to go. But the Communist war machine had other cards to play, far more dangerous to the American command than this gathering, which the B-52s or F-111s would make short work of. A few days earlier, the day after I was arrested, our little group was emerging from a *veal*, a small clearing, on our way to Ta Mok's village. We came across a much more impressive military unit: a group on bicycles, fifty metres apart, riding along tracks barely discernible beneath the trees. It was the key element of every offensive. Silent, mobile and undetectable, these older men – they were between forty and fifty years old – seemed perfect for the task. For decades, rapid action, camouflage and waiting between operations had been their daily experience. They carried everything with them: Kalashnikovs on their backs, carefully attached so as not to slip round or flip over;

cartridge clips and grenades hanging from their webbing; sacks of rice tied to their stomachs; a minute stove, matches and various utensils (bits of string, pieces of wire they had found along the way) in a haversack; pornographic photos (part of their official kit) in their shirt pockets; and all protected by a hooded nylon cape. The rusted handlebars and back fork of the bicycles were armed with soldered plates and reinforcing steel rods, and each one carried a mortar or a B-40 held to the frame with elastic or old electric wire. Ammunition was strapped on to the rear carrier with spare inner tubes, next to the regulation hammock for the night. This included a waterproof tent canvas for sleeping in the rain. Each fighter was a model of adaptability, simplicity and efficiency: they attacked powerfully, were practically invulnerable and cost next to nothing. They were level-headed professionals, with no illusions and nothing else on their minds except the next day's action – their wives and children reduced to cherished but distant memories – and they provided a fascinating response to Uncle Sam's excessive engagement in the region. This was the USSR (who pulled the strings of these sacrificial puppets) cocking an impressive snook at the contradictions of the West. Can anyone recall without a shudder Henry Kissinger's pathetic duel with the Vietnamese peace negotiator Lê Duc Tho? The former, hand on his heart, relying on the press, public opinion and the value of one's word; the latter, brandishing his "V" for victory sign, prepared to go to any lengths not to lose anything (apart from the hundreds of thousands of soldiers whom nobody cared about).

If the young men in charge of me had not been so very far from the anti-American propaganda that played upon the naivety of the richest nations; or if they had simply been asked what had happened during our journey, the Khmer Rouge leaders would never have risked allowing someone to leave who had witnessed such revealing proof of the presence, on Cambodian territory, of North Vietnamese troops.

But the Lacoutures still had a good many years ahead of them, for tides of opinion, however unjustified, are not easily diverted.

"I shall guide you myself, *at oy té* . . . Move on, comrade!"

Douch spoke to me gently, almost in my ear. His hands tapped my right arm, lightly punctuating his words. Our little group set off. Hesitantly, I began to move forward myself. In a high-pitched, almost excited voice, my cicerone began to steer me over every bump in the ground, moving me one way, turning me another, slowing when obstacles appeared and bringing me to a halt until they were removed. We gradually managed to coordinate our steps and I allowed myself to be escorted limply, blindly trusting his instructions. Moving without seeing, I began to feel close to the spirit of things, and their presence, no longer outside of me, came into sharp focus.

We took the route that so many others had already followed to misfortune . . .

Douch was excited. He must have worked out every detail of my return, anticipating all the difficulties, waiting for replies from distant command posts, the relay of guards along my route and the checkpoints on the roads as far as Oudong. I still did not know that his zeal had prompted him to organise a farewell meal for all the Khmer Rouge leaders in the south-west region. My freedom, obtained after a hard struggle, had become a sort of personal success for him, spurring on his career as a revolutionary.

We walked for hours on end. Guided by him, I strode towards my destiny, drawn into the cool moistness of a forest in which I could hear the rustling of insects and the song of birds. In front of me, I could hear the hurried steps of the guard clearing a path ahead of us. Occasionally, a soft, spiny rattan shoot, like some long prehensile tentacle, would bring me to a sudden stop as it fixed itself to my shirt. We were perspiring. Douch was breathing very hard through his nose. This proximity, the contact of his arm with mine, and my total physical dependence on him gave a new and indefinable consistency to our camaraderie which, I had realised with surprise over the last few weeks, was now undeniably real. To keep me from falling, Douch strained hard to focus on the path ahead, where I now strode with full assurance.

"Ah!"

I suddenly stumbled heavily. A high-pitched cry burst from his chest. His clenched hands grabbed me to give me support, but my weight pulled him down and we fell together. I went flat on my face, hitting my forehead against a stump. I didn't hurt myself at all. But it was clear from his shock and the anxious way he helped me up and enquired about the bump on my head that Douch had, in our relationship, gone beyond the bounds of basic courtesy, and was holding out a connection from soul to soul, a wider friendship, larger than the circumstantial fellowship that had arisen between us.

On the other side of my obscured horizon, I could hear faint sounds of barking, provoking even fainter barks. The familiar sound of dogs' voices echoing in the distance afforded me some relief. The presence of the good creatures one sees prowling around houses, ears flopping but corkscrew tails erect, immediately filled me with a sense of safety: the yellow dog barks only in times of peace, when the villages drowse in their daily routine and it can live calmly among men, women and children.

Douch stopped me and removed my blindfold. Night was falling. I opened my eyes without any difficulty. The sun was sunk behind a triple fissure of white on the golden layers of the sky. A fine mist on the pink line of the mountains split the light of its upper third like the faces of a crystal. We were standing in an area of regrowing thicket, against the bank of a red clay road. On the other side, in the light of early dusk, I could make out the black façades of a few closed-up houses built directly on the ground. Ahead, a *coucal* burst out into wild crowing. A glance from

Douch indicated that we had arrived, and I was untied. As we entered a large open space next to some old mango trees, I could see a door and some windows through which a pale brightness softly filtered.

A stout housewife, her bust squeezed into a short-sleeved blouse made of beige lace, was the first to notice us. She hurried out, turning around in front of the door to put on her flip-flops, and ran to the other side of the house, making welcoming gestures with her head. After a moment, she reappeared and invited us to follow her. The woman's smile was so sincere and courteous that it put me at my ease. But I didn't understand where she was leading us; Douch, for his part, kept silent. Behind the corner of the building, through a wide-open doorway, I caught sight of about ten Khmers Rouges in black pyjamas, caps and *krama*, who were standing in a row along one wall to welcome us. Douch pushed me in front of him and I went in, trying not to look disconcerted. At the very last moment, just as I was introducing myself, the leader standing by the entrance ordered one of his comrades at the end of the line to come next to him, while the others closed ranks and giggled like naughty choirboys. I exchanged a lengthy handshake with the first man. Then I shook the hands of the others in turn, doing my best to convey spontaneous joy while attempting to elongate my head, to open my mouth on to my upper teeth and to lower my ears, as each of my hosts did.

Above the cluster of moths and insects falling almost inaudibly on to the plates on the already-set table, I could hear the petrol hiss in the tungsten stem of the lamp hanging from the ceiling.

We remained there for a while, bodies swaying, complimenting one another, before I was placed at the end of the table and everyone took their seat. Douch, wearing a solemn expression, was seated further to my right; the artificial lighting made him seem even younger, without altering the naivety of his strained smile, which was in sharp contrast to the simple self-confidence of the others. All these men, at least half of whom had declared themselves indifferent to my death, looked at me with an expression of determined curiosity; they nodded with kindness and enthusiasm.

Bent double, the woman crossed the room, then came back after a moment, hastily carrying an enamel basin full of piping hot broth. Behind her, a girl in trousers brought the rice. I was ravenous with hunger. For some reason, I had not touched the lunch I had provided my fellow prisoners, perhaps because in any event – whether I was killed or set free – my stomach could wait. The smell of the marinade before me immediately gnawed at my stomach and released my gigantic appetite. I could have devoured the containers along with the contents.

I laughed as I smelled the soup, which gave off an aroma of boiled chicken stock and an intoxicating fragrance of citrus-flavoured herbs: it was *kroch nam ngao*, one of the Chinese dishes eaten on feast days in Cambodia. The lemons, pickled in brine and made into a hot stew, make the chicken taste like venison . . . my favourite! Watched by my delighted hosts, I gobbled it all down, including the withered, disintegrating lemon, which is not supposed to be eaten.

When my hunger was satisfied, one of the leaders coughed discreetly and there was silence. The expression on the face of the man who was about to speak, at first awkward and contrite, was poised between sudden inspiration and gravity. I remember him shifting around in his chair and fidgeting with the spoon and plate in front of him, while his expression alternated between joy, astonishment, doubt and regret. But this facial mobility no longer held any mystery for me, since Douch (who imitated his masters) had already demonstrated how authority was portrayed among the Cambodian partisans. A subtle combination: elation, sandwiched between a layer of naivety and another of mischievousness, the whole capable of achieving a complete lack of expression.

"Elder comrades, *mit bâng*, today is a great day!" he began, lowering his voice on the last syllables.

Within a few seconds, his expression had changed surreptitiously and he turned briskly to Douch: "Does he speak Khmer? Can he understand?" His mind instantly set at rest, he reassumed his grave manner.

"Ahem! We are celebrating the liberation of Comrade . . . Bizot —" he hesitated over the pronunciation of my name — "of French nationality. In the name of our revered Angkar and of all our revolutionary brothers, who constitute the armed forces of a people dedicated to liberating and protecting our beloved nation, may I be permitted, at this solemn moment, to express our sincere regrets for the discomfort he has experienced during his stay among us. But our glorious Kampuchea is struggling against the oppressive and unjust war of the capitalist aggressor! His captivity was thus inevitable and legitimate. Today, thanks to the generous and emphatic persistence of the Angkar, and as proof of the friendship between our two peoples, we have the immense joy of bringing it to an end and of saying, 'Return home, comrade, go and rejoin your family.' *Bane!* So be it. Now it is time for me to turn to him and to ask him, in the name of the Angkar, if he would like to express any particular wishes."

After allowing a moment's silence to pass and adopting as expressionless a demeanour as I could, I placed my hands on my knees and began to speak. "To all the grandfathers here present — "

Apologising for interrupting me, one guest stood up to pump the incandescent lamp, whose light was beginning to fade.

"To all the grandfathers here present," I began again, "I say a big thank-you! And especially for this lemon soup, which I shall never forget. [*Laughter.*] It's the first good thing to happen to me for three months! Well, elder grandfather, since you offered, there is actually something I should like to ask. First, I am leaving behind two very dear friends. I respectfully and insistently request that the Angkar grant them normal conditions, for they are not guilty of any crimes. I have given Comrade Douch all the money I had. I should like to request that half go to the Angkar and the other half to my two colleagues. Second, my work is concerned with the study of Buddhist traditions. But today the majority of the roads are cut off and much of the land of the Khmers is independent. I can no longer go anywhere without risking being arrested again. That is why I ask for authorisation to travel in the free zone, in order to continue my research in remote villages. In Phnom Penh, all the ancient customs have already altered. Everything has changed! You can no longer tell east from west. In some areas and on different levels, comrades, my motives and yours have points in common. But my personal aim is merely to highlight the genius of the Khmers in the religious history of South-East Asia. In all instances, this aim is legitimate. It is in no way contrary to the illustrious aspirations of the Angkar! I ask the Angkar to consider my request favourably. So be it. Thank you."

Comrade number one took up his spoon once more and heaved his chest several times to indicate that he was about to speak again; but he remained silent, glancing at his neighbours one by one, as if to show his embarrassment and seek their opinion. The higher a man in the hierarchy, the less his views are discussed. Spurning all pride, it behoves him to show frequent signs of hesitation and wavering, as if to prove his modesty and his willingness to accept an authority derived entirely from the collective will.

"As to the first question, I can say that there is no difficulty," he said finally. "Comrade Douch, here present, will himself guarantee that these two people are no longer treated as prisoners."

He turned and looked questioningly at Douch, who signalled his agreement with a firm nod of his cap.

"As for the second request," he continued, "we cannot give an immediate response . . . everything in its time. Today we are giving permission for our French comrade to leave the free zone. We did not imagine that we would also have to authorise his return, eh? This is not a normal request! Eh? Now, is it?"

He looked about him with his friendly expression, which faded after a moment, and continued in a nasal, scarcely audible tone. "For the time being, all we can do is advise him to wait patiently for the resounding victory of the United National Front of Kampuchea over the American imperialists and their lackeys" – spontaneous tapping of one foot – "which, thanks to the great and far-reaching solidarity of our brother peoples, united in one flesh, will lead us to independence, peace, neutrality, territorial integrity and democracy. Then Comrade . . . Bizot will be able to visit our villages as and when he likes! Eh? But does he doubt this victory, since he wants to continue his research without waiting?"

The ball was in my court, and everyone was looking at me.

"What can I say, comrade?" I asked with a laugh. "I – "

My reply did not satisfy him at all. He interrupted me sharply, still smiling but no longer looking at me, his wide-open eyes staring.

"Who is going to win? Eh! Will it be Lon Nol's men? I wonder if Comrade . . . here present is forecasting, on the contrary, a victory for the people's armed forces, which are divided into three groups, namely, Chhlop's village troops, Damban's district troops and Sruoch's provincial troops. Thanks to their revolutionary and patriotic spirit, thanks to their love of and respect for the people and their hatred of the enemy, they dare to attack and conquer any adversary! They command the admiration of the entire world, fighting against the aggressive manoeuvres of the American imperialists. So will they or will they not succeed in defeating the dictatorship of their lackeys, led by Lon Nol and Sirik Matak? That is my question!"

His last sentence had been spoken irritably and was prolonged by a series of arrogant little laughs. Then, settling his frame against the back of his chair, arms folded over his chest, he surveyed his colleagues with a jovial, self-satisfied look, glancing at each one, his eyebrows twitching nervously. I was overcome with confusion and could feel myself blushing.

"Comrade," I replied in embarrassment. "First of all, I should like to apologise to all the grandfathers here present and ask: Am I allowed to speak frankly? The senior grandfather has asked me a question. Does he expect me to express what I feel without fear?"

"Let the comrade speak!" he replied, his neighbours serving as witnesses. "*At oy té!* We are among friends, eh!"

Douch, elbows on the table, head set firmly between his shoulders, was silent and expressionless.

"Very well, comrade. I would say this: to my mind, the courage of the Khmers, whichever side they are on, is unrivalled. But the soldiers recruited by Lon Nol have been transformed into GIs! They are badly prepared for a war that is all about positioning and harassment. In fact, they are particularly averse to leaving the road and venturing into the paddy fields, to avoid dirtying their fine combat boots, which must remain beautifully polished!"

My joke relaxed the atmosphere, and amid the laughter and approval I could see Douch breathing normally again.

"Furthermore," I went on, "although their aircraft machine guns make a terrible noise, they are ineffective. The planes fly too high, for fear of exposing themselves when they fly too low. And all their artillery do is kill civilians in the villages! Nevertheless, comrade, I fear for Cambodia. I fear for her because with every victory of one side against another, it is always Khmers who die. I fear, too, because the Vietnamese brothers who support the Cambodian guerrillas will be tempted never to leave. I put the question: Is not Kampuchean independence rather fragile when seen from the point of view of her Vietnamese and Chinese neighbours?"

Though he looked worried, the Khmer Rouge had listened

without batting an eyelid. He replied straight away. "Those brothers who serve the imperialist aggressors and turn on their own kin are traitors who must be fought against and eliminated. As far as the Vietnamese troops are concerned, it is up to us, eh! They will remain just as long as we ask them to and no longer. As for little Kampuchea confronted by her big neighbours, well, instructive models exist that can inspire us: Albania, for example. The shining success of the People's Republic of Albania shows that when the leaders of a country genuinely represent the nation and the people, and when they institute freedom and democracy within its borders, a tiny country can establish its autonomy and its independence in the eyes of the entire world."

Then, with a look of total astonishment, he turned towards me and asked courteously, "Would our comrade like to express any other wishes?"

"No," I replied eagerly, relieved to see that we were changing the subject.

"*Bane . . .*"

Countless insects were spinning around us, the largest of them falling on to the table. The senior leader glanced inquisitively at a buzzing cockchafer that had fallen on its back, its metallic wing-cases wide open and glowing, then looked up briskly. Stretching out his chin, he pinched a hair on his neck between two fingernails and suddenly tore it out.

"We, for our part, have something to ask," he said eventually, absent-mindedly rubbing his fingers on the spot from which he had extracted the hair. "Is this possible? Eh? Can we trust him with this? At the same time, the comrade must feel free to refuse. That's essential!"

"Of course!" I replied immediately, not knowing what I was letting myself in for. "*Bane!* I agree in advance."

The Khmer Rouge stared at me theatrically with his tiny eyes, from deep within the swollen pouches beneath the tight arc of his lids.

"*At oy té!*" I repeated with a nervous laugh.

"Look at that! The comrade has agreed already, without even knowing what we want!"

With his colleagues there to watch him, he entertained himself by going around repeating, "Eh? How about that, eh!" as if to say "That's foolhardy consent for you!" Then he explained, "We had considered entrusting Comrade . . . Bizot with some documents to deliver to his own country. For it is very difficult for the partisans to dispatch anything to Phnom Penh. We have many friends there who support our revolution and await final victory against the fascist, racist aggressor, but it is dangerous for them to convey confidential documents to an embassy. They don't dare. Could the comrade here present undertake such a mission?"

"Yes. *Bane. At oy té!*"

"Ah!" he said in a tone of surprise. "How can he be so sure? Isn't he likely to be searched?"

The Khmer Rouge official's request amounted to having me drive across the front line in a truck laden with explosives.

Then, with an ineffable smile that lengthened the tight veil of his eyes, and as if to imply "He must have contacts among the CIA to be so confident", he asked, "Where does this fearlessness come from?"

"I don't know," I retorted. "But you mustn't ask me too many questions. Right now, it's the elder comrade who is making me frightened! I am quite willing to pass documents to the French authorities, as long as they are not too bulky, of course; I shall have to conceal them about me . . . I think, I hope that I won't be searched. There! That's all."

I caught Douch's eye; he was gazing at me proudly.

Thoroughly engrossed in his act, the senior leader acquired a slight frown on his brow, to indicate the busyness of his thoughts. Finally, without turning around, he held out his hand to the man on his right, who gave him an envelope that he passed to me.

Inside was a folder containing photographs and a pamphlet of some thirty pages in Khmer entitled "Political Programme of the United National Front of Kampuchea." The photographs showed Khmer Rouge soldiers standing to attention; different types of modern armaments; and several pictures of top dignitaries, including Comrades Hou Youn and Hu Nim, GRNUK ministers and resistance leaders whom enemy propaganda claimed had been assassinated by their own Communist brothers but who, I was told, were alive and well. I put the packet inside my shirt.

An end-of-meal atmosphere fell over the table. We looked at one another, nodding our heads in approval. My hosts were smoking and picking their teeth. One of those sitting near the top man leaned over the table to enquire amiably, "Have all the comrade's personal possessions been returned to him?"

I quickly tried to reassure him, but Douch interposed with a laugh.

"Yes, but Comrade Mok is very cross . . . now he doesn't have a watch!"

The quip made everyone burst out laughing, starting with Ta Mok himself, whom I hadn't recognised before. He shifted about on his chair, his good-natured laugh revealing the decay in his teeth.

A man appeared in the doorway, figure slightly bowed, hands crossed beneath his stomach; he said nothing. Douch, enquiringly, half stood up from his chair. The leader turned around and then said, "So that's it, eh? The car's ready? Good. Come on. It's time to go."

Douch immediately went outside. I shook hands with everybody. A white Peugeot 404 estate was waiting by the door. It was lit up by the moon pinned on to a part of the sky which, at this time of night, poured down the icy humidity of winter. The pale naked circle gave out a silvery glow which traced areas of soft shade in the surrounding half-light. The stars were twinkling. The sparse grey contours rising from the ground about us looked forlorn. Neglected trees held out the bare profile of their branches.

The vehicle had neither lights nor windscreen wipers, and was bashed in along the whole of its right side. The driver was standing at the far side, holding the one door that still opened. Douch crammed himself in first and had me sit beside him on the back seat, whose broken springs kept us barely above the floor. As I sat down on the dirty plastic, I suddenly pictured, as if in a dream, the awful desperation of the last occupants of this poor taxi at the moment it had been hijacked, probably during an ambush. An armed man climbed into the front and put his head out through the open roof. The Khmer Rouge leaders were assembled in front of the restaurant door. When the car started, they waved farewell.

We set off, bumping along the pitted road. The total lack of shock absorbers made our progress laborious, but the driver knew the route well and navigated by zigzagging between the ditch and the paddy fields.

"Do you feel reassured now?" Douch asked.

"Yes," I replied. "Thank you, comrade. I owe my life to you."

We were both clinging to the back of the front seat, jogging and swaying about in every direction.

"I acted according to my conscience," he defended himself, "and with complete conviction."

"Comrade," I exclaimed, "how could you be so sure?"

"I verified what you said with Lay and Son, whom I questioned individually and at length. Anyway, at my modest level, all I did was give an opinion – while trying to influence the final outcome, of course."

The Peugeot came to a stop, trapped in a rut, back wheels up in the air. We got out to push, as well as to take the weight off the chassis.

"As I told you," I reminded him, "I shall try to have medicines sent to you. I don't yet know how, but it ought to be possible. To whom should I send them? Just to Comrade Douch? I don't even know your full name."

"You can put the initials 'S.M.'* in front, if you wish," he replied.

"Is there anything else I can send you? Don't hesitate, comrade, it's the least I can do."

Douch thought long and hard and eventually said to me, with the look of a child writing to Father Christmas, "The complete collection of *Das Kapital* by Marx, though it's probably too big and too expensive."

We had arrived in an empty village, where some men were waiting for us by the side of the track. One of them came up hesitantly and directed the tired beam of an electric torch at us. The driver got out of the car.

"We have arrived," Douch told me. "Now you will continue on your own. Guides will take turns to lead you as far as Oudong. Good luck, comrade!"

We gave each other a fraternal embrace, and went our separate ways.

*The initials "S.M." stand for *sama mit*, "comrade of the same rank" or "comrade companion".

# 9

Gérard Serre displayed all the natural qualities of the cautious diplomat. He had been appointed chargé d'affaires in Cambodia after France recalled Ambassador Dauge in August 1971, in response to the *coup d'état* against Sihanouk. His wife, Charlotte, was a pleasant, elegant woman. I did not know either of them at that stage and had no idea that we would become friends. Anxious to be rid of the envelope the Khmer Rouge had entrusted me with, which I had nervously kept since the previous day, I decided, without further ado, to ring at the gate to the sumptuous colonial villa the Serres inhabited, opposite the Phnom.

I had walked all night long. Just as dawn was breaking, the last of the Khmer Rouge relay team that had guided me along the route left me to complete the last leg on my own and to cross the advance post of the government lines under the astonished gaze of the sentries, who were lying face downwards in their earth bunkers. They said nothing and allowed me to pass. I immediately squeezed myself on to a crowded bus and safely negotiated the two roadblocks guarding the capital. Soldiers had climbed aboard and searched all the baggage without asking me anything, although my beard, long hair and dirty clothes caused them to cast me a few suspicious glances. Then I walked through the town with deliberate slowness, measuring each step and breathing deeply, aware of the uniqueness of this moment and extending for as long as possible the joy of returning to normal life. I watched people moving about the street. My heart leapt. I felt I was living in another age; distances seemed different from how I remembered them. At certain places – the esplanade of the royal palace, for example, where I had often walked with Hélène – the past intersected with the present as if in a maze. When I arrived at my house, I stood transfixed on the opposite pavement, watching for any signs of life that might escape from the windows or the door, picking up familiar noises. I gazed at the columned patio that formed the entrance to the house, where I liked to sit and read. Among the trees in the garden, whose shapes I could remember clearly, I noticed immediately that the little latania, which had had such difficulty getting started, was sprouting a new palm; and that the incomparable crimson flowers of the erythrina were already budding on its bare branches. One of the house girls caught sight of me from the balcony with her sharp eyes, hesitated for a time, frowning comically, then suddenly raised the alarm. I entered through the little side door, covered with soft branches of flowering jasmine, and it seemed to me that I had never smelled its scent so powerfully or so deeply. Overwhelmed by emotion, Hélène's mother had fainted. Hélène did not recognise me; she was frightened and started to cry.

I was wearing the flip-flops that I had looked after so carefully all this time. Since the skin on the soles of my immobile feet had grown so tender, all my secretly cherished plans for escape, which had given me the courage to survive, had depended on their existence. They had become talismans. They were what I had clung to desperately when confronted with the swirling waves of despair. If I pulled through, I had sworn, I would keep them for ever. So I was amazed to discover that, in the confusion of the hugs and tears that greeted my return, they had disappeared. By an astonishing coincidence, Jean Boulbet, the ethnologist – and my very absent-minded colleague – was at the house that day, getting ready to go back to his home in Battambang, and had inadvertently slipped them on and left. Not for a moment could he have suspected what tears and distress, what solitude and panic, what immense terror those bits of rubber represented.

Engrossed in the joyous effusions we had all abandoned ourselves to after such a long separation, I had still not eaten anything when I walked into the chargé d'affaires' office in the early afternoon. I was accompanied by Bruno Dagens, my colleague from the École Française d'Extrême-Orient (EFEO), who had taken it upon himself to inform my mother and who, together with Michel Brunet, had unfailingly taken care of my family while I was gone. Set in the middle of a beautiful garden, the steps led up to the villa beneath a peristyle partly hidden by a clump of bright purple bougainvillea.

It was Boxing Day. Monsieur Serre was still at table with his wife, and our impromptu visit caught them having their dessert. Thoroughly taken aback at my liberation – no-one had really believed I would be released – as well as by my surprise appearance at their home, still bearing physical traces of my captivity, his wife hovered around me, gazing at me compassionately and insisting with the utmost kindness that we sit down and take coffee with them. I immediately declined the coffee, citing my empty stomach as an excuse. Highly embarrassed, she hurried off to the kitchen, loudly accusing herself of neglect, and returned very upset that she had nothing to offer me apart from the leftovers of their own meal. The notion delighted me, and I sat down in the beautiful pale-blue dining room framed by two curved columns whose palm-leaf capitals formed elegant scrolls on the high ceiling. The *bèp*, or cook, set my place, then brought in the delicious remains of vegetable soup and duck à l'orange.

enough to satisfy all my former companions left behind in chains in Omleang.

The soup was served. It was cold. I was so disappointed that I promptly devoured the duck and put the soup bowl to one side, untouched. This shameless scene still makes me blush, but at that moment I saw nothing abnormal in refusing soup that no-one had taken the trouble to warm up. Even worse, my response to Mme Serre's embarrassed enquiry was quite direct: "No, it's cold; but the duck is very good."

I was not really annoyed, just piqued by the cook's lack of awareness of the impact of such negligence: I had acquired a sacred relationship to food during my imprisonment. At this solemn moment, when I was resuming contact with existence, meals had attained the rank of a divinity, and I did not want to hurry the worship. I had sacrificed too much, too painfully, over the past months to be satisfied now with nonchalantly gulping down cold soup, as though it were unimportant, as one might in normal daily life, joking about it politely.

My reaction, which almost amounted to rudeness to my hosts, when their only wish was to please me, deserves some reflection. Over and above my own impoliteness, which the mistress of the house graciously ignored, I could sense the paradoxical mechanism that causes a man who has endured hardship to become an exacting and extremely sophisticated creature, little inclined to squander his essential skills or his capacity to find happiness in the simplest things; persistent in his yearning for a real quality of life. He must evermore live in full awareness of the transience of things, according to new and unformulated rules, which emerge from this sort of situation.

I remember in particular an episode that occurred five years later, in 1976, when, following the capture of Phnom Penh and the exodus of all foreigners from the country, I went to live in the north-east of Thailand, where I often met people, mostly volunteer workers, who came to help the Khmer refugees at the Khap Chhoeung camp. Fleeing the appalling massacres committed by the Khmer Rouge – to which the West continued to turn a blind eye – peasants emerged on to the Korat plateau in flocks of twenty or thirty. Males came first, females and young followed. The claws on their bare feet were full of earth. Panting in quick, halting breaths; their skin torn by t' orns and branches; their faces expressionless; and ready to set off again at a moment's notice, they surfaced from woods through which they had had to run the last few miles. They had miraculously escaped the lookouts who had been hunting them at the border, forcing them to abandon, here and there, a wounded companion, a bundle, a child they could no longer carry . . .

One day, ten or more of these starving fugitives rejected the rice they had been brought on their arrival on the pretext that it wasn't good! It was rice provided by American aid, entirely edible, but tasteless. The witnesses to this scene, officials from a non-governmental organisation – themselves capable of bravely consuming "anything" – were dumbfounded by their attitude, all the more incomprehensible in people they could never suspect of merely being difficult. At the time, I did not think of telling them that you have to be happy and at peace with yourself to eat cold soup. For starving people, wherever they come from, ever since the dawn of mankind, it has been a biological necessity, an essential link with life, to eat well. Today, thank God, I can once again eat food that is poorly prepared or that I do not like.

Mme Serre had a taste for fine clothes. A few years later, in 1975 – after that first meeting when I delivered the fateful packet to her husband – at the time of the partisans' victory over the government troops and their entry into Phnom Penh, I would realise this with wonder, to the advantage of a young Vietnamese girl . . .

On 17 April 1975, the first Khmers Rouges entered the capital from the north, making their way along deserted avenues. The previous evening, the new deputy prime minister, His Excellency Hou Hong, appointed to replace Long Boret, announced the surrender of the army several times on Radio Phnom Penh. Once issued, the order was irrevocable. The city's defenders, armed to hold out for months, were immediately struck at the very source of their strength.

I remember that the decision to enter from the north – which meant that the victors passed in front of our building – delighted the consul, who had been appointed chief of mission at the embassy. According to him, it was a clear acknowledgement of the revolutionaries' gratitude for French support. At the time, many felt that this was a popular uprising organised by the Khmer Rouge against American intervention in Cambodia. The complexity of the situation, the ignorance and incomprehension of the most prominent Western representatives when confronted by this atypical country, and the prevailing ideology, which tended to support the oppressed – everything contributed to an interpretation of the events which was skewed by attitudes towards Vietnam. Yet the greatest confusion reigned in people's minds. The following day, while the uninterrupted flow of revolutionaries entering the city wound its hesitant way past the embassy gate, one of the leaders, walking alongside them, harangued his men as follows (I was standing just behind the railings with one of the gendarmes): "Watch out now! This is the American Embassy: you mustn't touch the tyres of the cars in the courtyard."

In the streets of the capital, the tyres of vehicles abandoned all around were removed by the new arrivals, who cut out the rubber to make new sandals (called "Ho Chi Minhs") and replace their worn soles on the spot. The Khmer Rouge soldiers, who were all very young, advanced without any local maps, asking their way and faint-heartedly accepting the water and dishes offered them by the townspeople they passed. Neither they nor their leaders, following behind, could have imagined entering Phnom Penh without enormous losses or a siege lasting months. Others were now arriving in the capital by different routes, and they all converged in the centre, unsure where to go and lacking any precise instructions. The puzzled inhabitants stared and chatted with them. They found that they were children, equipped so basically that Lon Nol's soldiers, highly trained, overequipped and ordered to surrender, laughed and cried simultaneously. The disorganised rush of the Khmers Rouges met with throngs of refugee peasants travelling in the opposite direction, who had been waiting for this moment to go back to their villages. At the same time, all the inhabitants had been ordered to leave the city before the "American bombardments". It was the Communists' method of spreading deliberate lies, which no-one believed but everybody accepted. Soldiers dressed in black forced their way through the crowds, sitting in requisitioned vehicles with their drivers, using loudhailers to deliver the urgent order to evacuate. Huge jams formed at the end of Phnom Penh's long, shady avenues. Crowds massed in front of improvised roadblocks, where all vehicles had to be abandoned; people could take with them only what they could carry.

A few days earlier, from the top of the cathedral, fires had been spotted in the surrounding areas. At a short walking distance, to the north of Tuol Kok, shooting could be heard, a slow, fear-inspiring accumulation of explosions. Thick clouds of smoke dispersed gently into the sky. The sound of the fighting reached us with a slight delay. Far away, men were pursuing one another, ready to finish each other off with a knife. On both sides, the fighters had lost all sense of proportion. They scarcely regarded one another as human beings: the bodies transported back from the front bore wounds that only blind rage could have inflicted on an enemy who was already dead. Some of these corpses may have belonged to men from the same village – if not from the same household – as the people who had mutilated them without recognising them. Each family in the liberated zone was required to provide one son to the Revolutionary Army; but General Lon Nol's army offered each new recruit a salary equivalent to the loss of earnings from two sons, so brother would find himself armed against brother. During commando raids, the inhabitants of briefly occupied villages were abducted. None ever returned, and what we heard of their fates filled us with terror.

For months in Phnom Penh, the more than two million refugees camped on the pavements, peeling away the bark of the great century-old kokum trees by the side of the roads in order to cook dogs and cats there on the asphalt. The nose-to-tail lines of tanks from the elite divisions, which were still intact, formed a number of impassable concentric barriers.

A hundred or more rockets fell on the city every day. More than two hundred dead bodies had been counted the day before. Two rockets had fallen, in quick succession, on the racecourse, which was densely crowded with people. After the explosion, passers-by collided uncomprehendingly with groups of the breathless wounded, their clothes in shreds. At the same moment, in front of the Royal Palace, a peaceful, elegant crowd strolled along the Tonlé Sap. This was the constant reality of the fighting.

I returned to the embassy myself on 19 April, just after midday. The entire area was crowded; three thousand people, perhaps more, were packed beneath the trees; in the buildings; in the service corridors; in the car park, between the cars and inside them. The representatives of the United Nations Development Programme (UNDP), UNICEF, the United Nations and the International Red Cross had moved into the ambassador's residence; members of the press and the group Médecins sans Frontières had installed themselves in the reception rooms; the French community was camped in the vast premises of the Cultural Centre; embassy staff and their families, as well as the honorary consuls of Spain, Italy and Belgium, had taken refuge in the chancellery. The mass of Cambodians, Vietnamese, Chinese, and so on, had occupied the outbuildings, every inch of the gardens and even the space beneath the porches.

I telephoned Jean Dyrac, who was in charge of consular matters and the last person in a position of responsibility remaining on the premises, to ask him to make sure that the gendarmes guarding the perimeter of the much-sought-after locality were forewarned of my arrival. From the school, I could see so many abandoned vehicles in front of the embassy gate that I was not sure I would be able to get in.

I had been determined to stay to the last at the EFEO, where I had barricaded myself alone, like a proud captain unwilling to abandon his ship. Avi, the dog, had barked all night, while opposite us some Khmers Rouges were burning the house of Bernard Prunières, the cultural counsel, who, two months beforehand, like the majority of other officials, had been forced to leave the besieged city. Bands of scavengers were climbing over the corrugated-iron fences of the garden to loot the villa belonging to the school, which they thought was empty. Since the previous day, a corpse with its throat cut had been blocking the gate of the main entrance.

Hélène was in France. I had put her in the care of the Blatmans, who had left with the last of the aid workers to receive orders to depart. Her mother, the housemaids, the staff of the school and their families, and the Prunières' serving boys, as well as a few neighbours, had all gathered in the EFEO building before finally deciding to set off by road, afraid they would attract the attention of the hordes of Khmers Rouges who were roaming the streets with loudhailers, ordering the population to evacuate the city.

On the morning of 17 April, at about eight o'clock, His Excellency Hou Hong, the minister of state in charge of religious matters and acting prime minister, phoned to ask, without much conviction, for political asylum at the EFEO, arguing that since the building constituted French soil it benefited from the law of extraterritoriality. He was the former governor of Siem Reap, a man of great integrity with whom I had been on friendly terms over the years. This devoted student of philology could spend hours standing in the courtyard of a pagoda, searching for a reference in a manuscript, without noticing that it was growing dark. We used to spend a great deal of time together working on texts. The trust he placed in me was a precious gift that I still value today.

Hou Hong arrived a little later, driven in a black Peugeot 403, and Hélène's mother welcomed him amid the chaos with all the respect due to his rank. He moved into the library. But he, too, eventually made up his mind to leave, and gave me a bag.

"*Lok* Bizot! Here . . . in this bag are the things I inherited from my father, my grandfather, and so on, from Angkor. There are statuettes in bronze and in gold, horns, *khuc*,* elephant tusks, boar tusks, daggers, conches, boxes . . . everything you've seen on my altar at home, in Siem Reap. Today my sons are fleeing and go to meet their fate . . . peace to their souls! Keep these precious relics for me, if you can. And if, as I fear, something happens to me, keep them for yourself – if you can!"

I walked a little way with him, surrounded by the throng of refugees pushing to leave.

"Don't stay with me any longer," he told me. "It's dangerous. Go back, now!"

---

* *khuc* (bezoars), stony concretions found in various animals. Those from the salivary glands of elephants are particularly highly prized.

Hou Hong was murdered at Kilometre 6, on the lower side of the road, at the first roadblock he encountered; he had not concealed his identity.

A few months later, in the suburbs of Bangkok, when I was sharing an empty house with Boulbet, I had a visit from Dufieux, an old Cambodia hand who had left before the start of the troubles and who knew where Hou Hong's wife lived in France. Not without a certain regret, I had him take her the few precious heirlooms, which I had succeeded in getting out of the country along with my other possessions in the one suitcase we were permitted. Then, in the next few days, we were visited by Thai burglars, who stole the little we still had.

At dawn on 19 April, about ten soldiers had smashed in the gate of the EFEO with the butts of their rifles. The schoolhouse was the only building in the area that was still undamaged. The fierce rumbling of that gloomy night had kept me awake in a corner of the entrance to the villa. The ever-vigilant dog had not stopped growling. Distant explosions, echoes impossible to identify, the grating noises of bicycles and rickshaws, murmurings interspersed with groans, sporadic bursts of shooting, shouts of abuse, the muffled sound of jeeps going past, scrapes against walls, loud voices in the street, the creaking of cartwheels – all this had combined to bring up terrifying images from deep within me which obsessed my thoughts . . . I hurried to open up before they destroyed everything.

They immediately swarmed over the garden and the outbuildings, then went into the house, paying no attention to me. They were genuine Khmers Rouges, dressed in black pyjamas and *krama*, with green caps that elongated their faces: real country folk, free of all arrogance, but with slow-witted expressions and incapable of overcoming the disgust that filled their hearts at the sight of an "imperialist lackey". They searched everywhere, opening cupboards, going into the bedrooms, grabbing here and there a trinket, which they examined with a puzzled and innocent laugh. In a corner of the sitting room, one of them noticed the fine xylophone that I had brought back from my village of Srah Srang and which I liked to play in the evening. He transferred his cigarette to his mouth, pulling a face as he pressed it between his lips, then borrowed a second Kalashnikov from his companion; kneeling in front of the instrument, he shoved the butts of both rifles under his armpits. Using the barrels of the gun like two drumsticks, he smashed the keys to pieces, causing the bits to fly all over the room.

Meanwhile, a van had parked inside the courtyard of the school. Other partisans, who did not know the first group – I could see them warily sniffing one another out – burst into the library and began to empty the shelves, tossing bundles of books out into the back of the van. The collections on the first floor were hurled out through the windows. The van made several journeys, overflowing with precious volumes that we had deliberately kept in Phnom Penh, anxious to show our dedication to future generations of Khmers. (It was fashionable at the time to entertain the view that a country's intellectuals, Communists or not, would always need a collection of rare books dealing with their own history and culture.*) Caught up in her own inconsistencies, France realised too late that the Khmer Rouge, unschooled in the art of gathering wool, did not know to shear the sheep rather than skin it alive. All these books belonging to the school, laboriously collected and indexed by generations of scholars, were burnt with others in a pathetic auto-da-fé to provide thrills for a handful of adolescents.

Along with the books from the first floor, one of Hélène's

*Although, on 12 April, the ambassador had forwarded a telegram from Paris signed by Jean Filliozat, the director of the school, asking me – somewhat late in the day – to pack all the books in chests ready to be sent back to France.

dolls had been hurled on to the garden lawn. A soldier saw it land, grabbed it with both hands, and drop-kicked it in my direction. For an hour I had stood on the staircase, speechless, until that moment. But faced with this provocation, the howl of a wounded beast came from my chest. Without knowing what I was doing, I rushed at the astonished Khmer Rouge; all sense of time had vanished. In the middle of my furious charge, I began to look for a way out. As I approached him, my hands grasped his shoulders so as to move him sideways – though I did this cautiously, reducing the force of my thrust – and, with fury in my eyes, I yelled into his face, "Comrade cadet! What revolution do you represent here? Do you dare suggest that it is in the name of the Angkar's efforts to construct a prosperous and democratic Kampuchea that you trample the cherished goods of a progressive and industrious people? Do you think you are serving the community and making yourself useful to the people by this intolerable arrogance? No? Very well then, comrade, move along then! Stop treading on the sugar palms that I planted last year, thinking of your future children and grandchildren! They will provide them with sugar, palm wine, fruits for delicacies or medicines, fibres to weave, bark to make baskets, pillars to hold up their houses and palms to cover them, matting, partitions, joists, floorboards, canoes . . . Get out! Right away!"

Rooted to the spot, his complexion greyish, the Khmer I had just rebuked bent down and discovered the new shoot of a *Borassus* palm emerging from the earth.

"If you don't care about having children," I continued, "then think of your brothers all around you, comrade, for it matters to them!"

Stunned by my speech, which caricatured the jerky delivery of the Communist leaders, the soldier went back down the path. His flabbergasted companions had watched without moving. Relieved that I had at last spoken out but anxious to maintain the advantage of surprise, I slipped away, closing the door behind me.

# 10

The gendarmes were waiting for me on the other side of the gate. They immediately opened the grille, and I parked the car in a corner. I had been wise to call ahead. The entrance had to be cleared and several cars that were blocking the access removed. Outside, a jeep full of armed soldiers was positioned on the pavement. I arrived just as the first meeting of the French senior spokesman and the Khmer Rouge leaders was getting under way. The meeting took place in a room on the ground floor of the chancellery. An official came up and asked me to come and join the people who were crowding freely around the negotiation table: journalists, planters, missionaries, honorary consuls, representatives from international institutions, delegates from non-governmental organisations United Nations officials, teachers, businessmen, company directors and so on. Six delegates were seated: four Khmers Rouges, the consul and an elderly priest who was acting as a translator. The low-ceilinged room was oppressively hot. The instructions of the vice-president of "the command for the northern front of Phnom Penh, responsible for foreigners" were read out in a barely audible voice that required total silence from the large audience: first, on the orders of GRNUK, the command for the northern front would do its best to ensure the protection of the French Embassy, whose site, as well as all the assets therein, were to be considered as "spoils of war"; second, only holders of foreign passports were authorised to remain in the embassy, and those Khmers who had entered illegally were ordered to leave; third, henceforward, no foreigner should leave the protected enclosure; fourth, these orders should on no account be contravened; fifth, further orders would follow. In fact, nothing had been anticipated. The revolutionary high command had been taken unawares. The problem of our presence had hit them like a bolt from the blue.

I approached the table just as Jean Dyrac was putting forward France's demands, which for the time being arose out of our urgent situation. To his mind, the most pressing danger threatening our disparate community, even if a more dangerous one could not be excluded, stemmed from the overpopulation of our campus: lack of drinking water, lack of provisions, lack of hygiene. He made an urgent request for medicines, water and food. And just to show that we were not making unwarranted demands, Dyrac was specific: "Rice and dried fish will be sufficient!" The interpreter translated the consul's words literally, and we saw the faces of the Khmers Rouges freeze: their mouths set in a forced smile, they sat in silence; they were troubled by something. There was an awkward pause.

"The Khmer people," began one of the four, "by command of its historic leaders, is ready to make every sacrifice to satisfy the needs expressed by the respected foreign community. However, they have not yet reached the end of the glorious march that will lead them to ultimate victory against the American aggressors and the Lon Nol–Sirik Matak gang who are in their pay. For centuries, they have been engaged in relentless struggles against colonialist occupying forces and their lackeys, who have openly made repeated moves to undermine sectors of the economy. Today they can lift their heads high. But the means at their disposal are still very modest. They are not sure, therefore, that they can respond fully to the three-point demand made by the

French delegate on behalf of the foreign community.

The soldier who came out with this stream of clichés was standing next to another man who said nothing. It was nevertheless on him that all eyes were fixed: a dry, bony Chinese man of sinister mien whose slit and sunken eyes were crowned with eyebrows that were almost invisible; the passage of smallpox had left his marbled pink face covered with a sort of grey semolina. He was terrifying: a character straight out of a crime thriller. We would encounter him once more, then never again.

The atmosphere in the room grew tense. Yet what could be more legitimate than our modest requests? Dyrac did not understand but was very conscious of the awkwardness. The interpreter, who was also embarrassed, repeated the consul's words more gently, putting further emphasis on the dried fish. Right away the misunderstanding became apparent: he was translating not "dried fish", but "smoked fish": a request as inappropriate as if we had requested smoked salmon from people who had been surviving on bread and water. Although any fish can be put out in the sun to dry, *trai ngiet* had become a rare commodity. It was a sought-after speciality of the Great Lake, a complicated preparation using only one or two types of extremely expensive fish.

"Comrade!" I said in a loud voice without thinking. "All we need is for the fish to be dry, '*sguot*', or edible in any way. This question is unimportant!"

The Khmer Rouge turned towards me, considerably relieved, making broad gestures of approval. Jean Rémy, catching sight of me, asked me to come forward.

"Bizot!" Dyrac called out. "Come and sit with us."

Feeling embarrassed that I had intervened in this unsolicited and impromptu way, I did my best to allow the interpreter to speak, but the Khmers Rouges now addressed themselves only to me. My outburst had been instinctive, but not very courteous.

The man knew the Khmer language perfectly, and this type of confusion was commonplace, if not inevitable, in such a pressured situation. Nevertheless, I had caused him to lose face. He held it against me personally. These were the circumstances that led the Khmers Rouges and the consul to appoint me as the official interpreter at the embassy and, eventually, as the only person authorised to leave it.

The city's new authorities had no medicine, of course. We decided to make use of whatever was stored at the Calmette Hospital, which was situated a block away and which the French army doctors had still not evacuated. Water was brought to us the next day, but it was delivered by a tanker truck that had previously carried fuel oil. As far as food was concerned, the Khmers Rouges asked for a few more days. In the meantime, it fell to me to scout for resources stocked all over the city and to bring back whatever I could to feed the hundred or so people who had arrived on the first day without any provisions and who had still not been given anything to eat.

At nightfall, I did not know where I was going to sleep. Avi, one of the last dogs in Cambodia not to have been eaten, had been rescued by Jan Migot, who was a good guardian. Rumours had actually reached me that the dog's muscular haunches were attracting greedy, eager stares. Eventually, I went and lay down with him in the decoding office where Michel Lorine, the coding officer, had kindly suggested I stay. Outside, the endless flow of outcasts surged past the gate, in the opposite direction to the armed columns that continued to roll on towards the centre. Fighting raged close to the station. We could hear the thudding resonance of heavy machine-gun fire.

Pierre Gouillon and Georges Villevieille, the embassy's ever-dependable gendarmes, took turns at their post day and night. Since they did not speak Khmer, we agreed that one of us who knew the language would always be available at night. We were so overwhelmed that François Ponchaud, a missionary I had often seen speeding along the streets on a racing bicycle, spent the first few days constantly at the gate.

We were instructed not to admit anyone except foreigners bearing passports. It seemed very likely, in fact, that the Khmers Rouges, who had immediately asked for a list of foreigners to have taken refuge within our walls, would throw everyone else out on the road. We feared that the fate of these poor people – also-rans, in some sense, who had tried to escape the revolutionary *diktat* by asking asylum from France when she was not in a position to grant it – may have been even worse than that of other Khmers. The misgivings that had prompted them to go to the embassy were damning proof of their distrust of the new regime and therefore of their "guilt". Many understood this and resolved to leave the capital immediately; more than two thousand people slipped away without further ado.

But the decision no longer to grant asylum to the Khmers – no matter how many were seeking it, standing there in front of the gate, holding onto the grille until the Khmers Rouges chased them away – stemmed from another calculation: we wanted as much time as possible to organise our own affairs behind closed doors. In other words, we rejected all Khmer Rouge police control, both at the gate and within our confines; we even wanted to bar access to all armed soldiers. Of course, the victors of Phnom Penh had not signed any surrender terms with France, and for them the system of extraterritoriality was a fiction whose legal existence we vaguely attempted to explain. Our determination to isolate ourselves, that is, to remain autonomous, made sense only with their support. In reality, it was unsustainable, and I still wonder how we managed to impose our will in the beginning and to keep up the pretence until 6 May.

We had particular difficulty containing the fury of some soldiers who were threatening to knock out the gate with bazookas (as they had at the Russian Embassy). I had to run across the street to ask for help from Comrade Nhem, the "vice-president" of the northern front of the city who had attended our first meeting and was the person responsible for foreigners. Despite his good-natured appearance, this man was capable of terrible fits of temper. You could see that in his tiny, cold eyes, which were always at odds with his jovial expression. He constantly broadcast this contrast, for all around him to catch, and everybody picked up on it.

So when I went to ring his doorbell, I watched him emerge from the South Korean Embassy opposite us, where he had set up his quarters, and nonchalantly cross the Boulevard Monivong. He assessed the danger absent-mindedly, walked over to the officer, who was infuriated by our obstinacy, and focused his impenetrable gaze on him; touching him with its keen point, without pushing it in. Taking him by the arm or holding his hand, he led him away; after a while, the officer withdrew and set off along the road, taking his men with him, without a word being said. This former teacher from the Battambang region, who had been given full control over us, was understanding to the very end. Throughout the twenty-two days when we depended upon his goodwill from hour to hour, I cannot count the difficulties of every kind that were sorted out thanks to him. In answer to each of my constant requests, he would shake his head silently, as if refusing; then, apart from one or two occasions, he would consent by signing for me a piece of paper detailing his instructions.

This period in France's history, though perhaps not very illustrious, did benefit from another happy circumstance: the appointment, a few months earlier, of the consul, Jean Dyrac, as our senior representative. A former Resistance fighter who had been arrested and tortured by French police on the orders of the Gestapo (the "Brigade des Anges" in Lyons), he was instinctively aware of the formidable weight of his responsibility. From the outset he approached the situation humbly, creating around him a group of informal advisers who helped him, in a collegial way, with every decision. The men who made up this group had not been specially convoked, but many heads are better than one. His circumspect approach was described by some as a lack of leadership capacity. But the majority believed that the opposite attitude could easily have transformed our raft of good fortune into a field of slaughter.

The doctors and the staff of the Calmette Hospital arrived in the evening. They were put into the reception rooms at the residency — which had been made into a dispensary — in place of the members of the foreign press corps, who were moved into the ambassador's apartments. When I entered the large room to have a chat with them, Bernard Piquart, a surgeon about my own age who had recently arrived in Cambodia, whispered between his teeth, "Hush! They're spying on us."

In spite of his youth, the newcomer was already an eminent and respected figure and the type of man who liked making a fuss; unfortunately, he was so very aware of his own superiority that he had a complex about it. We had crossed paths a few months earlier at a cocktail party, just when he was in the process of explaining in a facetious tone of voice that he, a *"professeur agrégé"*, could not possibly have been sent from Paris to take over from Dr Lepelletier, his predecessor, since the latter did not have the same qualifications. This distinction, unfair and hurtful to the person he did not wish to replace, was frankly ridiculous in the context. I ventured to say that such reservations on his part were to his credit, since a surgeon such as Lepelletier (whom I had woken up to save the life of Bernard-Philippe Groslier, the curator of Angkor, who had been stabbed repeatedly by a burglar) could not, in fact, be so easily replaced. A few days after this little incident at the residency, Piquart stopped me in front of the chancellery. I could see his eyes twitch, then his face became red; his mouth tightened as he tried to hold back the sobs that suddenly caused his shoulders to shake.

"I'm a bloody fool!" he panted. "This awful business . . . this wretchedness . . . all around us . . . I've got nothing left. I've had to leave our Cambodian interns behind . . . They were like children to me. I'm a coward! I can never look myself in the face again! If we come through this, my life will begin at zero. Forgive me for the other day . . . I'm not proud of myself."

The strength of Piquart's regret, prompted by the events we were living through, turned the knife in the wound. It was true that the spectacle of this mass death gave each of us the feeling of being reborn. His confession brought to mind something I myself had said four years before: "If I come though this, I will never be the same man." Unfortunately – as I told him – I had to admit that over the years the expected alchemy had not occurred. Be that as it may, I was touched by his sincerity, and we got along. We would have several opportunities to speak again before he became my teammate on the final convoy.

At daybreak, I left the air-conditioned decoding office, where I had been getting cold. I took a few steps outside along the extended first-floor balcony that overlooked the sandbag-covered patio. It was already warm, and I could feel the scent-rich humidity lingering on my skin. I went to see Dyrac in his office to tell him that I wanted to go to the EFEO and bring back at least the sacks of rice I had left beneath the staircase. I found him and his wife already in conversation with Colonel-Doctor Henri Revil and the headmaster of the Lycée Descartes, Alexis Maurin, two men whose views he always took into account. With them was Carlos Ripol, the Spanish honorary consul, a deserter from Franco's Foreign Legion who was practising medicine unlawfully in Phnom Penh. I had once taken Hélène's grandmother to see him: her child with Down's syndrome was unwell. "Aren't you going to charge me?" I asked him at the time. "I don't charge Cambodians," he had replied. Whenever he happened to join our discussions, he spoke with a lot of good sense and always gave excellent advice.

The villa belonging to the school had been looted by vandals, ransacked by soldiers from top to bottom. The sewing machines had been broken, the cupboards smashed, the sarongs, blouses and cushions tossed on the ground, the mattresses turned upside down and the Khmer pottery in the showcases stolen. The silk *sampots* had also disappeared. Pools of urine flooded the tiled floor of the dining room. In the first-floor bathroom, the bidet was half filled with excrement. More mess stained the floor between the empty shelves of the library. Deeply shaken, I took the jeep out of the garage and quickly filled the trailer while pondering how man will brutally seize every opportunity for gain, and is instinctively attracted to defilement and desecration.

On the other side of the road from the school was a large flame tree, which bloomed earlier than any other in town, and was the pride of successive cultural counsels. Its extraordinary conflagration of red flames stood out against the sky. As I came out of the school, I noticed, in its shade, the Prunières' turkeys. A staggered pattern of eye marks on their gaudy feathers decorated their rounded backs, swaying through the high grass, with scales of bronze. I instantly decided to grab them and have them roasted.

I stopped the jeep in the middle of the road, beside some metal beds that the families of the wounded had driven out of the Preah Khet Mealea Hospital and abandoned when the wheels eventually collapsed. Pedestrians walked along the pavements, pulling or carrying large, poorly tied parcels, accompanied by children who stared at me as they followed. I went in through the wide-open gate, not daring to enter the villa, whose blackened walls were still smoking. The four turkeys were pecking at a rubbish patch covered with tufts of greenery. I walked straight up to them and pounced on the first one, which started to gobble crazily, beating the ground with its golden wings, losing its feathers and throwing up bits of gravel. I was holding it with one hand when my attention was drawn to the loud scrambling of a redskin in battledress, dancing away in front of me and puffing out its throat: coloured blue down to its neck, with a shaven head and a beak adorned with red grapes, the turkey, in a trance, was making sharp clacking sounds with the fan of its tail feathers. It sounded a few beats on a tom-tom hidden beneath the bulges of its extravagant keratinous armour and charged at me fiercely. I was taken aback by its courage, and had the greatest difficulty imaginable in finding enough energy to wring its neck – a painful struggle that brought tears to my eyes.

I was returning with the large birds tied up as best I could in the jeep when I noticed, in the middle of the boulevard, an enormous Japanese sow, teats swaying between superb haunches, grunting and zigzagging among the crowd, a few yards from the embassy. I quickly had them open the gates and several of us pushed it into the precinct, where it was immediately felled with a blow from a sledgehammer.

Next to the sentry box, a man of about sixty was waiting for me: handsome head held high, brow cleared of his ash-coloured hair which fell waving on either side. The starched collar of his formal shirt was open, revealing a badly shaved neck.

"My name is Marcel Riner, Monsieur," he told me. "I'm the manager of the Brasseries Générales de l'Indochine. I've left my office, empty-handed, to come straight here. My house is just five minutes away. Would it be possible for you to drop me there on one of your outings and let me pick up a few things?"

I was jotting down his request in the notebook in which I wrote everything that was said to me when Nhem summoned me. I made my excuses and crossed the street.

"The traitors who belong to the fascist and racist gang hidden in the embassy must give themselves up immediately!" Nhem said to me as soon as I entered the dark, chilly hall where he had had a table installed. "A lorry will come to collect them at eleven o'clock."

"Excuse me?"

"Sirik Matak and the other lackeys! They must all give themselves up. No harm will come to them, but they must surrender!"

"I don't know what the comrade is talking about!" I said in good faith. "We don't have any of those people here."

Nhem handed me a list that he was holding. I was flabbergasted to read the names of some fifteen members of Long Boret's last government, among them Khy-Taing Lim, the minister of finance; Loeung Nal, the minister of health; and so on. There was also one of Sihanouk's wives, Princess Manivane.

"I'll pass on the request," I said dubiously, "but I'm quite sure there's some mistake."

I sprinted across the boulevard and the courtyard and went into Dyrac's office. I interrupted him and put the Khmer Rouge list down in front of him.

"They say these people are here and that they must give themselves up!" I exclaimed, looking at him questioningly.

"My God!" he replied at once. "How did they find out?"

His face had turned scarlet. The others, who had been talking with him when I burst in, lowered their heads.

"It's impossible! Impossible!" he repeated in a resolute voice, looking at me. "Look, this is an embassy, damn it! We can't just hand them over. They've asked us for political asylum! And in any case, this list is wrong. This name here, this one, this one . . ." he said as he ran his finger down the page, "I haven't seen them. They're not here."

"So?" I asked him.

"So it's no!"

"OK. But things are going to turn ugly, over the road . . ."

I did not believe for an instant that we would be able to keep them, since they were actually there. At the same time, it was natural to refuse. I left the office and crossed the street again.

"Comrade!" I said as soon as I arrived, in as firm a voice as possible. "Comrade, these people have the benefit of *droit d'asile*" — I used the French term — "that is to say, they are now under French protection. Furthermore, half this list is incorrect."

Taken aback at my intrusion, Nhem listened to me calmly at first.

"The comrade has not understood me," he said in a gentle voice.

Then, with his elbows bent, he pressed both hands on the table. "Either they come out, or we go in!"

As he uttered the last word, he tapped his pencil on his desk and glared at me. His lips puckered. A tremor in his cheeks caused the corners of his mouth to break into a shifty smile. Then he stood up, saying nothing, took a few steps, and added, hammering out each word, "Let the comrade make this quite clear: if they have not come out by eleven o'clock, we will go and turn them out ourselves. We know where they are!"

"Can I guarantee that their lives will be spared?" I asked, trying to find an argument in the face of the weakness overcoming me.

"Of course! They will be tried fairly."

I stepped out into the dazzling light of the boulevard. As I passed, I could see some Khmers Rouges busy towing away cars abandoned outside the embassy. To the south, a temporary road-block forced the tide of refugees to branch off at a right angle. The consul was waiting for me behind the gate with Maurin.

"It's out of the question!" I exclaimed. "He couldn't care less whether we're on French soil. He doesn't even want to discuss it. In any case, this is no longer an embassy but an international gathering place. In less than half an hour," I said, looking at my watch, "they're coming to get them. Have you seen the boulevard? They're removing everything."

As he listened to me, Dyrac turned round to go into the chancellery. We went up to his office, where five or six people were already seated. He settled in his chair and asked me to repeat Nhem's response. A discussion ensued. On principle, everyone was broadly in agreement that we should refuse to yield up people who had asked France for asylum. At the same time, we all knew very well that we did not have the means to enforce such a resolution. Since we could not delay for weeks, we made a decision to go and find those concerned and put the problem to each one individually. If any of them ruled out leaving of their own free will, we would have to see.

"Very well!" said Dyrac. "Bizot, come with me. We'll go and find Sirik Matak."

Maurin, Revil, Rémy and a few others took responsibility for the remaining individuals, many of whom were in the chancellery. Some had been planning to escape through the back but had been dissuaded by the Khmer Rouge guards, who had set up fairly strict surveillance to prevent anyone getting in. In the end, strange as it may seem, none of them tried to escape their fate. They all believed that if they showed themselves willing, they might perhaps receive a little clemency.

I followed the consul. As we stepped outside, we noticed several trucks with tarpaulin hoods parked in a fan formation. One was full of soldiers. There was a jeep immediately in front of the gate, which Migot and the gendarmes had kept closed. Elsewhere, the boulevard and the courtyard were empty. Nhem had protested to the journalists who were photographing him over the wall of the enclosure in his headquarters and had asked that all cameras, along with the film they contained, be handed over. Not wishing to risk further provocation of this kind, we took very strict measures to ensure that no press correspondents were present when the Khmers Rouges arrived.

We walked through the gallery that led beneath the large staircase to the cultural affairs offices, stopping at the door to a small room, just before the blocked toilets, which were emitting a foul smell. The consul gave a few knocks on the door in an agreed-upon code. Then we heard a key in the lock and the door opened. We entered.

In the gloomy light of a makeshift office cluttered with furniture piled against the walls, Prince Sirik Matak was standing behind a table. With him were two young soldiers in combat uniform, boots and undershirts, who were acting as his aides-de-camp. Dyrac, who entered first, found himself unable to utter a word. Sirik Matak looked straight at us. An intense stare rose from beneath his thick, bushy eyebrows. His powerful jaws were set onto a long, birdlike neck. In his face there was no tension, only a questioning look. His hands were resting on a half-open briefcase.

"Excellency," I eventually said, after a ghastly silence. "The Khmers Rouges are at the gate. They are fully aware of your presence here. They are asking for you."

"But . . . the right of asylum!"

I kept quiet, to let Dyrac speak. He said nothing.

"It's a concept they refuse to acknowledge," I struggled to articulate. "They have nevertheless promised that you and the other members of the government who are being ordered to give themselves up will be allowed a fair trial. If you do not agree to give yourself up of your own accord, they are determined to come and get you."

"I know what I have to do," replied the prince decisively.

Then he lifted the lid of his briefcase. I anticipated his movements and turned the key in the door, which the orderly had closed behind us. But instead of the revolver that his words and the glint in his eyes had led my harrowed instincts to expect, he brought out a pair of carefully folded trousers. Sirik Matak was in his underclothes. He slipped on the trousers of a beige suit, the top half of which he was already wearing. The two soldiers with him also got dressed. Dyrac pointed out that they were not on the list and that nothing prevented them from remaining hidden; but they proudly expressed the wish to accompany their leader to the end. The prince turned fleetingly towards them, and I could see tears welling up in his eyes.

We went out into the bright light. The gate was already open, and it had begun to rain. I noticed Sihanouk's daughter climbing up with difficulty into one of the lorries with her husband and children. Seeing Sirik Matak, the Khmer Rouge standing beside the jeep looked in our direction. I recognised the pockmarked Chinese from earlier on. He walked over to meet the prince, open-armed and with a smile on his pitted face, as if he knew him, which was most unlikely. After shaking hands for a long time, each holding the other's hand in both of his – Sirik Matak was laughing too, but the terror in his eyes was unappeased by his adversary's surprising greeting – they embraced each other, several times, moving theatrically from one side to the other. Then the Chinese, who was clearly the grand master of the delegation, led him towards the jeep as if he were a friend. The three armed soldiers who had got off climbed on again at the back, where Princess Manivane had taken her place. The Chinese invited Sirik Matak to sit in front, holding out his left arm to allow him to pass. Courteously, the prince did nothing and requested that his host go first. Smiling more and more, the Chinese insisted, before eventually thanking his distinguished guest and climbing up into the jeep. Sirik Matak followed, but there was little room left on the seat; he sat down, as best he could, on one buttock. Dyrac and I watched this comedy in amazement. The jeep moved forward a few yards, then stopped. The Chinese asked Sirik Matak, who was sitting much too uncomfortably, to get down. Addressing him as his "elder brother" (bang), he insisted that he move to the middle. The prince made as if to refuse but then realised that his host, without saying so, was afraid that he might take advantage of his outside position to try to escape from the moving vehicle. He complied graciously and moved over next to the driver. The Chinese then fitted himself in as best he could. Sirik Matak put his arm around his shoulder and clasped him warmly, so that he "wouldn't fall off at a bend". Everybody laughed. The jeep set off again. The prince waved goodbye to us with the tips of his fingers without letting go of the Chinese man's shoulder. Once past the roadblock, the vehicle disappeared into the crowd.

I pointed out to the consul the banners hung across the boulevard. They read, "Death to the traitor Sirik Matak."

The Chinese man's smiling amiability was not designed to inspire his victim's gratitude. It was simply an upmarket alternative to the prosaic *At oy té!* of the executioners in the Omleang forest.

# II

Thick brush strokes of dark ink trapped the sun, causing electrical flashes to streak up into the heavy air, zigzagging as they rumbled against the wash of the sky. An eddying wind shook the glossy pendants of the great banyan tree with a noise like the rustling of cardboard. Some cans were blown off a bench; saucepans fell off a little stove, whipped up by the tail of a tornado that picked up piles of dust, leaves and empty bags before surging between the walls of the buildings.

Screwing up my eyes, I was walking towards the chancellery when I saw one of the gendarmes gesturing to me. Seeing me veer off in his direction, he hurried back. Nhem was standing by the gate with three Khmer Rouge officers and a group of armed soldiers.

"Open up, comrade!" he called to me through the grille in a voice that brooked no reply. "We have come to inspect the premises."

Perturbed that they were armed — no Khmer Rouge had yet crossed the entrance of our embassy with a gun — I left him standing there without an answer and rushed to warn the consul. I feared that in spite of our precautions, some of the military personnel who had sought shelter within our walls might have left their guns lying conspicuously beside them. Dyrac immediately dispatched someone to warn the department heads that an inspection was imminent; then several of us hurried off to welcome our guests (as we persisted in regarding them), trying – unsuccessfully – to dissuade them from entering with their guns.

Nhem looked nervous. The men escorting him were not the ones he was usually with. They were answerable to three other senior officers who wore Chinese caps pulled down to their ears and carried Colt .45s on their belts. Dyrac set about showing them the ground-floor rooms of the chancellery, where we had stored the few sacks of food supplies that had been delivered to us. But the Khmers Rouges made their way, without regard for anything else, towards the park, where the crowds of refugees, and in particular the Khmers who had entered illegally, were gathered. Our group walked the length of the large, windowless wall of the north face of the cultural affairs building, coming out onto a vast, compact crowd of more than a thousand people crammed beneath the trees, filling the pathways with their jumble of bags, sheets, bicycles and cardboard boxes, forming an immense clutter of men and women, squatting or lying on the ground. Without further ado, the black-clad revolutionaries began weaving their way among the fearful throng, their faces sinister and frowning, provoking much jostling and shoving; some women in sarongs ran away screaming, terrified at the sight of their guns.

"Stop!" shouted a soldier. "Stop!"

The fugitives froze on the spot, but one of them, distraught, tripped over the mats and the baskets and continued on her panic-stricken way.

"Stop!" roared a second guard. He raised his rifle and took aim, his eyes blazing.

Orders and savage cries rang out on all sides. Everything happened very quickly. The woman's action prompted others to flee in every direction. A wave of panic broke out all around us. The soldiers were shouting and cocking their guns. I rushed over to Nhem and demanded that he do something. Berger and Rémy tried to intervene. I particularly remember the look on the face of Monsignor Ramousse, the bishop of Phnom Penh, whose eyes caught mine in the collective hysteria: shaken with fear, he had jumped to his feet from his chair beneath the tamarind tree.

"*Ban hay!*" Nhem called out sharply, in a high voice which set off a strange, high-pitched echo. "That's enough!"

The vice-president of the northern front moved forward, and angrily slapped a nearby soldier's rifle butt with the flat of his hand. His expressionless face abruptly grew cold. For a few seconds he said nothing, casting his eyes about him and breathing quickly.

"All Asiatics must leave the campus without fail!" he suddenly shouted. "Women separately from the men. The women will regroup in the stadium!"

With these final words, he turned on his heels. His body was quaking. His face was distorted with rage. I believe he would have killed anyone who had opposed him. I hastily followed him.

"Comrade," I said insistently, "there are perhaps two thousand people here! A hurried departure could lead to appalling chaos. Give us time to prepare. There are other people than Khmers! We have not finished drawing up the list of passport holders. The job probably won't be completed today. Comrade . . ."

Followed by the young warriors who had so quickly lost their self-control, Nhem passed through the gate without replying and briskly returned to his headquarters. The tragedy that we had narrowly averted – for this insignificant visit could easily have degenerated into slaughter – had exposed a violence so terrible and so explosive that I felt totally disheartened. I feared that we had merely obtained a useless respite, as if this first part of the tragedy already heralded its catastrophic conclusion.

I returned mechanically to the Khmers, who all looked terrified. Women were weeping nervously in each other's arms.

Fathers were bustling about among the crowd, offering "psycho-logial support", as Dyrac had asked them to do, and I tried to join their efforts. A pall of torpor fell over the park, bringing no relief to anyone. Many of those who had been unsure about leaving on the first day decided then and there to pack their bags and leave the embassy in small, discreet groups.

I caught sight of Father Venet in the distance and gave him a friendly wave.

"No, I'm not all right," he called out, his brow furrowed. "I have a headache. It's about to rain. A good thing too! We're baking."

Father Félix, one of the four Benedictine monks from the Subiaco congregation who had been driven out of the Chrouy Changvar peninsula, was calmly going about his daily walk, saying his prayers, unperturbed by the heaped bodies, which were now languishing again, stagnating in their inertia. Carrying a hoe and a metal spike, he inspected the ground, gathering the pieces of excrement and soiled paper scattered everywhere: beneath the hedges, between the mats, along the pathways. From dawn to dusk, you could see the outline of his black habit and white beard, combing the area, bending attentively, and briskly burying the foul waste matter.

A number of French people were still in the city, either stuck in their homes or too afraid to leave. Migot had compiled a list. The consul asked me to try to get in touch with them and bring them in. Nhem lent us a minibus and an armed guard, who was given orders. I also got permission for Devaux, a resourceful and energetic Frenchman who had just joined us, to drive the vehicle.

We immediately got stuck in traffic in the centre of town. An impatient crowd filled the market place, flooding the entire area and spilling out into the surrounding streets, cycles, cars and carts facing in every direction, while abandoned tanks and army lorries obstructed the traffic flow. The huge, confused babble of this multitude on the march buzzed all around us and blocked out the sound of the minibus's horn. Unable to advance, we branched off on the Potchendong Road towards the university, where, according to my list, some French academics remained. The avenue, lined with emaciated, blooming flame trees, seemed to have been deserted by the teeming fugitives. We were warned that it was closed off further up. The airport, which was surrounded, still held out.

Along the paths of the abandoned campus, I passed students hurrying by, carrying their possessions in boxes. They pointed out the wing that housed the teachers' lodgings, and I rushed down the empty corridors, calling out the names of those I was to bring back with me.

"Yes, what is it?" called a voice from the stairs.

Leaning over the banister, a young man with a crew cut was looking down at me from the third floor.

"Are you Martinie?" I asked, looking up. "I've come to get you. Come on, hurry up! Get your things. We're going to drive you to the embassy."

"Ah, but I'm not moving!" he replied. "It's out of the question!"

"What? You really want to stay?" I said, with an incredulous smile.

"Of course!" he said, evidently provoked. "I've been waiting for this blessed day for too long to leave now! I want to join with everyone else in the joy of liberation . . . it's going to be fun!"

It was neither the time nor the place for a discussion.

"You're free to do as you wish! Are there any other French people?"

"Yes, flat number 9. But they won't leave either," he told me with a sardonic sneer.

The wind was sweeping down the open corridors, scattering pockets of dust and bringing with it gruesome echoes of the terrible chaos in the city.

I knocked several times at number 9 before a woman's voice answered in a lilting tone, "Coming!"

A hand pulled the latch and opened the door. The young woman in front of me wore an apron, held a plate and a dishcloth, and welcomed me affably.

"Forgive me," she said with a charming smile, "you can't hear anything in the kitchen. But come in. Do you want to see my husband? Jérôme! Do sit down. I'll go and get him."

"No!" I protested. "I won't sit down. I've come to get you. I have orders to bring you back to the embassy . . . for your own safety."

"Oh, really? It's so very kind of you . . . Jérôme? What's he doing?" she apologised, looking embarrassed. "He hasn't heard. I'll go and get him. Do please sit down."

The flat was bright and tidy. Classical music came from a back room. A tall, bearded man entered, wearing shorts, and greeted me warmly.

"I'll get you something to drink," said his wife. "What will you have?"

"No!" I exclaimed again, trying to quell my indignation at their blindness to what was happening all around us. "I must leave. Follow me if you want to. But do so at once! I haven't a second to lose. Others are waiting."

They chose to stay behind and were terribly apologetic that I should have put myself out for nothing. I rushed off, furious at their naivety and annoyed to have wasted precious time on people who approved of the invasion, the arson, the looting, the murders, of everything that disgusted me so profoundly.

We drove back through the vast mêlée in the streets of the capital, and we had the utmost difficulty in forging through the crowds. First we went to Bassac, where we were able to rescue a young man and his wife, who had been raped over a period of several nights. Then we headed to the National Museum district, where four French people were anxiously waiting for us. One of them, René Laporte, was married in France but lived with a Cambodian girl whom he hesitated to take with him. She was clinging to him, terrified, and we had to order them to come to a decision. We also brought back d'Harcour, whose wife was secretary to the ambassador, Louis Dauge. She was in Bangkok and had been terribly worried; the Foreign Office had managed to send her a telegram about her husband.

At each crossroads, we had to negotiate with Khmers Rouges who wanted to confiscate our car, remove our watches and search our suitcases. Our guard had the greatest difficulty getting them to recognise him. At one point, a conversation with a group of very young and excited guerrilla fighters grew so lively that it degenerated into a violent disagreement between their leader and our guard. Our escort took aim at his opponent, with the immediate result that the latter's companions began pointing their rifles at us. A tragedy was averted only by our guard's self-control: he remained stoical and let them know that he was determined to fire first. He was a curious fellow, quite young and slim, with a dark complexion, the frizzy, almost woolly hair of some Malays, and the expression of a bad-tempered lapdog. He knew instinctively that at moments like these everything hinged on the final second.

We continued our slow progress through the crowd, which was being held back on all sides. I remember with tears in my eyes the little boy with a shaved head, like the *rishi* ascetics on the bas-reliefs at Angkor, and the three tufts of hair that had been allowed to grow over his temples and his fontanelle. He was ready for the ritual of "shearing the hair". Very inappropriately, I took his photograph, without thinking. The child gave me a long smile as he turned around and went on his way. Ahead of him, his mother forced her way through the mass of people surrounding them.

Worst of all were the expressions on their faces. All around us, the dark pupils of a thousand restless eyes, flashing against an apocalyptic sky, bored into ours, each for at least a second – enough time to land briefly before continuing their uncertain flight, bequeathing us a fragment of their fear.

We reached the embassy just as the low ceiling of the sky gave way. Squalls of rain, driven by gusts of wind, bringing with them a strong smell of earth, poured down on our sweat-covered bodies. I got out of the minibus and ran. Avi, who was waiting for me to come back, pranced around me. The gutters had overflowed, and water was gushing onto the square patio of the chancellery. Several people were there already, soaping down their bodies and shouting at the tops of their lungs. I took off my clothes and rushed down the long chicane formed by the piled-up sandbags. Romanie, naked, was also making her way out along the cramped passage. "Madame le proviseur", as her husband, M. Maurin, referred to her in all seriousness, leaned back against the sacks to let me pass; I did the same. But the insufficient width of the passage meant that we would rub against each other. We looked at one another for a moment, then turned around so we could pass in a more seemly fashion.

Suddenly overcome with hysterical excitement, we all jumped about like kid goats. Avi, who was also dripping with soap, gashed my back with his claws. We both tore out of the chancellery, bolted across the courtyard through the rain, rushed along the footpaths, between the cars, over chairs and past packing cases, cheered on our way by hundreds of merry faces beneath cardboard boxes, and bounded our way to the residence, where the large British and American population started chanting "Streaking! Streaking!" as we passed.

I was dressed and shaved when a gendarme asked for me at the gate. On the other side of the grille, a man in his seventies stood rather stiffly, wearing his Chevalier de la Légion d'Honneur medal. A steady stream of pitiful people, pushing or carrying their bundles of wretched belongings, with their children or old folks piled onto carts and now soaked by the rain, were strung out behind him in the boulevard. Some Khmers Rouges turned and looked at the old man as they went past. His head was covered with thick white hair, and his cheeks, faded about his eyes and gently rounded, fell onto firm lips and somehow lent his features an air of nobility.

"I am Prince Sisowath," he told me. "I have the honour to request political asylum from France."

I could feel myself blanch and become slightly dizzy.

"Excellency," I asked him respectfully, "do you have a French passport?"

"Obviously not!" he replied.

I immediately asked him to wait a moment and dashed off to see Dyrac. His powerlessness seemed to him even more despicable in this case, and he expressed it with anger.

"No passport, no key. Right? What else can we do?"

I returned quickly to the gate.

"The Khmers Rouges will not permit you to stay," I told the prince before I had caught my breath. "They do not recognise the right of asylum. They will come and look for you."

"Very well!" he said forcefully, with a trace of annoyance.

He turned on his heels, and I watched him walk away, without turning round, before disappearing into the pathetic crowd of the exodus.

Along with the clutter of vagabonds who were making their way down the boulevard in dense columns, there now appeared the city-dwellers who had waited until the last moment to take to the road, hoping perhaps that once the first few days had passed – and since no American bombing had occurred – the order for forced evacuation would be replaced by other directives.

You could see girls wearing clean sarongs, shop assistants

from the market, seamstresses and employees of all kinds, their mouths marked with traces of the lipstick that they had had to wipe off as they ran the gauntlet of insults from the disgusted revolutionaries, who considered them to be prostitutes. They had broken their varnished nails on the edge of the pavement. Their beauty inflamed deep hatred in the hearts of the young partisans.

A large Mercedes with smoked-glass windows drew up in front of the gate. The refugees, loaded with suitcases, moved aside in an automatic reflex as the car approached. The back door opened, and an elegant young woman stepped out. With her heels ringing out on the pavement under the nose of the Khmers Rouges who were passing by in front of us, she hurried up to me, holding a well-swathed baby barely a few months old in her arms.

"I am Madame Long Boret," she whispered in French. "Let me in quickly! Please!"

The gendarme beside me took a breath, closed his eyes and blew out through puffed cheeks. Among the refugees the rumour had spread that her husband, who had returned hurriedly from Bali to try to negotiate with the Communist leaders, had been beaten up at his home and thrown into his garden well.

I shall never forget that she was wearing black tapered trousers and a dark short-sleeved blouse, that her face was white, and that her dark-ringed eyes, with their lightly made-up, slanting eyelids, were terror-stricken. For a brief second her long, manicured fingers protruded through the latticework of the gate.

"Madame!" I asked her, already close to tears. "Do you have a passport?"

Casting distraught looks about her, her chest heaving, out of breath, and clearly not expecting my question, she gazed at me with an expression of panic as she shook her head.

"Without a foreign passport the Khmers Rouges will expel you," I said in a single gasp, not daring to think about what I was saying.

Some grimy-looking partisans had approached. One of them

was inspecting the car, the doors of which had been locked from the inside. He hit one of the windows with his rifle butt; it didn't break. The pale-faced chauffeur slowly opened his door. His khaki uniform was covered with dark blood flowing from his neck.

"Then at least save my child!" she implored.

I will never forget her cry: a protracted, heart-rending moan overlaid with harmonic trills, ending in a gasp.

"No! Don't do it – " I begged her, raising my voice as I realised what she was about to do.

Now frantic, the young woman took her baby in both hands, then held it out in front of her and, not quite sure how to go about it, swung hesitantly to one side; leaning forward slightly, with a rotating movement of her bust, she prepared to throw the child to me over the gate.

"Save him, I beg you!" she wept. "Here, catch!"

"NO!"

I could feel my body grow tense and my heart solidify. The gendarme walked away, stunned. My hands covered my eyes. And for a few moments I stayed like that, not moving, standing rigidly to attention in the darkness. I could hear soldiers calling to the driver and then the slamming of a car door. I lowered my arms just as the Mercedes set off, bearing Mme Long Boret and her little baby to their dreadful fate.

I was trying to get my breath back, walking round and round the courtyard, quivering and panting, when Piquart and Larègle (the chemist from the Calmette Hospital), accompanied by two journalists, came up to invite me to the barbecue they were organising jointly at the residency, at eight o'clock.

"There'll be no invitation card!" they warned me jokingly. "Dress informally. And be on time!"

Right then, Dyrac summoned me to say that I must urgently set off in search of food. Rémy explained to me where the planters stored their rice and how to get there. Others also gave me a number of addresses, and I jotted all the information down in my notebook. We were in the office that Ripol and his family occupied. It was full of people: one of the gendarmes, Mme Dyrac, Revil, Father Ponchaud, Father Berger, Fournier des Corats (the bursar at the Calmette), Cagnat (the vice-consul), Goueffon (the director of the Pasteur Institute), Jules Maire (the Belgian honorary consul), Espuy (from the orderly office), Zink (the military radio operator). Since this morning, I was told, Captain Ermini and Migot had no longer been welcome at the chancellery. I realised that there were cliques within the building. We were to stop providing them with information because they were working not just for the Foreign Office . . . but Migot was a friend and I was not going to get involved in these obscure considerations. To surprised acclamations, someone uncorked a bottle of Rémy Martin. I discovered that it had come from the Serres' packing cases, which had been blocked and returned from Kompong Som, and which the forwarding agent, Piquart, had put in the orderly office with the provisions. We filled our goblets with brandy and soda and clinked glasses without really knowing what we were drinking to. The first mouthfuls without ice made my head reel. Some people tried to make jokes, but their hearts weren't in it. I went out to get some fresh air.

The rain had brought a little cool air with it. Under a uniformly grey sky, darkened by the approach of dusk, long-eared bats, visible only in their wing movements, dropped from the tall kokis onto insects twirling in the light of the streetlamps. A lugubrious sadness rose from the boulevard, still peopled by shadowy figures moving along its length. Sitting in his doorway, Nhem was watching them file past.

I opened the gate and walked a few paces across the damp asphalt, in the grip of an uneasiness I could no longer describe.

"Comrade Bizot is sad!" Nhem called out with a laugh. "He's thinking of his family, on their journey!"

I smiled without replying. From the pavement, I asked

permission to stop by my home to pick up some clean clothes.

Both doors of the gateway to the EFEO were wide open. With a melancholy air, the large dipterocarp planted by Boulbet lifted its plumage into the night, its base dimly uplit by the lights from the boulevard. The pattern of tiles in the hall alternated a yellow and white motif with symmetrical figures in two shades of blue. Black streaks covered it where a fire had been extinguished with streams of urine. I went up to the first floor without stopping to survey the chaotic jumble of broken chairs, upturned sideboards and shattered glass mounts that reigned below. From among the tangle of clothes, sheets, pillowcases and linen of all kinds that littered the floor of the bedroom, I pulled out a shirt and a pair of shorts. In the bathroom opposite, I observed with astonishment that the bidet, which had been half full yesterday, was now overflowing with excrement. I fled as quickly as I could, mulling over this foul, little short of miraculous achievement, pondering the astonishing mental machinations that can make sense of such behaviour.

Nhem came to meet me, and we walked up the boulevard in silence, eyes downcast, our hands in our pockets, and our hearts heavy, like old friends who no longer need to speak in order to communicate. It seemed to me that our attitudes towards the present events were similar, pain and suffering stirring deep within us. We took our leave wordlessly in front of the gate, and I felt that these few minutes had, curiously, been more meaningful than a long conversation. We did not know each other. But the closeness of our footsteps in the night had prompted shared thoughts and introduced a sort of trust into our relationship that would play its part in later events.


I was already up when a livid bluish daylight stole across the sky. The weather was close and rainy, but less unsettling at least than the night had been. I immediately took my day's schedule to

Nhem for his endorsement. I carefully noted everything on a sheet of paper, as he had asked me to do: shopping trips to town (rice, canned goods . . .); a visit to the cemetery (for Migot); a search for someone holding a French passport who was wounded and hiding in his home (near the market); the recovery of a trunk from the Benoliels' flat (behind the Mission Technique); and so on. He wanted to be informed of my every movement and to discuss its appropriateness with me. As an exception, he agreed that someone could accompany me to help collect the sacks of rice, but he turned down the visit to the cemetery because he could see no reason for it.

Leaving the embassy in the jeep, I drew up beside the manager of the Brasseries Générales de l'Indochine, who was standing by the sentry box, as he did every morning.

"Come on, get in, let's go!"

He jumped in gratefully beside me.

"I'll drive you home and pick you up in an hour. You've got plenty of time to pack a suitcase. I won't come up. I'll sound my horn from below to tell you to come down."

I dropped him outside his home and immediately set off again in search of supplies. The tiny streets were empty except for a few ghostly shadows. I braked suddenly as I happened to pass Negroni's house. Negroni had been recruited on the spot as manager at the conservation office. One evening at Boulbet's house, this affable, unassuming man had, with tears in his eyes, told us his life story: he had been enlisted in the Milice* at Nancy during the war before escaping to Indochina at the time of the Liberation. Much later, he had married a Vietnamese girl and was the father of a boy, Charles, now seven or eight years old. When he said "my Charles", he said everything. All three of them had French nationality. I had dealt with the papers relating to his

*A paramilitary organisation created during the Vichy regime to assist collaboration and to track down Resistance groups. [Tr.]

185

meagre pension. Yet he had not turned up at the embassy. Just to be sure, I decided to cast an eye over the flat that he and his family occupied, free of charge, in a collection of buildings run by the nuns from the Daughters of Mary convent. No longer clearly remembering where he lived, I ventured aimlessly into a maze of courtyards, enclosing walls and half-landings, opening doors and vainly calling out his name. Hens and ducks with metallic plumage ran about through the deserted doorways. The smell of a samrong (*Sterculia foetida*) stood out above all others: the tree's tall, leafless branches loomed over the middle of a small garden, and its red-ochre flowers, spread over the ground along with the grainy husks of its fruit, emitted their foul fragrance. I found that in total solitude, cut off from any other presence, one can soon begin to feel frightened.

As I crossed a large room, a sort of communal hall or dormitory, I noticed a figure beneath a mosquito net. An elderly nun, still alive and clearly French, lay motionless on a mattress that smelled of urine. Her eyes smiled at me. I told her gently that I was going to take her to the embassy, where she would be looked after, and leaned down to lift her up. But she wanted to stay where she was and stopped me with a slight gesture of her bony hand. Her face remained impassive. She did not reply when I asked her name.

I set off again and after the Phnom passed the large ochre building of the National Bank of Cambodia. Tens of thousands of 500-riel notes lay strewn over the road and the pavements, which were cluttered with sandbags and barbed wire. What even yesterday had represented a huge fortune fluttered about in front of me, ephemeral banknotes that in a few hours had lost all their value. I was coming to look upon this destroyed world and these desolate avenues as a spectacle, and laugh at it all.

I slipped silently into an immense theatre of death. I thought that the apprehension of so much destruction would soon tip the fragile balance of my sanity. There was not a single child, not one living creature. This sudden suspension of life in the heart of what had been the great commercial centre of the Mekong Delta — this city famed for its many and varied activities, its colourful population, its cosmopolitan lifestyle — struck me as both so incredible and so straightforward that I imagined myself in a dead world, deserted in the wake of some cataclysm, where I, without knowing it, was the only survivor. I shut my eyes and went deep into the entrails of this empty stomach like someone in a futurist comic strip and I confess that I derived some kind of pleasure from this dark wandering.

The Khmers Rouges appeared to be in control of the city centre. They were erecting barricades at crossings, yelling at the last people to leave who were still running around in the streets, levying a fine on each of them as they passed. They stopped the jeep. I had to show my pass and explain where I was going. I went first to the house of Jules Maire, who represented the Roussel pharmaceutical laboratories and who had boasted to me about the abundance of supplies in his garage, as well as his first-rate cellar. But I also had to break into other people's houses, kicking down doors, going into their kitchens, looking at the paintings on the walls, penetrating the intimacy of their bedrooms — photographs of children, open drawers, lingerie, underclothes, trinkets, souvenirs — free to take anything, or to leave it all. Occasionally I came across a prowler filling his bag. Forcing the front door of one of the houses, I found myself face-to-face with a large dog, a cross between a Dobermann and an Alsatian, that had been locked in for several days and looked at me with a rather worrying expression. I hastily passed into another room and allowed it to escape. In the dining room, a meal lay served on an embroidered tablecloth; glasses were still full. Beside the open bottles, the remains of a chicken sat on a plate and had begun to stink.

Finally, with the trailer and the back of the jeep filled with sacks of rice, tinned goods, packets of spaghetti, lentils, sugar and salt, as well as some bottles of wine, I went back to pick up my Brasseries manager at his place. He did not answer my calls. Attracted by the little beeps of my horn, some Khmers Rouges came up and started asking questions. I made as if I were leaving and returned a little later. Still nobody. Not daring to sound my horn again, I rushed into the house, calling out, terrified that something had happened to him. The ground floor was an indescribable mess. Walking past the kitchen, I noticed next to the sink a magnificent angora cat whose grey fur gleamed with silvery reflections; I quickly walked over to look at it more closely, and a rotten smell penetrated my nostrils. I eventually found the manager on the first floor, sitting on his bed, his head slumped. When I entered the bedroom, he slowly got up, without any reaction, looking at me with lifeless eyes. Beside him, an open suitcase was still empty. I took a few toiletries and a change of clothes.

We returned to the embassy and I went to look for Migot at the consulate.

"I think it will be possible," I told him, "but not today."

His wife, Monique, was sitting next to him, both of them busy drawing up lists. A few weeks earlier, they had lost their youngest daughter in a terrible accident, and they wanted to go back to the cemetery for the last time. A former parachutist, an officer of the Foreign Legion and a geography teacher, he was the director of the Alliance Française in Phnom Penh. With an athletic physique and a robust personality, he was shaped like a cube. His doctrine was fierce anti-Communism; his obsession, always to be the first to bring out his wallet to pay for a meal or a round of drinks; his mission, always to do favours for everyone; his credo, work; his passion, wine. In short, an explosive mixture. But Migot had something else as well: two twinkling suns for eyes on which all the wrinkles in his cigarette-stained face converged. And the light that shone from these two lively orbs, which he turned on you the moment you shook hands in the morning, made you forget the previous day's arguments.

"It doesn't matter, old boy!" he assured me. "Don't worry about it . . . Hey, here's the gendarme! It's for you."

A covered lorry was parked in front of the gate, and three Khmers Rouges were asking us to take in eight foreigners who had come up to them on the road. The gendarme wanted me to check their passports before letting them in.

I went out to look through the side of the lorry and saw some Indians, who were talking away in Khmer, badly. Fortunately, they all had passports, which one of them handed to me. In fact, they were Pakistanis, and I made a show of examining their papers in order to prove to the Khmers Rouges that these things mattered to us. One of the travel documents was of a different colour and belonged to a woman of South Vietnamese nationality, whose poorly glued photograph had apparently been added at a later stage. I stood on the tips of my toes to look beneath the tarpaulin again. Two gleaming eyes stared at me from the back of the truck.

"OK! Fine! *Bane*," I said to the Khmers Rouges.

At the same time, I signalled to the gendarme to open the gate. One by one, the Pakistanis jumped down onto the road and the girl emerged from the darkness. She was a little over twenty years old. The creased material of her floral-patterned sarong was black with dried menstrual blood. I kept their passports and bade them enter the embassy.

Nhem crossed the road, holding in his hand a safe-conduct pass with a brown cover.

"What sort of passport is this?" he asked me. "This Chinese man has been here for an hour and speaks a little Khmer. But he says he's not Chinese."

I inspected the passport as I followed Nhem. It belonged to a shopkeeper who was in Phnom Penh on business. The man was in a terrible state.

"I am a citizen of Singapore!" he repeated in English, pointing a finger at his chest.

"Ah!" I said to Nhem. "He lives in Singapore. He's Malaysian."

"No, no!" insisted the wretched man. "Singapore! Singapore!"

Neither Nhem nor I knew that Singapore had become an independent republic, and we did not understand what he was talking about. I nevertheless took the woeful Chinese to the French Embassy, where, in the middle of the courtyard, the Pakistanis and the Vietnamese girl were waiting for me to find room for them. We needed to attach them to a group so they could be included in the food calculations. We decided to put them with the Indians from Phnom Penh, who were accommodated in the north-west sector of the campus.

But the Vietnamese girl was reluctant to go with them. She came up to me to explain, without using words, that she did not want to stay any longer with these men, who had been bothering her for the past two days. As she asked for my help, I could see her trembling. She seemed frail and lost, and tears welled up in her eyes. Her teeth gleamed brightly through full lips. Locks of stiff, sticky hair fell over an oval-shaped face whose features had retained the full charm of youth. But as she spoke there was a little movement at the sides of her nostrils, as if they were pulled by a thread, and this suddenly gave her whole countenance an expression of audacity and determination that made her look older. It was the hardness of her deep-set, dark black eyes that was most surprising. And I saw them trying to look into mine.

"Right. She doesn't want to be with the Pakistanis," I explained to the gendarme. "I'll look after her. Since the Chinese speaks English, we'll try to find a space for him near the residence."

Venet and Ponchaud were walking towards us, in heated discussion. They were worried about the inevitable expulsion of the FULRO* troops. These men, who had fought an

*FULRO (Front Unifié de Lutte des Races Opprimées): Unified Front for the Struggle of Oppressed Races.

anti-Vietnamese guerrilla war for decades in the mountainous region where three frontiers meet, had entered the embassy and were refusing to leave. Accompanied by M. Y Ban, the founder of their movement, and Colonel "Paul", their commander, they had arrived on the morning of the first day and had staked out territory next to the Indians. We asked the two missionaries to accompany the new arrivals to the far end of the campus.

"In the meantime, you'll wait over here," I told the Vietnamese girl. "Come!"

I set off along the corridor of the Cultural Department, thinking to find her a place in one of the ground-floor box-rooms, but they were all locked. We then passed the recess that led to the passage with the blocked toilets. I started down it and then turned around. The girl was upon me. Her mouth was open, and her lips seemed to be softening into a smile that was at once contemptuous and provocative. She flattened herself against the wall and stretched out her neck. Then, all of a sudden, her face took on a tragic expression. Everything inside my head became confused and jumbled. I pressed myself savagely against her. A cry, quickly repressed, rose from her throat, like a blast of wind that pervaded my senses. With a violent movement, she seized my penis from inside my shorts. Her half-closed eyes rolled upwards modestly, leaving only the silvery gaze of their whites.

I crossed the courtyard quickly and went into the chancellery, where I enquired about finding some shampoo. No-one had any.

"What do you need it for?" asked Lorine with a look of surprise.

"None of your business!" I told him, with a wink.

Eventually, I found what I wanted thanks to Romanie, who also gave me her perfumed soap. Without further ado, I moved the Vietnamese girl into Prunières' office, to which I had been given the key on the first day. I had, in any case, already spent a night there myself, on the large rosewood table. The square foam-rubber cushion from the armchair, which I had used as a pillow, was where I had left it. I pointed out to the girl the small adjoining lavatory with the tap attached to the wall. She said nothing, and I left her on her own.

I went to find Espuy.

"Where are the Serres' belongings?" I asked him.

"In the basement. But there's nothing left," he said derisively. "I've brought up everything useful. There wasn't much, anyway, apart from the brandy. Which I can't deny was good. I opened all the crates. There are only some books left, a few knick-knacks and some women's clothing."

"Exactly!" I exclaimed.

But all Charlotte had left in Phnom Penh was some evening wear. I searched through the abandoned trunks, among the elegant dresses, sleeveless and otherwise, some of which – very smart and mostly long, in red or green, plain or patterned, made of crêpe de Chine or silk and light as gossamer – were bare at the neck and shoulders. There were other short ones, made of embroidered cotton or multicoloured material, that had been cut to reveal the legs. Struck with wonder and unable to make a choice, I finally selected a fairly simple silver lamé fabric, not realising that the plunging neckline also left one shoulder bare.

The Vietnamese girl had shut herself in the shower room while waiting for her soiled sarong and shirt, which she had immediately washed, to dry. From the other side of the door, I let her know that I had left a dress for her on the desk and then went out again.

"Bizot! They're looking for you," the gendarme said to me. "That fellow opposite wants you."

Standing on the far side of the gate, I recognised the "Malay" who had escorted us to the university. We crossed the road together. Nhem was chatting to a few Khmers Rouges, some of whom I thought I had come across before in his company. He asked me to sit down in one of the post-art-deco armchairs upholstered in red-and-black marbled leatherette that he had chosen and placed in a corner of the gloomy den that had become his shelter. The Malay joined us, together with someone else I did not know and who was by far the oldest among us.

"All the Khmers must leave now, or they will be killed on the spot!" Nhem burst out in a firm voice, going straight to the point.

Disconcerted, I sat with them sheepishly, unable to reply. It was true that time had gone by and the refugees were still in the embassy – though far fewer than on the first day, more than a thousand having vanished without our noticing – in spite of the solemn orders we had received to force them all to leave. I had a foreboding that the character who was with us at the meeting had come to warn us that the Khmer Rouge high command was getting impatient. I could see that he was in a critical situation, almost as if he had been accused of not knowing how to go about enforcing the evacuation. The last thing on earth I wanted was for our gaoler to be replaced.

"They will leave, comrade!" I replied confidently, to appease his sudden aggression and reassure the other man. "But perhaps not this evening? It's late . . ."

"Tomorrow!" he affirmed, doing his utmost to show that at the end of the day it was he who made the decisions.

"Comrade," I said uneasily. "I am only the interpreter. It's not for me to respond. I need to go across the boulevard and return again in a few minutes."

"Tomorrow!" Nhem repeated drily as he rose to his feet, but having assented to my request.

I went to find Dyrac. By a curious bit of thought transmission, this unbearable obligation, which weighed day and night on our empty stomachs, was precisely the subject of heated discussion in the consul's office when I entered. Each of his advisers was subconsciously and persistently delaying this forced departure and had even begun to underestimate its urgency, hoping that the passage of days would lessen the problem.

"This is very timely," I announced immediately. "Because it's happening tomorrow. Nhem is in a stranglehold; he won't give way any longer. In fact, it's fairly straightforward: either we reject the idea or we accept it. If it's no, I'll go and tell them. If it's yes, it has to be done very quickly. At the same time it makes no difference to the Khmers: in either case they will be evacuated. Except, in my opinion, for this slight difference: if they resist, it will be far worse for them. And for us too, perhaps, but that's another matter. Anyway," I told Dyrac, "you have to decide. Nhem is waiting for an answer. I'll be in the courtyard."

Head in my hands, I sat down in the main entrance on the polished green steps which had glittering bauxite chips set into them. Devaux and Ponchaud were at the gate. Grey scarves of cloud stretched away above them, mingling with the white streaks of an aeroplane high up in the sky. I imagined the pilot huddled in his cabin, thinking of anything but us, like in the Omleang forest, when the distant noise of a lorry's engine would reach my ears and I would have given anything to be able to attract the driver's attention, because his vehicle was for me an epiphany of the outside world, and the sound of his engine an extension of the realm of freedom. Then I followed the two men's eyes, which were taking in the evening's mixture of tones. I observed with them the degradation of the colours, their changes under the influence of the dying light and the thickening shade. Not only the colours, but even shapes seemed to acquire a new energy; I discovered secret significance in the contours that loomed out of the twilight: the cars, the walls, the frangipani trees were rich with some unexpected substance. There is a hidden meaning in things: you just have to look.

But I also noticed that they kept turning around, casting occasional, almost furtive glances in the direction of the Cultural Department, where a silvery form was swaying in the still warm air which was now mellowing the cool shade of the car park. The Vietnamese girl had slipped on Charlotte's figure-hugging gown. She was walking hesitantly, not daring to draw attention to herself, both embarrassed by the rawness of her beauty and happy to be beautiful.

She was an unreal vision, yet one that emanated from a fierce determination to survive. When her body was against mine, I had felt her reach through concealed layers into the very depths of the universe, to extract that mysterious energy that has always linked man to the brilliance of the stars.

Afterwards, there was no longer any question of such things between us. We kept our silence, bound by the discovery of a secret that is buried for ever. I would see her again, a few days after our arrival by truck in Bangkok. Equipped with a safe-conduct pass – a genuine one this time, which Father Venet had procured for her – she was preparing to leave for France. Our eyes only met for a second.


The stifling atmosphere was unexpectedly shattered by a terrifying explosion from the centre of town. The tremor the displaced air produced made the chancellery shake on its foundations.

"Well!" exclaimed Dyrac, who had appeared behind me. "It's probably a gas pipe. All right. You can tell him that tomorrow morning we will do everything in our power to make those refugees who entered illegally leave the embassy confines. But we can ensure our cooperation – you must insist on this – only if he can guarantee that nothing will happen to them when they leave. They must all depart freely, regardless of sex, without any special supervision. This is very important. Show him that it matters a great deal to us."

Nhem was standing in the middle of the boulevard with his colleagues, watching the smoke spiralling up into the air. Above the grey cut-out of the city's rooftops twisted the material of the clouds, woven with scarlet lamé lines.

I went up to him. He had calmed down. I don't believe he had doubted my answer for a moment. We walked nonchalantly in the direction of the square, and as we walked I told him what the consul had to say. All around us people were still moving to and fro, skirting the barbed wire that blocked the passage beneath the Japanese bridge, sabotaged two years ago by a North Vietnamese commando force, making it spill its steel guts into the Mekong. Once we had reached the cemetery we turned back.

"Comrade Nhem, look!" I said, pointing to the tombstones and the iron crosses, some of them leaning wildly in the overgrown grass. "My friends' daughter was buried here only a few days ago. Her mother would like to come here to pay her last respects. This is a personal favour I ask of you."

As I said this, I looked at him.

"We'll see tomorrow," he replied. "It's getting dark now."

# 12

"Migot, Monique, we're off to the cemetery!" Dawn had just broken, and I had only half opened the door to the consular service to call them. They were still stretched out behind the counter of the long room where they spent their days and nights endlessly drawing up lists, together with two staff employees, Binh and Villaréal. They must have been up late, in the company of the consul, making counterfeit passports for those Khmers who would be likely to possess one and who could thus remain in the embassy without attracting too much attention: spouses of French nationals, ex-soldiers, hospital staff, teachers . . . Naturally, we had to be careful to make the false identities look reasonably convincing – not just the documents themselves but their attributions, to avoid giving rise to suspicion when they were checked. We therefore took a great many precautions, even falsifying the registers. These guarantees were absolutely necessary, since we did not know what level of scrutiny we would be subjected to. Fifty-three passports and passes were produced in this way on behalf of eighteen young Cambodian and Vietnamese men, twenty or so women, and about fifteen elderly people.

The Migots rushed to follow me. The Malay was waiting for us at the gate with two men holding their Kalashnikovs on their shoulders in the way one holds a rake or a broom, that is, by the lighter end. We quickly crossed the large square and passed some bushes and hedges, flattened by the recent rains, which enclosed lines of neglected tombstones. The ground was covered with overgrown vegetation that reached as far as the railings surrounding some of the tombs. The plot was at the far end, by the wall, but though it had been dug recently, we could not immediately identify the spot because it had already disappeared beneath the tall grass and the undergrowth. Migot squatted down and knelt on the damp ground, vigorously clearing the china pots and the dried flowers from his daughter's grave. Not understanding what he was looking for, one of the soldiers imagined he was uncovering a cache of arms. He panicked, immediately trained his gun at Migot and started yelling; in the confusion, the other two also took aim. Not realising what was going on, the broken-hearted Migot jumped to his feet ferociously, ready to charge them with his bare hands. A tragedy was narrowly averted, thanks once again to the Malay's composure: he managed to intervene in time and persuade the threatened man who was fighting back proudly, to step back; he then went and checked with his foot that there was nothing hidden in the grass. I helped my friends clear the little mound that formed a tender patch of green above the earth.

On our way back to the embassy, we greeted Mlle Carrère. The old lady had just come to sit outside, on the chair that had been allocated to her, beneath the awning at the entrance to the consulate. She had taught French in this country for years, and she did not want to leave. She was well known here: she wrapped her hair in a white lace mantilla, fastened behind her head with pins, that fell down over her shoulders; occasionally she wore a few flowers over her temples. All day long she would sit there, watching without curiosity whatever was going within the field of her tired vision.

The team of missionaries, the doctors, the planters and all the

French people who spoke Khmer were bustling about, tending those who had so ill-advisedly wound up with us and who now had to depart. Most of them were ready to go and were not surprised to find themselves preparing to leave, even if a few, blinded by the trust they put in us, would have liked to cling indefinitely to the tiny patch of French soil where we had allowed them to find shelter. The doctors, who had been alerted the previous day by Revil, had provided small bags of medicines, antibiotics and, especially, treatment for diarrhoea, of which there had been a hundred or so cases during the past few days. Since some of the Khmers had entered the embassy on the coat-tails of a resident, a specialist or a journalist who had been their neighbour, or colleague, or friend, many of these helpless protectors, with tears in their eyes, were now assisting them in their final preparations.

Several hundred people were gathered here, opposite the Cultural Department in front of the parked cars. They stood in a column, their bundles at their feet. Then this most terrible of processions got under way, everyone doing his or her best to smile. But it was an affected smile, the sort we give while biting our lips, when we are seriously ill, for example, and we don't want to worry our loved ones. For those who stayed behind, the worst thing was having to conceal our own sadness from those who were leaving. Surrounding the Khmers, hordes of men who had not wept for many a year were pressing up against them, spluttering, coughing, sniffing and turning round to take deep breaths.

Among those we were evicting were a Swiss, a Frenchman, a Vietnamese, an Italian, a Thai and a Laotian, who could have stayed but did not want to abandon wives, husbands or fathers.

At this final moment, all present tried to confront the situation with dignity. They could sense the hard life awaiting them, but they were ready to begin a new existence. Many joked in order to fortify themselves, to make the situation less dramatic, and also to minimise the shame we felt. I can see Mme Despres, in charge of the secretarial staff at the Dumarest Company and married to a Cambodian civil servant, putting on a determined frown and telling anyone who was prepared to listen that she, for one, had had enough of working in air-conditioned offices. The couple had packed their belongings into a wheelbarrow and seemed impatient to leave (though the husband at the root of their common misfortune, struck a tragic figure). A large, blonde Italian woman was making people laugh by saying that, Khmer Rouge or not, there was no way she'd let her man set off in search of adventure and find a younger woman on the way. And then there was the Thai woman who had lost her passport and was insisting that she would manage to seduce a handsome revolutionary who would look after her. But deep in all their eyes we could see their terror.

Nhem arrived at the gate with the Malay. The moment he appeared, a wave of agitation rippled through the procession, which he addressed with the help of a megaphone:

"Countrymen old and young, men and women, workers, civil servants, peasants! As vice-president of the northern front of the city, I welcome you all, workers of all strata and every social class. The Angkar has examined the great and historic victory gained by the people of Kampuchea, which has totally defeated the extremely barbarous war of aggression brought about by the American imperialists and their lackeys. This after five years and one month of valiant, relentless and resolute struggle, in the course of which the people, displaying sublime heroism and willing to make immense sacrifices, have endured difficulties of every kind. These difficulties are not over! We must still deal with the thousand and one urgent problems bequeathed to us by American imperialism and its lackeys. Our economy is destroyed. Our factories, meadows, paddy fields, communication routes, schools and hospitals, our homes and our pagodas in both the towns and the country are, for the most part, in ruins. Thus we must organise our resources to develop our production throughout the entire land in order to solve present problems as well as future ones. Comrades! Our beloved fatherland needs the efforts of each one of you and invites you all to participate enthusiastically in the nation's production, jointly with the cadres, from the ministers down to rural communes and villages, from senior cadres to soldiers, to cultivate both fast- and slow-growing rice and to harvest bananas, potatoes, manioc and more. This is why I ask you not to be afraid to leave the capital, to remain together and not to try to return to the centre, access to which is forbidden from now on. You must follow the instructions that will be given to you along the way, so that the Angkar can welcome you appropriately. I thank you!"

Nhem's inspired speech seemed intended not so much to reassure the Khmers as to satisfy the French authorities and the ideas of the foreigners who had gathered in the courtyard to listen to him. We were relieved to observe that he had kept his promise not to group people according to their sex. Behind him, on the boulevard, inhabitants of Phnom Penh were still moving forward with bundles perched on their shoulders. But there were fewer and fewer of them, and it was now going to be harder to disappear into the wilderness, as all our refugees had planned to do. However, nothing led us to suppose that the Khmers Rouges were going to mark them out in any way. I believe that the revolutionaries had been caught unawares and did not have the means to do so. We opened the gate, and those we could no longer keep because they were putting our frail ship in danger threw themselves into the sea.

We were closing the grille of the gate silently behind them when a minibus, bearing an embassy plate, drew up sharply beside us. Two jeeps, loaded with armed men, followed it.

"Here are some more foreigners!" shouted a Khmer Rouge as he jumped down from one of the vehicles.

He ran over towards me and handed me the passports of

those inside the vehicle. There were seven Caucasians, "guardians" of the Soviet Embassy. Three fairly stout women were sitting in the back with bags of food on their knees. One of the men had been seriously wounded in the arm. Caught off guard by the intrusion of the revolutionaries, who had blown up the heavy reinforced gate of the embassy with a rocket launcher, he had been forced to smash the lights and the quartz lamps of the radio transmitters with his elbow. The broken glass from the tubes had ripped his forearm. They were in a pitiful state but still managed to adopt a look of arrogance. They were fulminating about how these savages were incapable of recognising their allies, and were treating the Soviets like Americans. From the moment they joined us, they behaved so disagreeably towards everybody that many of us were glad to see their crestfallen faces.

There were still some 150 FULRO commando troops left on the premises who, according to the military tradition of these countries, would not move without their guns, their wives and their children. One of the young wives, who was anxious to give birth to the child she was carrying without further delay, managed to go into labour a bit prematurely, thanks to the doctor from Mimot's plantation, Dr Rémi Xualet, an extraordinary practitioner of Sino-Vietnamese origin who was both a Catholic guru and a bonesetter, as well as a master of kung fu. He delivered her baby in the nick of time at dawn, with the help of manipulation and prayers addressed to Jesus. She would leave behind the son she loved more than all else, so that he might have a chance to survive. The Lorines, who were childless, had agreed to adopt him.

These toughened men never wavered for a moment. They were the counterparts of the North Vietnamese cyclists, with some added panache perhaps (they all came from tribes where the men proudly wore headdresses, combs, necklaces, pearls and feathers both to attract women and for going to war). They obeyed no-one but their leader. And yet Colonel I Boun Sour, alias Paul, who commanded them, could not conceal his chattering teeth, for fear had paralysed him and taken away all movement from his arms.

Married to a Frenchwoman, the war had turned him into a playboy, handsomely paid by the Americans. They preferred to encourage him to live the life of a wealthy night owl in Phnom Penh (while his men were at the front), rather than stop providing for him and risk his joining the enemy. He was still young, with a mass of thick black hair divided by a parting, and in his open Asiatic face the charm of his fine dark eyes and the freshness of his features combined almost too perfectly. Fortunately, he was tall and powerfully built. As far as his temperament was concerned, he was a pure product of the Catholic schools in Ban Me Touot: an unhappy creature, well educated but artificial.

I believe it was the first time that I had witnessed such a pitiful collapse. He lost control of everything, his mind as well as his intestines. Sitting in the grass, numbed by fear and no longer ashamed, he could not get to his feet. Beads of feverish sweat stood out on his forehead. The very notion of setting off on the road made him behave like an acrophobe on the edge of a sheer drop.

And now this cowardly glamour-seeker, so eager to appear brave that he had sworn prematurely to his audience of nightclub cronies that he would "stay with his men to the end" – and who could, in fact, have fled before it was too late – was the only fulcrum for more than a hundred fighting men who were armed to the teeth (their weapons were buried beneath them, wrapped in oil cloth) and ready to do everything for him and nothing without him. It was obvious that they would not budge an inch without him and that they were prepared to wait for the Khmers Rouges.

A curious interchange then took place among the people crouched around this man, who heard and said nothing.

"Look, come on, Paul! You've got to decide!" said one of the old fellows with a white goatee, who appeared to have known him since childhood. "Think, for goodness' sake! If you refuse to do anything, you're murdering your men, and you're not giving yourself any chance either."

"Paul!" someone else continued. "Have you really thought about what it means to stay? For all the people around you?"

"Colonel," someone from the embassy intervened, "time is moving on!"

"Shit! Supposing they turn up now," muttered another.

"Well, if they do," replied a fourth, "we're talking about a massacre! If they enter," he continued, "your men will shoot at them. I don't want to think about the carnage."

"Paul!" the first man resumed. "It's true! You must realise how serious the situation is. Bloody hell! Do something! Clear out of here with your men, for heaven's sake! Outside, you can all disperse incognito."

The *padre* who was whispering these exhortations into his ear gently let his smooth forehead drop onto the head of the young commanding officer, and we watched as a few silent sobs shook his shoulders.

"Paul," he went on, recovering himself, "it's what you have to do."

Drops of rain began to fall spasmodically, one by one, so heavily that all you could hear was the sound they made as they landed on the cardboard boxes strewn over the grass. All of a sudden, the colonel stood up, shook himself and looked around him like someone returning from the other world.

"Do you have anything to drink? A small glass of brandy?" he asked the old missionary. Five people were turning quickly and asking the others, who stood around waiting, not understanding.

A journalist ran up bearing a crystal brandy glass filled with some orange-coloured cognac. I Boun Sour readjusted the coat of his uniform, brushed a hand over his hair and his face, took the glass between two fingers, held it for a moment at eye level, then downed it smartly. His mouth and cheeks creased into an expression that reflected either the somewhat powerful pleasure imparted to his gullet, which had immediately caused his eyes to turn red, or the determination that he now wished to manifest. He took a few steps forward, turned to face his soldiers, who were already lined up and awaiting his orders, and called out in a steady voice, "Come on, boys! Let's go!"

Of all the emotional moments we experienced during that period, Paul's exemplary courage certainly provoked the most tears.

The dark mass of cloud and rain that had hung over the city was blown away by the wind, suddenly revealing a sky that looked like a large blue veil dotted with silver sequins. The newly cleared ground created a large void in the middle of the park that we no longer dared look at. Without further ado, Father Félix set about his meticulous task on the flattened, litter-strewn lawn.

There were now just over a thousand refugees left, including seven hundred French nationals, a quarter of whom had originally come from metropolitan France. The others were foreign passport holders of twenty-six nationalities. The banishment of the last of the Khmers was the occasion to implement certain arrangements we had put off, such as the rationing of provisions; the storage of supplies in the strongroom of the pay office; the destruction of all the bottles of alcohol in the cellars at the residence, to put a stop to excess consumption (except for a batch that we consigned to the dispensary); the sharing of cleaning duties (until then, only Migot had swept the courtyard each morning); the slaughter of stray dogs that were wandering around the campus; the digging of latrines; the organisation of night rounds; and so on.

Nhem judged this to be the right time to assert his authority over us. For a start, he asked us to heap up in front of the gate any weapons on the campus, as well as any photographic equipment, cameras and rolls of film, exposed or not. Even though we had already got rid of the FULRO weapons by burying them at the bottom of a dry well that had been dug with a pickaxe on the very first day, there were still a good many guns. The second part of the instructions came as a heavy blow to the fifteen press photographers among us, with their profitable array of pictures of the "liberation of Phnom Penh", to which they seemed to attach more value than they did to their own lives.

I helped Ponchaud and Rémy share out provisions, and in particular the several cartons of cigarettes the Khmers Rouges had delivered us. Then it was time to hand out lunch, which took place at around the same time in the different sections. Mealtimes were frequently an occasion for arguments among the refugees, who were all hungry and dissatisfied. Within a few days, our campus had become a breeding ground for all the basest instincts: theft, jealousy, selfishness, aggression. Old quarrels between clans and families resurfaced, without anyone knowing what they were originally about. I had spent my childhood at a boarding school, where I had had to endure the spitefulness of boys my own age. It was now that I discovered what a community of adults could be like when caught in a trap: a flock of stubborn sheep who exaggerate every difficulty and complicate every problem; their claim for the right to survive making them grumblingly accept as their due the benefits that the initiative of a few others has acquired on their behalf. In the different sections, it was always the same few individuals who took the necessary decisions.

But our flock included yet another category of people, the discovery of whom was a lesson as striking as it was useless: those who request things and brook no refusal of their demand, legitimate or not. If denied, they keep on trying; if turned away, they stand their ground; if driven back, they return to the attack, politely but stubbornly refusing to be discouraged, not caring a bit about the contempt they inspire and oblivious to any sense of pride or propriety. These people got everything they wanted, from forged identity papers to toothbrushes to an antique they had left behind on their sideboard – to the detriment of more dignified people who asked for nothing and who, confronted with the unfolding tragedy, did not dare disturb the community with their personal desires.

About a hundred refugees stood in a line in the middle of the courtyard, holding a mess tin or a plate. Devaux, armed with an aluminium beaker, was dipping into a tin bucket steaming on a small earthenware brazier. He served each of them a helping of soup that smelled of warm oil. In the queue, which stretched as far as the arches of the Cultural Department, I recognised Albert Spaccesi, the owner of the Café de Paris, "the best restaurant in South-East Asia", as he himself liked to proclaim. With his bare torso, the poor man looked pitiful: his big varicose-veined legs protruded out of an enormous pair of woollen underpants. Large scars on his stomach and back from an operation in France were still pink. I heard him explaining to his neighbours in his falsetto voice that they had removed more than forty kilograms of fat . . . and he kept moaning, stifling his sobs as he spoke about the fortune he had invested in his fine restaurant, "where General de Gaulle and Prince Sihanouk used to come", and which was now lost for ever. He had nothing left.

"Look, it's Borella!" said Rémy, glancing towards a man of about forty who was patiently waiting his turn, leaning against the blue mosaic wall with one leg tucked under him.

"Borella?"

"Yes, you know him. Dominique Borella. He's only just arrived. He's been holding Potchentong airport for the last week

– it's been under siege. The Khmers Rouges needed it so badly, probably so the Chinese could land there, that they negotiated his withdrawal with all of his men last night, no strings attached. Those guys disappeared into the countryside, but Borella arrived here this morning, on the quiet, through the back entrance. Incredible, isn't it?"

I peered eagerly at the man the Khmers had christened *sok ksa*, "white hair", and about whom I had of course heard much. He looked like Robert Redford, with red hair that had indeed turned dirty blond. The oxidised skin on his still-youthful face had the indescribable burnt autumnal colour of certain dead leaves. His china-blue eyes sparkled beneath eyelids feathered with white.

So this was Borella, "the mercenary"! The crusader for anti-Communism who had come to Cambodia to fight alongside the republicans. His bravery and professionalism had made him mythical. The men of his parachute battalion reckoned he was invulnerable and swore him blind allegiance. Along with his innate sense of strategy, he knew everything about handling weapons and methods of close combat. Moreover, while he himself refused to be paid, the soldiers under his command were the only ones in Cambodia to receive their wages on time. Throughout the embassy episode, this legendary man was ready to take on all kinds of duties and found a thousand discreet ways to make himself useful.

Dyrac sent me to arrange a meeting with Nhem as soon as possible. He wanted to speak to him about certain urgent problems. To begin with, everybody was hungry and we wished to have better supplies. My excursions were clearly not enough. We were reduced to two ladles of rice per person, per day. We also needed strong disinfectants such as lime or cresol, as well as matting, mosquito nets, buckets, cooking pots, boilers for washing clothes . . . Second, since the airport was now accessible, the instructions from Paris (which we continued to receive via Berger, camped next to the telex) were to obtain permission from the Khmers Rouges for a French jumbo jet to land. The Ministry for Foreign Affairs had set up an emergency unit that was in radio contact with us day and night, relayed via Bangkok, Saigon, Singapore and other cities. The plane would be packed with medicines and supplies, and it could evacuate some of the foreign community, starting with children, women and the sick. Finally, the consul also wanted to ask Nhem for news of our compatriots who were scattered about the country (about two hundred, according to the registers), in particular those in Battambang and Pailin.

The "president", as the consul referred to him, received us in his quarters in the early evening. The still air that hung over the embassy was burning hot, further accentuating our feeling of tiredness. Dyrac, who was no longer young, sweated and panted with exhaustion as we crossed the boulevard. I myself was worn out; the moment dusk fell, despite my anxiety, a wave of sleep would hit me, and I would go out like a light.

Prior to our meeting, I had sent Nhem two official letters summarising the French demands point by point, in order to give him time to consult his senior colleagues. When we arrived, he shook the consul's hand warmly and invited us to sit in the leatherette armchairs. Two brand new standard fans blew the air behind our backs. The Malay sat down next to him and passed a pack of cigarettes around. A young guard with big peasant fingers and dirty nails clumsily poured tea into magnificent Korean china teacups.

Rather than addressing us too solemnly, the "president" began speaking with the combination of swaggering pomposity and clumsiness that I was so familiar with. It was obvious, too, that his expression came from mimicking somebody else; one doesn't live with impunity in the shadow of the same leaders without adopting a few of their postures and mannerisms. For instance, like the majority of other revolutionaries I had seen going about their work, he kept his lips pursed before speaking, time enough for them to extend into a flat, cheek-creasing smile.

Nhem greeted the representative of the French Republic on behalf of the Government of the Royal National Union of Kampuchea and categorically refused the request for a French plane to land. Similarly, he ruled out the suggestion that refugees should be evacuated by air. On the other hand, he gave us assurances about our supplies and expressed his confidence that the Angkar was making efforts to round up the French people marooned in the outback, "starting with the specialists working in the new coffee plantations in the Pailin area," he specified, in order to show us that he knew what he was talking about.

We went out into the glare of the boulevard. Dyrac appeared very put out by these refusals. "Good heavens! What are they up to? They can't expect us to leave on bicycles."

We stopped for a moment under the shade of a large tamarind tree, from whose lacerated trunk pieces of bark hung pitifully, like frayed rags. From its topmost branches, a syncopated plucking and a washboard scraping covered the distant, high-pitched trill from the pond behind the embassy, which had overflowed after the rains.

We had no sooner walked back into the courtyard than an uncovered GMC truck pulled up in front of the gate. Standing up and clinging to the sides, some revolutionaries were raising their arms and cheering like excited fans acclaiming their team's victory. I noticed Jérôme Steinbach's beard at first glance, but looked again in surprise: he was dressed like a Khmer Rouge! Among the young revolutionaries surrounding him, dressed up in the same way, I recognised Jocelyne, his wife, who had welcomed me so kindly at their home, and Jean-Pierre and Danièle Martinie. Predictably, the partisans had been keen to get rid of the French Communists, since they had nothing to share with them.

One of the guards seated next to the driver got down from the truck and handed me their passports. The four teachers from the literature faculty gave a great many demonstrative embraces to their somewhat embarrassed escorts, who responded to these effusive gestures with laughter. Then they jumped down onto the tarmac with a clack of their Ho Chi Minh sandals.

This display by Parisian intellectuals of fraternising with poor Khmers Rouges struck me as ridiculous and misplaced. What did they understand of their motivations and their language, their history and their revolution? Scarcely anything, as the well-written little book that the Steinbachs published on their return to France demonstrates. Their dangerous naivety, based upon some idealistic vision, in the face of events that were to mark the pages of history in red and black, made me shudder. It was all part of the heavy responsibility of the West, which had heaped its models and its ideas on a totally alien world, unable to anticipate, prevent or recognise the perverse effects it was having. I have felt hatred, as I have felt sympathy, for some of these dreamers, guilty yet motivated as they were by a sincere sense of brotherhood. Today, now that the point of no return has been reached, and they are silent, I feel merely a bitter compassion, and an infinite sadness.

The shouts of joy coming from the truck had attracted the attention of a few curious onlookers. They observed the scene from the courtyard, and at first did not understand what was happening; then they understood, and kept quiet. The gendarme opened the gate and, concealing their vexation, the new arrivals entered, though not before they had looked back several times to clap and cheer on their brothers in the struggle against the class system.

Wearing his Chinese cap, a *krama* round his neck and a pair of black pyjamas that were too new and puffed out at the knees, exposing his ankles, Martinie was the first to step forward bravely. He had a cynical look in his eyes and an impudent expression on his cheerful face; he was trying to conceal his embarrassment at being forced to seek the protection of the French authorities. The refugees who had gathered behind us felt humiliated at the cheek of the young lecturer in attiring himself in the uniform of the revolutionaries; it was as if he were deriding them. One, André Dessain, who was fairly hot-headed, could not contain his indignation. After arriving in Indochina with the expeditionary force, he had been demobilised in the area. He had had time to assess, day after day, over a period of thirty years, the extent of the chaos and abomination that Communism had brought to the peninsula. He was a stocky, well-built fellow; several days' stubble covered his face, delineating his jawbone. He leapt forward at him.

"Have you no shame?" he yelled at Martinie, drawing himself up on his short legs.

And he gave him a resounding slap.

The intellectual in fancy dress was stunned and raised his forearm to ward off another blow that never came. Dessain's eyes were burning. He snatched the khaki US Army haversack down from his shoulder and forced him to change. The others removed their caps and *krama* of their own accord.

Dusk fell. We found a place for them behind the parking lot, by the arches, where they got on well with the East German diplomat Erich Stange, who had dashed out on the last plane from Bangkok to reopen his embassy and celebrate the victory of the Communist forces. Like them – and the Russians – he abhorred the capitalist milieu in which, very much against his wishes, he found himself.

Retracing my steps, I passed Pascal Grellety, whom I had noticed sitting against a wall, bent over a sketchpad, his pencil moving over the paper with concentration. When he saw me, the young Red Cross doctor quickly turned over a few thick, noisy pages, looked up at me with his cheery eyes and wordlessly handed me his sketchpad. The page was covered with vivid characters, coloured lightly with a brush. I recognised myself in one picture, followed by my dog, who was jumping around in the rain among some bathers. Another, meticulously drawn, depicted the boulevard, with refugees pushing carts and Khmers Rouges observing them. There were also sketches of the embassy, showing Sirik Matak and the French flag, some with gendarmes and the consul standing in front of the gate; and others featuring journalists, doctors and delegates from the international bodies, all looking unhappy but well accommodated, with the Khmers around them on mats and pieces of cardboard. I was struck by how the draftsman, with naive imagery, conveyed the hidden truth of our situation simply by juxtaposing circumstances we ourselves had ceased to find remarkable. It looked as if he wanted, in his drawings, to find compositions which would portray things with more clarity than in real life. And each little drawing strangely rekindled my anxiety: all the misery that had befallen us was concentrated here, in the perspective of a single moment. There is no higher art than an image which can capture life in this way.

I went to find Avi, who had been waiting for this moment all day long (Migot used to say that he shed tears every morning as he watched me leave). I took him to the courtyard and we sat down on a step, the dog between my knees. His little tail was wagging. It was one of those evenings that are the apotheosis of the Far East, the soothing moment when the pace of surrounding life grows languid and all the troubles of the day fade away.

In the damp breath of a sky that had suddenly darkened, pearl-coloured sparrows were tracing elegant spirals as they overtook one another in pursuit of their elusive prey, describing tight circles in the still-warm air. The dog followed them with his eyes, moving his head in fits and starts, and then suddenly unleashed his boxer's jowls with a suction noise whenever one skimmed past us. I amused myself by getting his attention and making him listen carefully to the quiver of their motionless wings; with their imperceptible fluttering, it seemed they were saluting the last rays of the setting sun.

# 13

" *Chop!* Stop!"
  Vigilant, eyes peeled, ceaselessly scanning every corner of the bleak alleyway, I rushed through the debris littering the ground, pretending I hadn't heard. Warm vapours and clammy smells rose from the soft, rutted asphalt. Broken windows and battered-down doors cracked the walls, criss-crossed with barbed wire . . . on the pavements, articles of clothing, smashed objects festering among the rubble, empty cardboard boxes moved about by rats . . . pools of water and mud everywhere leaking out of fire-damaged waste pipes . . . In front of me, in the middle of the alley, its lips curled in a grimace of suffering, bluish legs sticking up like a snail's horns, hide swollen by the recent hot sun, lay the pallid corpse of an enormous boar, covered with flies and emitting a revolting stench.

  Suddenly, the indistinct sound of a chest being moved alerted me: I stood stock still and stopped my breath. I turned my gaze to a Chinese-made cabinet in the Portuguese style, with slatted panels which stood half open; it was set back in an alcove. Emerging from behind it, a shifty-looking kid was glaring at me slyly down the barrel of a gun. He was about to shoot.

  I had left before daybreak without a word to anyone. I parked the jeep at the EFEO and continued on foot so as to make myself less obtrusive. If I avoided the main thoroughfares, I reckoned I could complete my expedition in three hours; I would come back as if I had never been away. I first wanted to call on M. Yang Sun, a specialist in the rituals associated with the casting of Buddha statues, and save the precious work he had done over many years for a colleague from the school, Madeleine Giteau. Then I would go up to Vat Maha Metrei, a temple in the Serei Roath district, hoping to pick up some texts left at the home of my old teacher, You Oun, an endless fount of knowledge who had taught me everything: Pali, Khmer, rigour, doubt, curiosity, boldness . . . I especially wanted to retrieve a small exercise book where we had compiled a strange treasury of around forty Khmer words constructed by a transposition of consonants (*dangkap* → *kangdap*). I did not want to miss any opportunity to recover these irreplaceable documents while perhaps there was still time.

I had mentioned my plan to Nhem two days before, but he had dismissed it out of hand with the excuse that he could not guarantee my safety in a city still haunted by uncontrollable vagabonds. But now Phnom Penh appeared to me to be empty, and I believed I could avoid the barricades at the main intersections.

Straight after leaving the school, I was twice ordered to stop by soldiers from a distance, but I drove on, merely giving expansive and authoritative waves. I knew that they would be deaf to my explanations, whereas in the absence of any precise instructions they should merely be disconcerted by a show of self-confidence. Guns (mainly wielded by government troops) had already been pointed at me on several occasions since the outbreak of war, and a few days earlier, on the morning of 17 April, a Khmer Rouge officer had rammed the barrel of his revolver into my stomach. But I had never experienced what I felt here, in this empty, narrow alleyway: the fear that roots your feet to the spot, that freezes your blood.

The child held me in his sights. The left leg of his filthy

trousers was rolled up clear of a bandage spattered with mud and blood. I had been in his aim for several seconds; he followed me, like a moving target. Little by little, my corpse-like stillness — which I was not putting on — took his eye off the task.

"I'm on a mission for the Angkar!" I stated as calmly as possible. "The young comrade must let me pass, for I'm in a hurry!"

The young guerrilla finally lowered the gun he had been holding, with some difficulty, up to his eye at arm's length. He drew a hand over his forehead, which was half hidden by a greasy fringe, as if to remove a veil whose opacity was clouding his intelligence. He was a solitary, unresponsive youth, unpredictable and totally impervious to anyone else's thoughts or intentions. I looked at his grubby little face, raging at having stumbled across an insuperable barrier: his insanity. He came towards me, lurching through the rubble, and, without a word, kicked me. His pallor indicated that he had a vitamin deficiency and was probably suffering from chronic malaria as well. Despite his fifteen years, there were tiny wrinkles on either side of the pear-shaped bags beneath his eyes. He made me walk in front of him, pushing me along dark side streets and muttering inaudible words that were addressed to no-one. We passed houses whose porches had been knocked about; others had been destroyed by rockets; some were nothing but craters filled with yellowish water. In these still-unchecked passageways we twice had to circumvent isolated bodies, their limbs swollen beneath stretched clothing, their faces blackened and covered in city grime.

We reached the brightness of a boulevard, in the middle of which a squad of Khmers Rouges had set up an ambush; they were dozing in armchairs and a radio was crackling. Beside them, on a drawing-room table, were an AK-47, some cartridge clips, cigarettes and empty beer bottles. In the dull, still morning, we drew level with them. The as-yet-invisible sun filled the air with diffused light. With its rows of wild guava trees and empty houses, the flat avenue stretched away silently towards the

Independence Monument, which stood out in the distance against the motionless sky. In the other direction, the early dawn light had formed a gleaming halo around the turrets of three abandoned tanks that lay on the yellow grass of the long esplanade leading to the racecourse. In two sharp, short sentences, my guardian announced that he had found a Frenchman, and then he left me there. Unable to believe that my expedition had so quickly come to nothing, I wanted to be on my way again immediately. They tied my hands behind my back.

I was furious. I had failed so narrowly, I had almost been shot, I had foolishly missed my last chance to find my papers because of this kid. One of the soldiers was excited by my arrest and showed himself very keen to have my watch . . . In short, for much the same reasons as four years before, I found myself a prisoner of some Khmers Rouges who understood nothing at all about my story. In a long speech, I tried yet again to influence the younger elements in the squad, but I was wasting my time. One of them was dispatched by bicycle to find Nhem. Three hours later – I was becoming mad with impatience – the "president" arrived in a car; he wore a reproving look. I climbed in beside him, annoyed with myself, aware of my own helplessness, overwhelmed by the sense of absurdity that this appalling operation had imbued in me, and rather more ashamed of my disobedience than of my failure. Nhem was silent throughout the return journey, and I felt extremely grateful to him for not asking embarrassing questions. We arrived at the gate.

"Comrade Bizot!" he said, holding me back by my arm as I was getting out of the car. "We must now make arrangements for foreigners to be repatriated at the border with Thailand. I want to discuss this with the consul this afternoon."

It was ten o'clock. I entered the embassy as if nothing had happened. The gendarmes were gazing at a four-engine Chinese jet that was circling above the city, waiting to land at Potchentong. Dyrac came out with Maurin; both were lost in speculation about Sihanouk's return. I joined them and told them all of our imminent departure: "Do you want the scoop of the year? We're going back by truck!"

At about midday, Nhem sent the consul the following letter:

*Very urgent.*

> *To: 01-ra. ra. ka. bha. ba. 75.*
>
> *Addressees: the representatives of France, Switzerland, Spain, Germany, Italy, the USSR, Belgium, Holland (via the consul of France).*

## MEMORANDUM

*At the meeting that took place on 25 April 1975, the Cabinet of the Government of the Royal National Union of Kampuchea decided the following:*

*Given that diplomatic relations with other countries have not yet been established owing to the fact that the GRNUK is busy restoring stability,*

- *The Government of the Royal National Union of Kampuchea has decided to invite all foreigners still residing in the city of Phnom Penh to leave the country as of 30 April 1975;*
- *Later, when the situation has stabilised, the GRNUK will examine the question of re-establishing diplomatic relations;*
- *The GRNUK has decided to convey all foreigners by road from Phnom Penh to Poipet, and each of the countries concerned must take responsibility for their own nationals from Poipet onwards.*

*Issued at Phnom Penh, 25 April 1975.*

> *The Vice-President of the Northern*
> *Command Front of Phnom Penh*
> *with responsibility for foreigners*
> *Signed: Nhem*

"François . . . François!"

I looked around in surprise. No-one called me by my first name. Chantal Lorine was hurrying after me just as I was getting ready to cross the boulevard. The decoding clerk's wife was fresh and pretty, with lovely myopic eyes encircled by large spectacles that left a mark on her cheeks.

"Would you agree to be Olivier's godfather?"

"What?"

"You know we've just adopted a wonderful little boy!" she continued, seeing me hesitate. "Father Berger is going to baptise him, and Madame Dyrac will be the godmother. And so now I'm looking for a godfather."

I accepted wholeheartedly and then hurried off to the former Korean Embassy, where Nhem had sent a message to the gendarmes that he was waiting for me. All of a sudden, I caught sight of my motorbike. It had been "requisitioned" by the president's men and brought into the courtyard. Fast and sturdy, it was a fairly powerful machine, and I had always taken great care of it. It was ideal for sandy tracks. I noticed immediately that the headlamp was broken: they had pulled out the electric wires to form a contact and make it start.

"Comrade!" I said to Nhem, exaggerating my annoyance and pointing behind me. "I deliberately left the key in my motorbike so the revolutionaries could use it easily, without needing to damage it. I'm not one of those Americans who puts out of action whatever he leaves behind him! Well, look what happens: it appears that it's been smashed, like everything else."

Nhem took a few seconds to divine what I was talking about. His expression remained impassive, and he came to his point without batting an eyelid: "The embassy must suspend its broadcasts and receptions at once. I want a meeting with the consul before this evening."

He employed a neologism for "broadcasts and receptions" whose precise meaning made me pause. Since the French station had a reasonably comprehensive radio infrastructure, I was not sure I understood what it was he wanted us to suspend: the Teletype, the telegraph or the BLU one-way transmitter. On the other hand, it was quite clear to me that he had something important on his mind. I may not always have been able to translate his words very well, but I was used to interpreting his gestures and codified facial expressions: to begin with, he looked at me with steely eyes, staring at me awkwardly; then the muscles in his face grew tense, and their involuntary fluctuations would cause the corners of his lips to curl up and twitch. I was inclined to think that he was once again obeying an order from the high command that (as with the refugees) had to be carried out without delay. If this order, which was a total violation of international agreements, was intended to sever completely the umbilical cord that still linked us to our mother country, we were dealing with a real catastrophe that would affect the morale of every one of us, not least the consul's.

Dyrac, flushed and motionless, pondered this for a long time, dreaming up and rejecting all sorts of explanations, unable to remember anything we had done to justify such a decision, except the foolish behaviour of one of the American "journalists", whom he had actually warned several times. With his own powerful secret transmitter-receiver, the man had been sending messages to a plane flying high above our sector, intending to organise a surprise evacuation by helicopter.

"I should have confiscated his radio straight away!" the consul moaned. "You can bet your life they've got detector vans! Of course they have! And then their Chinese experts must have come and unloaded a whole load of equipment . . ."

He decided to open the ambassador's offices on the first floor, so as to lend the meeting a more solemn setting. The president arrived in the afternoon, accompanied by the Malay who never left his side, two taciturn-looking officers and another character of fairly unpleasant appearance. Thanks to the gendarmes, whose uniforms meant a great deal in the bluffing game we continued to play with all our visitors, we obstinately insisted that their armed escort remain at the gate. Having said that, we pretended not to notice the two officers stuffing the revolvers they had carried on their belts inside their shirts.

We entered the office adjoining Louis Dauge's former study with tense smiles and set expressions. The atmosphere was not good. Nhem's attendants consisted of disparate elements that seemed hostile. Dyrac had brought along Revil, Maurin and the coding officer, and I had asked that the interpreter who had been there on the first day be present too, so as to be sure of a proper translation. We sat down around Clotilde d'Harcour's desk, which Mme Dyrac had asked to be moved into the middle of the room. She had placed a pack of cigarettes on it and some bottles of cordial. Light streamed in from the large window, which was hung with dark, damask curtains, tied back. A cold draft issued from the holes in a noisy air-conditioning unit that was sunk into the wall, sending a musty smell into the damp air of the room.

In a solemn voice, enunciating each word in a sort of inaudible murmur, Nhem repeated the request I had already reported: an immediate stop to all radio broadcasts and receptions. He added that this was a decision taken by the GRNUK's council of ministers in response to the untruthful communiqués that had recently appeared in the press in Europe and the United States. I turned to my colleague in order to compare what we had understood. So that there should not be any misunderstanding, we asked him to specify what type of radio transmission he was referring to.

"To every single bit of your equipment!" he replied, at the same time letting it be known that our hesitation in the face of a clear order was causing a certain irritation.

Dyrac shuddered at the notion of being cut off from the ministry. Already inundated with difficulties, overwhelmed with responsibilities and exhausted by fatigue, he was filled with dread at the idea of losing contact with the outside world.

"No! Tell him it's impossible," he answered. "I insist on daily contact with Paris. Anyway, there is no question of seriously contemplating any sort of evacuation, especially by road, without coordination with Bangkok, via Paris."

Nhem, who understood our language (Maurin told me that a few days earlier he had had a long one-to-one conversation with him, entirely in French), immediately turned a telling shade of grey. He waited, however, for the consul's words to be translated before giving vent to his anger. The blood ebbed from his lips; his mouth, then his cheeks and his forehead, grew pale. The expression in his sparkling eyes tightened like jaws, sending a paralysing alarm across the room. Revolutionary fervour, which authorises all crimes, had suddenly filled his gaze with the very basest instincts, from malice to sadism, cruelty to madness. The president began to smile; his show of forced calm became terrifying. We realised that he was irrevocably embarked on a course of anger, and that no self-respecting warrior could repeat such threats without carrying them out.

"The French are no longer in a position to refuse or to enforce anything!" he hammered out, nostrils flared, teeth clenched.

He slowly released his hands, which were clasped over his stomach, placing them on his knees, and I could see they were shaking.

"You must stop *everything!*"

His face was pale. He lowered his gaze and, suddenly rising to his feet, he shouted out, "No more need be said! Let us see the transmission post."

We went out, and Dyrac showed them the radio installation in the military office, then the decoding room where the Teletypes were plugged in. The Khmer Rouge ordered that from now on an armed sentry would keep watch over the two doors, day and night. This decision hit us like a bomb. Dyrac, vexed, hissed at me between his teeth, "We must avoid that at all costs!"

I mumbled as I walked over to Nhem, making a supreme effort to control my anxiety, "Comrade! Er . . . we have heard the Angkar's instructions. I have a request, however, that I should respectfully like to put forward . . . on behalf of the consul, as well as all the French officials here present. Does the comrade president agree to hear me?"

He slowed his pace, casting his eyes over the things around him with a steady gaze, like a child dreaming. This man, though far from innocent, had an air of naivety that reminded me of Douch's dreadful inconsistencies. Refusing to grant my request — there was nothing left to discuss — but also not wanting to repudiate me, Nhem set off again down the corridor at a slow, dithering pace, without saying a word, as if inviting me to follow him.

"The elder comrade has ordered us to suspend all broadcasts," I resumed. "The representative of the French Republic has no alternative but to abide by this, and he does so unreservedly and without any ulterior motive. Everything will cease this evening; definitively. The doors of both rooms will remain locked. Given these conditions, why put guards in the chancellery, when we already find it hard enough to live together for lack of space? The presence of armed men among us will inevitably give rise to fresh difficulties and is not without a certain risk. Had we not agreed on this point? What good will it do to humiliate us further, comrade? Trust should prevail between our two peoples! You must believe us! The French don't make long speeches: when they say they will stop, they stop. I personally undertake to do this; you have my word of honour! Keep your sentries outside our walls. I promise you that everything will be closed down, from six o'clock this evening."

The president slowly crossed the courtyard, bent forward, staring at his bulging toes, seemingly enthralled by the comings and goings of the thick yellow half-moons at the bases of his toenails. I had done my pleading over his shoulder, hopping along behind him. He passed through the gate without waiting for me to finish, obliging me to conclude my sentence hurriedly. It seemed like a good sign.

As dusk fell, we waited anxiously for the slightest movement from the boulevard . . . The sentries did not come.

Like a losing football team, we were genuinely delighted with our only goal and started to crow about it, trying out touching little dance routines in the first-floor hall and congratulating ourselves, attempting to purge ourselves of our crushing defeat. I felt very tired in the evenings but never slept for long. The unforeseen emotions, the strokes of bad luck and all the hostile reality kept interrupting my rest; my cocooned spirit emerged from its refuge, passing from sleep to a painful certainty of the dreaded Khmer Rouge victory. Then I opened my eyes in the darkness and went out to immerse myself in the stifling patch of the universe that fate had assigned to us: the perimeter of the embassy, enveloped in gloom. A dull glow came from the pallid globes attached to either side of the gate, matching those from the Cultural Department and making the shadows in the parking area overlap like long, dead phantoms. The grainy accent of insects superimposed itself onto melodious notes from an amphibian reed section, allowing a few beats rest here and there between the Ellingtonian riffs. Those few bars of silence seemed to swallow up night itself. The effect was so beautiful and melancholy that I let my own fears fall in after it.

The next morning, in the reception room at the chancellery, the consul and his advisers gathered the representatives of the press and the international organisations, the honorary consuls, the doctors and the department heads, to establish the list of people to be evacuated in the first convoy. The Khmers Rouges could muster only around twenty trucks (Chinese Molotovas and GMCs). We therefore had to plan at least two journeys and their requisite sanitary and logistic arrangements. The operation would last several days and cover about 280 miles, most of it on bush tracks, since the bridges had been blown and the roads were pitted into the shapes of piano keys.

The population of the campus amounted to precisely 1,046 people, of whom 656 were French and 390 were foreigners, including 84 recently arrived Chams.* A first list of 513 refugees was drawn up, on the basis of twenty people per truck.

Many refugees were immediately gripped with terror. They saw this incomprehensible departure – the airport was usable – as a well-constructed pretence designed to get rid of us all. This is what had happened at the Olympic Stadium, where civil servants and military personnel had been assembled on the first day, selected according to rank and profession, and finally executed in separate groups.

But a greater number, impatient to be rid of the intolerable situation at all costs, were eager to leave the embassy as quickly as possible. Among these, mainly for reasons of rivalry, were the press correspondents (apart from two or three, who had resolved to cover events to the end). There seemed to be a network of secrets among them that went beyond the rules of propriety. These competitive interests created the sort of rivalry which could turn nasty. But those concerned were restrained by their professional conscience. They all agreed to an embargo on information, intended to avoid premature disclosure of alarming news stories: numerous eyewitness accounts of atrocities were beginning to filter through. All this risked provoking Khmer Rouge vengeance on those left behind in Phnom Penh:

*The Chams, or Khmers-Islam, are one of Cambodia's ethnic minorities. They are Muslims and speak their own language. [Tr.]

*We, the undersigned, newspaper correspondents, freelance writers for the press, radio and television, and photographers, currently at Phnom Penh, undertake not to publish in any news media or to give any statement or testimony whatsoever before receiving confirmation that the last passenger from the last convoy has crossed the border to Thailand.*

*Furthermore, we undertake to use all our influence to prevent other news media from publishing news and accounts of events in Phnom Penh since 17 April, until the evacuation of persons sheltered within the precincts of the French Embassy is completed.*

*It is understood that the embargo on the broadcasting of news, articles, films, photographs and magnetic tapes will remain in force from arrival in Bangkok onwards.*

The statement was ratified by eighteen journalists and opposed only by two American correspondents, Lee Rudakewych (ABC) and Denis Cameron (CBS), who, for reasons of their own, refused to sign. On the other hand, twelve of the journalists (mainly Americans, Germans and Swedes) put their signature that same day to the following protest, which was also delivered to the consul:

*We, the undersigned journalists, protest against the French consul's decision not to include the only German correspondent, who also represents Eurovision, on the list of correspondents leaving with the first convoy planned for the thirtieth of this month.*

*We are astonished to note that half the list is composed of Frenchmen, two of whom are from the same press agency.*

*28 April 1975*

Father Berger was not the kind of priest who distributed the sacraments far and wide. He had nonetheless agreed to baptise "little Fulro". In the circumstances, it would certainly have been untimely to make the usual investigations of religious legitimacy. Is not baptism, after all, to do with the faith of the parents, adoptive or not? Yet for two days he had not stopped brooding over the notion that this child had already lost everything and was about to have his own religion, his only true identity, taken from him.

We were walking together towards the chancellery, where, with all due solemnity, Olivier's baptism was to take place.

"What are you talking about?" I said with exasperation. I was intrigued by his militant and paradoxical convictions. "His own religion! As if it were something innate ... Come, now! The only appropriate religion is obviously that of his new country. Does the Church now deny pagans purifying ablution? Their right to cast off original sin? It's completely upside down!"

"My dear friend," he replied solemnly, "should I, in your view, behave like a vending machine? Have you not frequently told me," he added in a mischievous tone, "that I was here just for the converts, not for the Buddhists or the animists?"

I knew that the man loathed this way of confusing religion with social, cultural and human considerations, but I could not help stirring him up at the slightest opportunity. His simple faith in a single universal God – our own Christian one, of course! – drove me up the wall.

A former priest at Saint-Denis Cathedral outside Paris, Berger had arrived in Phnom Penh wearing the sheepskin jacket of the worker-priest rather than the missionary's beard. Driven, devoid of humility or hypocrisy, not at all the zealous evangelist, solely dedicated to the needs of the oppressed, this rebellious figure was all the more attractive because he did not try to beguile anyone. Above all, he never cheated, neither with himself nor with others, which made him a difficult, bitter and lonely man whose life somehow seemed fairly unhappy. His commitment to love his neighbour was equalled only by his intolerance of the well-to-do, as indeed of all those who were spared life's suffering. From this point of view, my rising every morning with joy at the dawning of a new day was extremely suspect. Whenever he came to see me at the EFEO or when I paid him a visit at the presbytery, we spent hours arguing. In short, we soon became firm friends.

A great many of us were gathered in the vast, bright room that had until then been reserved for the permanent representative of the French State, whose ministerial desk, covered with a sheet, had been transformed into an altar by the addition of a cross, two candles and a silver platter. On the walls were photographs of Angkor, an engraving of the Bayon depicting potters at work, and, occupying a large space, one of those Aubusson tapestries — beige, yellow, grey and black — that the Mobilier National loans to our embassies to display the work of French artists. The chairs, lamps and smaller pieces of mahogany furniture had been pushed back to make room for the silent congregation. Hair awry, shabbily dressed, they had solemnly come to pay homage to this little fellow's tragic yet fortunate destiny: becoming both Catholic and French in one fell swoop. Turning his back on the menacing creatures that adorned the wall hanging — a mass of swords and horns, teeth and claws — that seemed to come out of a Picasso sketch for *Guernica*, the man who was to become the last priest at Phnom Penh Cathedral poured water over the newborn's forehead. He intoned the first words of the prayers that I still knew by heart from boarding school. I noted with surprise, however, that fashions had changed since then: it had become appropriate to address the Lord quite informally.

I left the new mother, already cosseting her child like a grandmother, under the doting eyes of some of the faithful who were bent over the little creature. I set off from the embassy with specific objectives, already checked out with Nhem: to roam the deserted streets in search of addresses that had been scribbled down for me on a map, where I should find, between a destroyed shop and a looted commercial firm, one of those Ali Baba caves that still abounded in the city. Greedy as a pirate, I used an iron bar to break down the doors of a storeroom, a factory, a shop, and helped myself to dried vegetables, cans of corned beef, ham . . . to say nothing of the bric-a-brac I must have moved, stirring up odours that were indefinable in their complexity, somewhere between damp hemp, ashes and mouldy cheese.

Initially exciting, such excursions soon became harrowing. I increased them, however, to as many as four or five a day, because ultimately, despite my weariness, they took my mind off the miseries of our confinement. But as I carried these heavy food parcels on my back, I often had to make my unsteady way to the trailer through slippery refuse still floating on the water, blocked by the sandbags piled all along the walls. Alone amid the debris, I laughed out loud at the grotesque difficulties of the situation.

During these temporarily diverting moments, I would allow my thoughts free rein. They would rebound off a child's bicycle, or a neat row of tools, or they would fly off some carefully folded floral-pattern sarongs. Sometimes they would fly off so far into the sky that I would find myself suddenly alone, lost in my frightened body, weighted down like a coffin, a multitude of corpses piled up on top of me; and sticking out of the mass grave, the mangled bodies of Lay and Son.

In the embassy, the refugees were getting ready for their departure. Each of them was carefully sorting out his or her possessions to fill the one piece of luggage that was permitted. Those who were due to leave first were already waiting and talking among themselves. Suddenly, there was pandemonium at the gate. No-one had foreseen the danger: Nhem was demanding immediate access, together with a dozen soldiers armed with bazookas and machine guns. He wanted to make sure that the radio station was no longer operating. I calmly ran over to meet him, while the gendarme on duty went to warn the consul. Nhem, who was very aggressive, set off almost at a run in the direction of the chancellery. Dyrac encountered him on the staircase. He looked so shocked at the sight of the Khmer Rouge commando that I felt deeply worried myself. Paying no attention to what the consul said, the president charged down the corridor and stopped in front of the door of the military broadcasting office.

"Open up!" he said, beating at the door and turning to the consul.

The guerrillas, with their weapons, had gathered on the gallery of the floor above and were watching the scene with unpleasant expressions on their faces. Dyrac looked as if he was losing it. He gazed vacantly at the Malay, who was looking back at him questioningly and holding out his hand to him, turning an imaginary key backwards and forwards. He started to walk off, then suddenly turned back.

"Tell the president that the keys will be here in a moment," he told me.

Dyrac had pulled himself together and was smiling and nodding reassuringly. In fact, he had every reason to be anxious, for the broadcasts – a fact of which I was completely unaware – had never stopped. Somebody brought the keys and tried them in the lock. The door opened immediately, on its own, released from the inside. Zink was in the room, trapped. Terribly embarrassed, he looked at us, trying to find a face to hide his fear. It was obvious that the two transmitters he was in charge of had just been switched off; they were still warm.

I was transfixed as I walked into the room with the Khmers Rouges. I couldn't believe my eyes: an ashtray was still smoking on top of one of the transmitters. Zink became bogged down in confused explanations: with staring eyes and wide gestures, he maintained that he was merely carrying out maintenance work. I stammered as I translated his remarks. Nhem was breathing rapidly; he said nothing. Then he ordered the electric supply to both transmitters cut, and went to the decoding office. We looked him straight in the eye and swore to him that he was mistaken, even if appearances suggested the contrary.

I felt betrayed and humiliated. After the departure of the Khmers Rouges, I immediately demanded explanations. "How could you . . . you let me give my word that everything would be closed down . . . yet you had no intention of doing so, did you?"

On the embarrassed faces of the Frenchmen I saw surprised expressions that bordered on commiseration. Faced with my naivety, some of them preferred to go on denying everything. I remember that Ermini turned on his heels without saying a word, thoroughly upset to see my disappointment, although I was unable to tell from this whether he felt the slightest desire to reassure me. I learned later that we continued secretly to receive and send messages right up to the final day, and that there was even another radio station concealed behind the consular offices.

# 14

A Peugeot 203, crammed to the roof with all sorts of stuff, drew up with a screech of brakes in front of the gate. Not only had we heard the noise it made from afar, but its worn-out engine emitted spirals of smoke that could be seen from the Japanese bridge. A man in shorts, bathed in sweat, managed to extricate himself by pushing the door with both feet, causing parcels to fall out with him. He burst in upon us.

"My word, they're all mad!" he bellowed without any preamble, approaching as if he knew us. "You should see the shambles at Kilometre 6! And they all wanted to pinch my car."

"Where have you come from?" I asked in astonishment.

"A long way away! I live in the country," he replied, gesturing abruptly. "My family's still down there. So! What's it like here? Are you coping? Good God, I thought I'd never get through! They fire at you for the slightest thing. You should see the dead bodies along the road!"

Somewhat taken aback, we advised him to bring his car in before he attracted attention. But the thing was in a terrible state, and had only just managed to get as far as us, before packing up and refusing to start again. We pushed the car into the courtyard.

The man had friends among the group of Vietnamese old boys who, along with their Asian wives, formed an exuberant and lively lot housed beneath the arches of the Cultural Department. He was immediately welcomed with jibes.

"Oh! So you've eventually decided to come and look around town!" one of them called out. "Manage to find the way, did you? It's an ideal time to do a bit of shopping. There are some great bargains at the market. And the beer's free!"

"Not a bit of it!" someone else interrupted mockingly. "He's not buying, he's selling. He's come to sell you his old crate! Hey, guys! Now there's a real bargain . . . ha, ha!"

He went straight from one person to another, laughing along with them, shaking hands, feigning punches. Too much sun had gouged his skin, and now furrows of affability were adding themselves to his face. He had an amazing mug, which would have looked perfectly happy if it weren't for the trembling crevasse dividing his forehead in two. The material spread out on his rocky skull, with folds here, pushes there, seemed to have been scraped by a chemical agent, and a bony puffiness deformed his nose, shining like an arch pitted by the rain. His head was perched between wide shoulders, on a hollow chest. A grid of thousands of fine lines cross-hatched the flaky skin of his neck.

"You're just jealous!" he answered. "Come on now and help me unload it!"

Everyone began to unpack his junk and we joined in. Then he started speaking at the top of his voice, rather like a madman, not looking at anyone. "Right! Mustn't hang around! My wife and daughter are waiting for me! I have to go back for them. I'm just the advance party!"

"What? But where are they?" I asked him.

"At Kilometre 27. I hid them there. They won't budge."

"Hang on! It's not that simple," I replied. "Once you're here, the Khmers Rouges won't allow anyone to leave! You'd need a special permit, and I can't really see — "

"But this is my wife and my daughter. They're French. I'm going to get them, and no-one's going to stop me!"

His friends watched him perspiring and working himself up as they helped him unload the paraphernalia wedged into the back seat. They were all casting glances at one another and nodding, looking worried. No-one understood why he had come alone or dared to believe that he would be able to collect his family.

"Where are they, exactly?" I asked him. "Can you be specific? I'll see whether it's possible to try anything," I said, turning to the gendarmes.

"No-one will find them without me!" he exclaimed humorously. "It's in a little village . . . on the outskirts . . . I can't explain where they are just like that! In any case, they won't come out of their hiding place unless they recognise me, unless it's me they see, understand?"

I crossed the boulevard with the intention of asking Nhem if I could go and look for the Frenchwoman and her daughter. We had no idea what was happening outside Phnom Penh, and I found the prospect of taking the Nationale 5 road along the Mekong for thirty or more kilometres very exciting. Above all, it wasn't totally unthinkable that I might find Hélène's mother and be able to bring her back with me. But I was immediately gripped by such excruciating anxiety that I hardly dared think of her or the house girls along the road. I also didn't want to get too excited, for I didn't think Nhem would allow me to make such a trip.

Two kids were cleaning some rifles in a corner of the hall. The Malay was dozing in one of the leatherette armchairs, his legs stretched out one over the other, kept half awake by the humming of a fan. Nhem had gone off somewhere, and he had been left on duty. I was cursing this unfortunate setback and preparing to return disappointed, when I glimpsed a possible advantage in the president's absence.

"Comrade, I have to go and get two French people!" I said confidently. "They're cut off on the road, near Prek Kdam. There's not a moment to lose!"

The Malay pouted and hesitated, then slowly rose to his feet, shrugged and asked me to wait until his boss returned.

"Impossible!" I maintained. "There's heavy traffic on the road. I need to leave right away. I must ask you to allocate me an escort with the necessary documents."

The Khmer Rouge stood in silence, looking puzzled and deeply confused. He then paced about the room, his eyes cast down, expressing his disapproval with continuous nods of the head.

"It is my duty to remind you that you are responsible for our safety!" I said resolutely. "In the absence of the president, if anything happens it is up to you to take the necessary steps. And nobody else. You're in charge, aren't you? I ask this of you, just as I would ask it of Comrade Nhem. Come now! We've already delayed too long."

Forced into a tight spot, the Malay gave way with a look of irritation, for fear that he might be making an even bigger mistake by refusing. This is the weakness of all totalitarian regimes. This instinctive man knew that responsibility was a surer way of killing the Khmer Rouge than the B-52s.

I emerged in triumph from the former Korean Embassy, left the young guard who had been designated to accompany us in the jeep, and dashed off to look for my Asian settler.

"Well, you've really had a stroke of luck. Come on, we're off to your place! I've got a permit . . . unbelievable!"

Surrounded by his pals, the old fellow had just finished unloading his car and was looking at me stubbornly. At times, his twisted features would crease up in an agony of worry.

"Yeah, wait, we're almost done!" he replied, as he went on struggling to close the boot.

"Hurry up!" I reiterated. "You can do that later. The jeep is ready, and our guide is waiting."

"Ah, but I'm going in my own car!" he vowed, looking daggers at me.

I couldn't believe my ears. The fellow was crazy. There was something so incurably stubborn about him that it was alarming. We all stared at him in amazement.

"What? You must be joking!" I replied, bewildered. "Look, it doesn't make sense!"

"I promised to leave it to my brother-in-law!"

As he said this, he jumped into the car to make it start. Nothing moved. The battery was dead.

"Fine!" I said to him. "Never mind. Come on now, quickly!"

But he refused to listen and went on working the starter to no avail. He then called out to his friends: "No, we're going to push! Come on, guys!"

He got out like a creature possessed and set an example by bracing his feet on the ground and pushing with all his weight against the half-open door. From his chest, glistening with sweat, there came repeated grunts that were so painful to the ears that several people came to give a helping hand. The 203 gathered a little momentum; he hopped in behind the steering wheel and engaged second gear but was unable to get the car going; it bumped along into the car park. He insisted on trying again with greater speed, and those who were pushing changed sides so as to move the contraption back to the middle of the courtyard.

More than half an hour had passed. Exasperation boiled up inside me. I turned my eyes to the heavens, grinding my teeth furiously, fists clenched in my pockets. The Khmer Rouge was peering from his jeep, not understanding what was going on. The gendarme looked annoyed as he held open the gate.

*Brrm . . . brrm . . . brrm . . .* With much misfiring and vibrating, the car finally started. It then stopped suddenly, releasing a cloud of smoke over the old boys who were wearily pushing before putt-putting away again. With the first roar of the engine, I started up the jeep and we drove round, past the Malay, who was crossing the street to find out what was going on. At this precise moment, the president's minibus arrived in the boulevard. Nhem gestured to me. I ran over to explain the situation to him.

"It's out of the question!" he snapped. "The Angkar takes care of everything. We ourselves will go and collect the woman and the girl."

"But – "

"*At oy té!*"

Disheartened, I decided to pack the whole thing in there and then.

The gendarme ordered the poor wretch, who was waving his arms around, not knowing what was happening, to come back.

"What? What is it? What's going on?" he asked.

His friends took him away with them. Nobody wanted to explain to him. He left Cambodia alone and was repatriated to France, where he had not had family for many years.

The night of 30 April was short. The Khmers Rouges had brought twenty-seven trucks in front of the gate well before daybreak. The vehicles were covered in yellow tarpaulins flecked with red from the mud on the tracks. It had taken them hours to manoeuvre in the stillness of the avenue, and park them in a single neat line. A Molotova that had broken down was immediately towed away from the smoking column. Nhem was supervising operations himself; it was he who would advance the convoy to the frontier. On the French side, Maurin had been put in charge.

We had agreed that at the last moment before entering Thailand, André Pasquier, the delegate from the International Committee of the Red Cross, would hand a letter to Nhem. It would give us precise indications about the current conditions of the journey, in coded words which we had already agreed upon. In the worst-case scenario – and this was what a number of us feared – Nhem would not have any message to give us on his return.

Alerted by the loud cries of the assistant drivers, who were directing operations, the first group due to leave had gathered in the shade with their belongings. As well as the obligatory supply of drinking water, each traveller carried a single piece of carefully filled luggage. The Khmers Rouges would frisk everyone when they came to check the passports. The volunteer stewards did their best to deal with the crowd that had formed outside the chancellery, and stop them getting in the way of the loading.

By the light at the entrance, Nhem was leafing through the final inventory of names, typed on onionskin paper. Surrounded by armed reinforcements who stood watching us assemble, Migot was walking back and forth, nerves snapping with fatigue, buried in the lists that he and Monique had spent the whole night correcting and revising. At that very moment, behind the throng of people, I remember seeing their daughter, Vinca, leaning against the chancellery wall, alone and angelic, struggling to survive her sister's death.

The least mistake could set off a drama. Our guards paid minute attention to the slightest error in the names, the spelling of which had to be identical to that on the passports. The copies given to the Khmers Rouges had to correspond precisely to the originals we retained. They wanted them impeccable, carbon-copied in quadruplicate, without the slightest amendment made by hand. More than a rubber stamp or a signature, the type-written form of the document mattered to them, and this alone appeared to guarantee authenticity.

Nhem allowed us to proceed with boarding, truck by truck. The refugees responded glumly when Migot's gruff voice called out their names and they went to the boulevard to join their allotted vehicle. I myself had to carry out a further roll call as they boarded one by one, under the gaze of the Khmers Rouges who checked the pile of passports. Then I clambered on board myself, forcing my way to the back of the truck, bending under the dusty red canopies, amid the stench of grease and damp iron that the canvas hoods gave off. I loudly counted the passengers one last time, ticking them off as I did so, supervised by a team of soldiers who scrutinised them from beneath the side panel: one, two, three, four . . .

With difficulty I made my way through tucked-in legs, bags and containers. My unsteady feet trod on impervious hands and bumped against motionless heads protruding from under the slatted benches. Frightened stowaways had crept beneath the packets and the baskets, right down on the greasy floor; photographers desperately anxious to avoid being searched, to the great displeasure of those passengers who had their papers and who were glancing at me anxiously; a certain number of trapped Khmers, mostly young women who had bravely stayed behind with their lovers, staggering with fear as they slipped through the rows of the "legally entitled" and climbed in with them under the tarpaulins, trusting to police inefficiency.

In fact, just as the military supervisors had shown themselves incapable of maintaining a protracted and methodical surveillance of the embassy, so the fanatical caution they displayed and the meticulous air they adopted as they picked over each list was nothing but a show designed to conceal their impotence when confronted with more than five hundred people whose papers and baggage had to be checked all at once.

Were they relying on our own efficiency in properly coordinating each of the tasks they allotted us? Did they ever really trust our arrangements? I believe that, above all else, they wanted to get rid of us quickly. In the end, we were not subjected to any serious examination.

The convoy moved off in a cloud of smoke. The light of dawn added a shimmering sparkle to the eyes of the occupants of the last truck, as they looked back solidly at us.

Everyone who was now setting off (we could see them in the distance, disappearing behind the cathedral) was going willingly; none of them, right up to the very last moment, would have given up his place. Yet precisely when they were about to be launched into the unknown, they looked back at us there in the protected perimeter; many of them, without daring to admit it, may have felt that they had acted precipitately.

Light flooded down the straight line of the deserted boulevard, casting a blazing radiance under the fabric of the clouds. Huge streaks of gold trailed along the bluing sky, smearing a light diamond dust for the sun's first rays to disperse in an instant.

We found ourselves in unfamiliar new surroundings, suddenly deprived of a part of our community. We would feel their absence, like an amputated limb, for a long time to come, not merely because of the void left within us but because of the amount of newly vacant room.

It was the occasion for a major upheaval. All of a sudden, nothing had any value, and everything was turned upside down: our identities, our habits, our ways of making ourselves useful, our sleeping patterns. Then, beneath the sky's impassive gaze, in the stillness of the passing hours and the constantly fine weather, the routine resumed.

I returned to the EFEO to decide what to take and what to leave behind. Amid the surge of mutilation that sickens me to this day, I resolved to abandon the two hundred rubbings, several metres high, that I had begun to make upon my arrival in 1965. At that time, I had wanted to study the iconography of the historiated rinceaux or foliated patterns that adorn the piers of monuments at Angkor, hoping to find clues to the origins of local traditions.

Six years later, when Douch had released me – and my sense of freedom regained gave me a renewed vigour – I had returned to my research into Khmer Buddhism, this time in a new direction. My prolonged isolation and the obligation to define a clear subject of study which would convince my captors, had triggered fresh enquiries. I had immediately embarked upon the study of texts written in the local language, thus reducing some of my interest in the rubbings. From my liberation in 1971 to just before 17 April 1975 – three good years, that is – I had never stopped roaming around accessible areas of the ancient kingdom, collecting and copying Buddhist texts preserved in villages and pagodas, and as a result neglecting my first pre-war love.

"Hey!" yelled Laporte, who noticed me in the courtyard. "I'm leaving with her, finally! That's it, it's decided," he said with undisguised satisfaction, in that slightly chastened and relieved tone that serious people adopt when they admit to yielding to an unreasonable but (to them) necessary pleasure. "We're leaving together. The problem is that she hasn't any papers. At the consulate, they say it's too late to add her to the lists. Nobody said anything to me. And then there's the little girl!"

Totally immersed in his own problem, as if resolving the difficulty depended on his decision alone, he had failed upon arrival at the embassy to draw attention to the presence of his partner and his child, or else had resolved not to mention them.

Tanned, with sleek hair and a thin Errol Flynn moustache, the man was famous because of his voice, which could be heard every morning reading the news on Radio Phnom Penh.

I had met his Cambodian wife even before I made the connection with him. She was a pure-bred Khmer, with that typical, unforgettable beauty. I had photographs of her dancing, possessed by the gods she represented, during trances inspired by a medium. Her feline grace made her movements ripple. The whites of her eyes were the colour of ripe corn, her teeth white as ivory; her lips framed the opening of her mouth like a red ribbon dappled with azure. Just as Nature had pulled up the corners of her slanting eyelids, it had simultaneously turned up the tips of her eyebrows, the wings of her nostrils and the corners of her mouth. Their little daughter was ravishing; like her mother's, the darker area around the blurred base of her nose merged with the very top of her lip, disappearing into the contours of her mouth.

During the late afternoon, I asked Dyrac about the Laporte family.

"Of course," he replied with an air of consternation. "But what can I do? He only registered his Khmer wife and daughter yesterday! The lists are now closed. And you know what they're like across the road. They would never accept a last-minute addition."

"You know his problem," I intervened. "He's married in France, with children, and even if he no longer lives with his first wife, the idea of the second one becoming his lawful wife paralyses him. I think he wants her to leave Cambodia with him, but not as his wife. Later on, he could divorce and acknowledge the little girl . . ."

"Sir!" One of the gendarmes rushed up, slightly out of breath.

"We have some new visitors at the gate," he confided wearily, setting off again immediately.

We hurried off behind him.

"I want to see!"

We had not yet met the revolutionary speaking to us in French with a stern look in his eyes. His radiant smile beneath his Mao cap made him look like a Red Guard. He was proud, neat, tidy, and in good health. Two shoulder straps met across his bulging chest beneath a kind of cartridge pouch of faded fabric. He carried a revolver on his belt. The men behind him were also armed.

Agreeably surprised to see the Khmer making an effort to address us in our language, the consul himself replied, politely inviting him to come in, not forgetting to ask the men to leave their guns outside. In actual fact, the revolutionary knew only a few words of French, and I had to repeat our demand in Khmer. The young rebel leader immediately looked surprised and uncomfortable, and the thought of having to try to convince him again suddenly made me feel weary.

To my great relief, one of the president's men, whom I had not recognised among the soldiers, came and whispered in his ear, explaining that this strange practice was now law. No guns in the embassy. Extremely ill at ease, but not daring to contradict Nhem himself, he selected five men, without their weapons, to accompany him. We urged him to keep his own gun, afraid to see him lose face in front of his men.

He strode across the courtyard with us. He had received orders from on high. His mission was to search our baggage, and in particular that of the journalists, to make sure that we had neither films nor photographs. Knowing his purpose now, Dyrac looked somewhat relieved. He was concerned about the fate of the photographers' work, but he knew that those who had stayed behind had entrusted some of their rolls to passengers on the first convoy and that the rest had been carefully hidden away.

We walked quickly over to the offices and at a sign from the Khmer Rouge, whose men were discovering our premises with great curiosity, the consul asked a gendarme to open a drawer, a cardboard box and a suitcase. We moved to another building and visited the Cultural Department's offices, where the occupants were now enjoying a little more space, before making our way to the residency, at the other end of the park, where some of the international delegations, the doctors and the press correspondents were based.

A little bored with finding nothing but underwear and souvenirs that were of no interest, our young inspector, whose primary objective may have been merely to keep us on our toes, gradually cooled. He and his escort scanned the rows of luggage lined up in the rooms, beneath the windows and on the benches, and he became much less demanding than he had been at the beginning. We reached the room where the journalists were; along the walls they had set up cubicles, small individual spaces partitioned by assorted clutter. The Khmer Rouge stopped at random beside a large, flat bag made of a stiff fabric lying on the floor. Its owner, Denis Cameron, was standing in front of us, and he was asked to open it. The reporter calmly bent down, without the least embarrassment, to show what it contained. I did not react immediately myself, and I realised what I was looking at only when I heard Dyrac choke with indignation. "What is this?"

The case was full of the embassy's antique silverware, engraved with the arms of the French Republic. The expression on the consul's face was transformed, and his body swelled with rage. He picked up the heavy suitcase as if it were a wisp of straw and tipped its entire contents out over Cameron, standing speechless in front of us: a ewer, a candlestick, a gravy boat, a platter and a huge silver sugar bowl came clanging down and bounced onto the floor, watched by the Khmer Rouge, who had no idea what was going on.

On the morning of 5 May, we still had no news of the first convoy, even though we were meant to leave the following day. However, it wouldn't take us long to climb aboard; we were all ready, waiting for the moment to arrive, our belongings reduced to a minimum. We, too, would surely hurry off into the trucks, even without the guarantees we were expecting from Nhem, who should have returned the previous day. He did not make his appearance until the middle of the day, but he bore reassuring messages from Maurin and Pasquier, who were now in Thailand.

Revil came to find me. The surgeon-colonel was a small, bald, pudgy man with very alert eyes, in which you could read his authoritative manner, and a playful smile, where you could read his wit.

"During the trip," he told me, "a baby died of dehydration. Many people fell sick and there were many injured, though not as seriously as they might have been. But we also have a pregnant woman, who could give birth prematurely through fatigue. I have asked the president to put an ambulance at the convoy's disposal. He seemed to agree. We thought of your Land-Rover. It's the only long-wheelbase diesel with a winch we've got. It could be fitted out with intensive-care equipment and converted into an ambulance. If you agree, you would be accompanied by a medic."

After a moment of silence, he added, looking directly at me, "I believe, er . . . that it would please Piquart to leave with you."

I had inherited the brand new vehicle from Roland Mourer, a friend who was a prehistorian and who had been forced to leave Phnom Penh a few months earlier, unable to ship it out. Within a few hours, the doctors from the Calmette had transformed it into a mobile hospital, with all the instruments and equipment necessary to carry out operations on the way.

An overall restlessness, mixed with emotion and excitement, came over our community both indoors and out. The Chinese trucks would come to collect us during the night, ready to leave first thing in the morning. At ten o'clock that evening, Dyrac ordered a small gathering, as brief as it was poignant. On the flagpole in the middle of the courtyard, which was sunk into a muddy lawn and surrounded by white pebbles, the French flag still fluttered. The gendarmes stood to attention as the colours were lowered.

We did our utmost to leave behind clean buildings and to take care that everything – doors, chests and cupboards – was left open. Symbolically, the consul handed over the keys of the embassy to Nhem.

*

246

We left Phnom Penh on the Nationale 3 road. In a few moments, the dawn behind us gave way to the sunrise. The rays of light projected their colours over the immense felted blanket of the sky.

The wide avenue was empty. We drove along smoothly, at the head of the slow-moving convoy. Along the roadway, the blooming flame trees had unfurled their languid vermilion petals over the asphalt. Stunned by this beauty but shocked by so much indifference – the fiery crimson was more an invitation to light-heartedness than an image of a wave of blood – I suddenly began to cry, pouring out all the tears that had accumulated in my body. Piquart's hand, tapping on my shoulder, came to my rescue.

Within a few minutes, we drew level with Potchentong airport, which had been virtually razed to the ground. Gaping with holes, the red-and-white control tower barely stood above a heap of rubble; the rockets and sprays of gunfire had failed to obliterate it entirely. It reminded me of an occasion that had profoundly affected me. At this terrible moment, I had a memory of immense resentment. Every detail of what happened came back to me and I rapidly unburdened myself to Piquart.

It took place, I believe, in January 1973. Spiro Agnew, vice-president of the United States, was expected to arrive at Phnom Penh at ten o'clock local time. For weeks no-one had spoken of anything else. The area around the airport was under constant surveillance; spy planes circled in the sky. The Khmer police, who had infiltrated everywhere, had made it a point of honour to control access to American areas very strictly. Together with the Criminal Investigation Department and the Intelligence Unit, they kept the American chancellery, the diplomatic office, the residency and the campus under tight supervision. The American policy office had even imposed double protection, under the authority of a group of experts who had been sent over. Several possible routes between the airport and the embassy had been studied secretly, signposted, cleared and searched, and in places even gravelled and asphalted. Additional troops had arrived from Saigon to give the GIs a helping hand. For days, soldiers had been camping out in the streets, keeping watch over paths and approaches that were considered suspect, observing shops, the windows of buildings, tops of trees . . .

Faced with such paranoiac activity – comical when compared to the real dangers the government faced – the Khmer had not wanted to be outdone. Such a costly deployment meant that the sneers were somewhat silenced, to be replaced by the most genuine respect. They pulled out all the stops to welcome the prestigious guest, whom they had imagined as an imposing figure. All the traditions of Cambodia, from the oldest customs practised in the ancient kingdom to the most recent procedures, were to be represented for the occasion. They called upon the most renowned traditional masters of their crafts; if unable to locate them, a search was made in the remote villages of the hinterland. The largest orchestras, the best ballet and dance troupes, had rehearsed together day and night in productions conceived with airport and security constraints in mind. On the big day the ministers, dressed in their sumptuous ceremonial garb – white coats, loose green trousers, white stockings and shiny black shoes with buckles – were supported by several *phimpeat* orchestras, singers with wooden *tatrao* drums and flageolet players. Alongside the military chiefs in full regalia were hundreds of schoolchildren waving American flags and all standing to attention. The tarmac was covered with delicately woven matting. A red carpet led to the place where the presidential plane was meant to come to a stop. Some Brahmins had taken up their places, conch trumpets in hand, opposite trays laden with offerings made of lacquer and silver. The cars for the procession were ready, headed by an armour-plated sedan that had been flown in the previous day. Dozens of dancers, who had been sewn into gold-embroidered bodices, stood gracefully with baskets of petals. Across from the ministers, gleaming brass instruments played a fanfare with great pomp and ceremony as the sun rose in the sky.

The eagerly awaited aircraft appeared, a little earlier than expected, coming to a halt at the exact spot that had been agreed upon. At that same moment, the sounds of the orchestras and the buglers, the voices of the singers and the words of welcome yelled out by the choruses of schoolchildren resounded in a fantastic cacophony. Even the long wail of the sacred conches could hardly be heard. The dancers started to perform while the ministers and generals solemnly stepped forward. The door of the aircraft opened, and some girls dressed in silk advanced with gold-painted steps, bedecked in flowers. At that very instant, and in less time than it takes to say it, the whirring of a helicopter's blades could be heard in the air, accompanied by a great deal of crashing and banging. Half a dozen GIs burst out of the plane and fanned out in front of the steps, pushing the schoolchildren and the dancers out of the way, their automatic weapons sticking out in front of them, their legs apart and a fixed expression in their eyes. Within a few seconds, the vice-president of the United States, carried by two giant men, was ejected from the plane and ushered into the helicopter, which took off instantaneously (to land later on the roof of the American Embassy) in a whirlwind of dust mingled with flower petals and paper flags, leaving the ministers, generals, Brahmins, dancers and musicians looking on.

Once we had passed the airport, a place of desolation in my memory, we turned northwards, cutting between the plots of rice and following tracks barely visible beneath the fallow fields. Sometimes the trucks drove through peat bogs filled with stagnant water and rotting vegetation, sinking into potholes from which we extracted ourselves only with the greatest difficulty; at other times we had to skirt tiny streams that flowed through the fields between impassable ruts. On several occasions, we came within a hair's breadth of having to abandon the vehicle, the terrain was so obstructed. Yet we also felt an exalting feeling of freedom regained, as we struggled to manoeuvre through the *Licuala* bushes and the gnarled *Streblus* that grew out of mounds of white clay, trimmed vertically by the rains.

Without realising it, we bypassed Oudong and travelled through a village where men were digging under the supervision of a commando of Khmer Rouge women. We stopped there to regroup. I could see some soldiers in lively discussion with the soldiers escorting us. They approached the Land-Rover.

"There's a Frenchwoman in this village!" they announced solemnly, as if it was an order. "She must go back to France."

Beside the road, which passed in between the houses, a rather pretty girl was holding a city-dweller's suitcase with both hands in front of her. She might have been sixteen, but she had a strikingly stern and sorrowful expression, much in contrast with her age. She was dressed like a market trader in a close-fitting blouse that revealed the tops of her arms, and cotton trousers of a dark material gathered by elastic at the waist, whose creases twisted round her legs. Her somewhat square jaw gave her face a broad look, but her deep-set, widely spaced almond eyes covered the entire surface of her temples and stretched as far as her hair, which was not quite black. There was an almost imperceptible pinkness where her smooth lips met her teeth. When I looked at her, her childlike features took on an expression of tragic determination. She was trembling.

"I am French!" she announced in Khmer. "My aunt's house is here, my mother lives in Phnom Penh, my father's in France. I'm frightened. Please, I want to go to France."

"What's your name?"

"Malie."

"Marie?"

"*Tcha.*"

"And your father, what's his name?"

"Er . . . I can't remember," she said, smiling and shaking her head.

"Do you have any papers? Do you know his address in France?"

"No, but Mummy knows!"

"Do you speak French, Marie?"

"No . . . but I'll learn quickly!"

The Khmers Rouges, who must have been young people from the village, were following our conversation and nodding their agreement to the young girl's replies, proud to have taken the initiative in making her existence known.

"She must leave!" they asserted.

"She hasn't any papers," I replied.

"*At oy té!* Her father is French."

I wanted to consult Nhem immediately, but he was at the back of the convoy, which was about to set off again.

"Very well!" I said without giving the matter much thought. "We'll see . . ."

There could be no question of taking her with us in the ambulance. I made her climb into the back of the first truck. People made room on the bench, and she squeezed in between them.

We set off again through an area of intermittent bush alternating with patchy forest. Here and there, we passed small islands surrounded by swamps and dominated by large scattered trees. The trucks took up the entire width of the tracks, which disappeared beneath the mass of sagging shrubs and huge fallen branches. We passed through clusters of dwellings populated by "liberated" folk who lived in poverty, subsisting in a wartime economy, scarcely looking up as we went by. The row of their cabins was set directly into the sandy earth beside rare crops that had been abandoned and lay fallow. Still, small gardens of sweet cucumbers, dotted here and there with stumps charred by bushfires, seemed to have benefited from the storms that heralded the new season.

On the horizon, the orange disc was fraying at the edges as it dropped behind the forest-covered summit of Mount Aural. Suddenly weighed down by touches of gold, the carded wool of the clouds stretched into the outlines of a Chinese junk, then turned into some serene, majestic wave over the shore of the mountains, lapped by a sea of snowy peaks. In the west, the sky grew dark. In the east, the radiant moon was already high in the firmament.

Once night fell, we were forced to follow rough tracks thoroughly unsuitable for motor vehicles, bumping along by the light of our headlights. The majority of the twenty-two hunks of metal that constituted our convoy had no lights; they bounced about like water running over the rutted ground. The roar of their engines drowned out the noise of the Land-Rover. Above us, the moon disseminated a glow that shrouded the holes in the road.

We finally arrived at Kompong Chhnang at about eight in the evening. A group of soldiers on mopeds was waiting for us at the gates of the dark, deserted town to guide us to the old prefecture building, where we were to spend the night. The exhausted passengers emerged slowly from the trucks, shaking themselves as the burning, clanking engines released the last stenches of fuel before being switched off.

Against the light, bathed in pale reflections, the lofty architecture of the colonial building, which may have been ochre or blue, rose from the level foundations on which it had been built. Embellished with French windows and shutters, its façade towered over the columns of the porch, which housed a broad staircase. On either side, square-shaped wings, each with a four-sided roof, flanked the first-floor terrace. Piquart was immediately monopolised by dozens of people who were suffering from bruises or feeling faint. I opened the muddy bonnet of the steaming vehicle to check the water, oil and so on. Marie was behind me with her suitcase.

"Ah! Of course," I said, turning around. "Come on. We'll go and ask the person in charge of the convoy, and you can explain yourself. Leave your case in the car."

Nhem was getting into a jeep next to the Malay, who was driving. I ran up to him and produced the girl.

"She joined the convoy during the course of the journey," I explained to the Khmer Rouge. "Her father is French. She no longer has any papers."

The president asked her a few questions, but then the Malay started to question her in a nasty way.

"Comrade!" I interrupted. "You can see she's of mixed race. She has lost her mother. Let her at least find her father! What difference can it make now?"

"The difference is that she doesn't have any papers and she has to stay!" he cut in.

The jeep shot off and left us standing there. I had already observed how, in a few weeks, this little man, so full of energy, had gained greatly in confidence, and it now began to occur to me that he seemed to exert influence over his leader. He was the sort of man who is never deterred by obstacles, but as a consequence, like so many power fanatics, he looked on the suffering of weak and anonymous creatures with total contempt.

I deliberately turned round to the girl in front of them.

"Think carefully," I told her. "I don't know what to suggest. If the Khmers Rouges don't allow you to leave the country, you'd better retrace your steps straight away, before we're too far away from your village."

"It's not my village, and my aunt is dead," she answered. "I am from Phnom Penh."

I couldn't stop myself heaving a weary sigh. I silently returned to the car, dogged by despondency. Not wanting to waste time, I went and splashed my face with some water from a cement pot I had noticed in the courtyard. Piquart was getting ready to go to sleep in the car. I decided to settle down on the floor of the prefecture, taking with me a surgical sheet (we had brought a whole pile) to use as a blanket.

In the darkness of the room, where other motionless bodies were already spread out, Marie came up and lay against me for protection. I froze, just as Avi used to do when Hélène placed a kitten between his paws, who would begin to sniff him, innocently exploring the folds of his muzzle. She fell asleep immediately.

It was the infernal noise of the engines that roused everyone the next morning. Seven more trucks had attached themselves to us during the night, laden with numerous Pakistanis, Indians, Filipinos, Indonesians and Laotians who happened to be in the province. As soon as I rose, I went to inform Dyrac about the girl who had haunted my sleep. During the night, a light dew had formed on the tufts of grass that protruded from the gravel. All around us, the six-wheelers were already shunting to and fro, the thrusts of their accelerators causing them to jerk forward, and we had to shout to make ourselves heard.

"Pfff . . ." he sighed, his lips vibrating exaggeratedly. "How does she reckon she's going to find her father when she doesn't even know his name? How sad! Personally, I'd like to take her with us, but I'd be amazed if it's that easy. It's like that journalist from ORTF – his wife and child climbed aboard with him. But I don't know what the Khmers Rouges would say if they realised . . ."

Squatting amid the blue smoke from the engines, which the soldiers warmed by revving them in spurts, several refugees were polishing off some tins of food that had been opened the previous evening before taking their places beneath the tarpaulins. Followed by Marie, who would not leave me, I set off without further ado to find Nhem and told him that France would accept the young Eurasian girl. The president replied, addressing himself to her, "Why do you want to leave? You have no education. What's the point of going to France to serve other people and become their slave? Your country is here!"

The last trucks were taking up their positions in the convoy, reverberating with the hollow sounds of their perforated exhaust pipes. I turned to the girl and forbade her to go any further. I just had time to see a sudden flush come over her face, causing her eyes to redden. I ran off to join Piquart, who was waiting for me in the ambulance.

We set off again, sometimes at the back, sometimes at the head of the thundering column, fording streams and negotiating the mud of the potholes, rattling about in the middle of hoed fields, through villages that had been razed to the ground, past burnt pagodas and destroyed bridges. As far as the eye could see, there was nothing but collapsed dykes and flooded craters where putrefying buffaloes lay. And then in places there were cars, motorcycles, mattresses and suitcases lying abandoned at the side of the road. We came across groups of Khmers Rouges, left to their own devices, who would often stare at us with expressionless faces, and numerous civilians pushing their possessions, hanging around in clusters along the tracks and waving us greetings as they moved out of the way. Empty-headed, we drove for hours, with brief stops, beneath a burning sun that caused the particles of dust we swallowed to glitter. The pregnant woman felt faint. Piquart made her lie down in the back and gave her an injection. I can see her, beads of sweat forming on her brow, trembling, eyes withdrawn, oblivious to everything apart from the child she knew lay curled up in her womb. I found myself envying her animal selfishness. Woman has this that man will never have.

At dusk we were within sight of Battambang, which we had to bypass in order to spend the night at the exit to the town. The trucks pulled up in the middle of the road, which at this point ran alongside the old monastery of Kbal Khmoc, now converted into a military headquarters.

With the aid of a torch I borrowed from Piquart, I set off to look for Avi. I myself hadn't done anything about him, not so much because I didn't have time but because I had too much else to think about. I was leaving my family behind: I could hardly think of taking my dog (even if, in the sight of the stars, there is no difference between man and dog). But without saying a word to me, Migot had found a chaperone for him in the person of Rémy. In the midst of the bustle of travellers and drivers calling out to one another from between the trucks, I noticed Avi methodically engaged in spraying a tree.

"He's perfect, really!" Rémy assured me. "He's obedient and he keeps still. No problem. But this dog is sad. It's amazing how he manages to show it. Ah! I almost forgot. Here's his vaccination certificate for Thailand."

He handed me a roneoed form that he had already signed and carefully completed himself: "I the undersigned Yves Goueffon, Veterinary Surgeon, Director of the Institut Pasteur in Cambodia, certify that I have vaccinated against rabies a dog named . . . *Avi*, aged . . . *4 years*, coat . . . *tan*." I admired this man and his direct, straightforward character. He had managed the Compagnie des Terres-Rouges, and his hevea plantation produced the highest yield per hectare in the world. We exchanged a few remarks about life, in words whose simplicity did not in the least detract from their strength. (I have since learned that simple words sometimes convey more intense truths than others.) I did my best to respect the linguistic sobriety of colonial people, who use the same dull stereotypes to speak about their emotions or express a feeling, to describe a change in the weather, the ecstasies of love or the pangs of death. It's a universal phenomenon, but I am not sure whether, from one generation to another, language can always deal as pertinently with the profound expression of the commonplace.

"Bizot! It's done!" said Dyrac, who emerged out of the darkness and approached us. "I've married them. Nhem agreed. The wife and the child have been added to our two lists. Under the name of Laporte. It was the only solution."

By the side of the road, in the paddy field, all around the trucks and beneath the tarpaulins, the refugees were rolling out their mats and hanging up their mosquito nets for the night. Avi and I entered the precinct of the pagoda, where the courtyard, surrounded by a cloistered gallery that concealed some naive prints of the lives of the Buddha, was already full of people. The temple roof was shining in the moonlight; the large preaching hall, the tall stupa with its tinkling bells, the chapter room, the library, the large residential buildings and the smaller ceremonial ones; we might have been in a small, fortified village. I found a place for myself by the edge of a low wall that ran alongside the ambulatory.

When we got up in the morning, I came across Laporte, who was holding his Khmer wife affectionately around the waist. Sitting with her legs to one side, she was purring quietly with happiness, deftly combing her long hair out in front of her. She looked radiant. They had left the little girl with neighbours and had themselves slept on the pavement.

"Not very comfortable for one's wedding night!" Laporte called out, smiling contentedly.

"I know, Dyrac told me. Bravo, and er . . . well, congratulations!" I replied with a knowing air, caught somewhat unawares by the happiness they displayed.

At that moment, behind them, I noticed Marie weaving her way among the trucks. Taking pity on her, some refugees had offered her shelter in their meagre space.

After four hours on a narrow edgeless road made of ballast, full of potholes, more testing than any of the tracks through the paddy fields (we abandoned a GMC truck whose engine had fallen out), we stopped at Sisophon. We were nearing our destination. However, we needed a short break before embarking upon the gravel road, across arid bush country, which led to Thailand.

A team of Khmers Rouges were waiting for us at the entrance to the town. They had prepared food to help sustain our community of almost eight hundred people: buffalo meat, rice, tubers, coconuts, bananas and pineapple. Two new trucks and a more comfortable bus were also put at our disposal.

Summoned back to Phnom Penh, Nhem was about to leave us. He asked me to come over so he could introduce me to his successor, a smiling younger man whom the Malay would make short work of. Before bidding farewell to him, I decided to take him aside to discuss the girl of mixed race.

"Comrade," I said to him, dragging him along by the hand, "our roads part here."

It gave me no pleasure to hold his thick, soft fingers in mine and to touch their callused top joints.

"I genuinely wish you the best of luck!" I began again. "May you, too, be allowed to live in peace and to return to your family. I thank you for what you have done for all of us – "

"*At oy té!* Comrade Bizot will soon not think any more about all that!" he said in a friendly tone, teasing me in the Cambodian way. "In France, he will forget about the suffering of Kampuchea!"

"Do you really think so? I'm leaving my family behind . . . In any case, I shall not forget Comrade Nhem, without whom our ordeal would have been still more distressing! I am sure we shall meet again," I said, "even if we have to wait ten years!"


As I had often done during the past few days, I thought of my father. I saw myself once more back in Nancy, on a fine afternoon, as we were crossing the rue d'Amerval. With his hand on my shoulder, he stroked my ear. "You'll see the year 2000!" he said cheerfully. "Well, so will you!" – "Oh, you know, in my case it's not so sure . . . although I hope to live some good years yet!" – "How many, Papa?" – "Ah, I can't tell, but ten years at least!" he assured me, hugging me several times as we walked along the pavement. "So few!" I exclaimed, troubled. Now, in the weariness of that long morning, as the azure sky grew pale in the heat, high above the convoy and the refugees who were eating their meal, I could see his dark eyes gazing at me from beneath silvery eyebrows, filled with love. I looked at him, as I had done countless times, sitting at his work table, bent over a pen-and-ink drawing; then, three years later, on his deathbed, his frozen features plunged into an unbelievable silence whose emptyness has never left me.

"But before saying goodbye," I continued, "I would like to ask one last favour. Comrade" – I took care to wait until there was silence – "I beg you to allow the Eurasian girl to come with us. It has been her dearest wish ever since she was little."

"She belongs here," he replied automatically. "Helping rebuild her country, working in the fields and taking part in collective offensives, in order to achieve national reconstruction. What use can she be to France? Here, her strengths are vital."

"She's only a child, and I'm not talking about usefulness!" I retorted, baulking at so much drivel. "I ask you about her, and you answer me with Cambodia. Let's leave the job of raising up the country from its ashes to the revolutionaries, and let's allow this little girl to rebuild herself in her father's footsteps! At the end of this war of brother against brother, can I not hope for one last outpouring of humanity from the comrade-president?"

I was fully aware that the Khmer Rouge leader had a short temper and was easily irritated by any opposition. Beneath his eyelids, which he had lowered so as not to see my anger, I nevertheless noticed more embarrassment than fury. He was silent for a while, absorbed (as always) by the sight of his feet, then looked at me for a few moments. He finally left me without saying a word, making only an awkward, unfathomable gesture which could equally mean "You haven't understood", "I don't give a damn", or "I'll see".

The scrubland stretched away in endless waves as far as the eye could see. Here and there, occasional clusters of gnarled bushes sprung up, choked with spurges, a bird of prey hovering over them. In the early afternoon, from quite a distance, we caught sight of the red flag flying over the border post. The air was stifling and humid. The heat of the day shimmered above the road. Tired of driving through the dust, Piquart and I had decided to position ourselves at the front of the trucks and to remain there. Between the abandoned paddy fields and the pollarded clumps of the sugar palms, there were now a few trees to shelter us, indicating that we were at last leaving this burnt and infertile region.

The entrance to the minute town was shut off by two rows of barbed wire stretched between wooden posts. It was defended by a small earthwork fort, reinforced by sandbags whose worn sacking had left shreds of material on the walls. The place seemed deserted. We got out of the car and entered. Along the sides of the circular embankment that formed the centre of Poipet, there were a few abandoned shops and restaurants built on stilts. Their backs overlooked an area given over to rubbish, chickens and pigs. On one side, some demolished barracks served as a billet for fifty or so soldiers whose uniforms could be seen at the back, drying on a wire. On the other side, the post office and custom-house buildings, with their tiles and their blinds, constructed with long-lasting materials at the time of the protectorate, still stood. In front of the immigration office was a barrier made of a long piece of bamboo and a block of stone that served as a counterweight; it guarded a patch of raised ground leading to a bridge whose framework, made up of three lengths of steel and a parapet, supported some heavy, bolted planks. The stream marked the border.

On the other bank, we were gratified and relieved to observe a festive crowd milling about behind cameras and telephoto lenses. We suddenly became aware of the international importance of the events we had lived through. All around them, cars, buses and tents waited there in the sunshine. The red cross on a dedicated tent stood out against the pale colours all around. At the far end of the bridge, the Thai police had set up tables to check the evacuees. We recognised the representatives of the French consulate in their civilian clothes.

In the burning light, some Khmers Rouges came forward, almost reluctantly, to meet us. They greeted us with a smile and took down the barbed wire, allowing in only the lighter escort vehicles so as not to clog up the area. I took the opportunity to drive the Land-Rover in as close as possible to the bridge, hoping to be able to drive it away. Once they set foot on the ground, the refugees spread out into the ditches. Exhausted and dirty, eyes blinded by the dust, they formed an immense throng, adults and children swarming around, meeting one another, searching for shady corners in which to compose themselves and repack their cases, and advancing in indescribable disarray towards the leading trucks. A real fracas broke out among the first arrivals when the Khmers Rouges tried to make them go in one by one, according to the order on the lists. Many people found their way to safety in the resulting, uncontrollable mêlée. Unable to cope, the revolutionaries' control was ineffective. And those whose names were not on the lists – women, friends, children – miraculously slipped through the net. They then crossed as far as the bridge, where the guards, overwhelmed by the crowds and perhaps constrained by the camera lenses and the Thai authorities on the other side, let virtually everybody through without much difficulty.

Dyrac managed to cross the bridge, talk with his French counterpart from Bangkok, and hand over the list of immigrants to the Thais. France and the other countries involved, had sent along their representatives. These nations would stand as guarantors of the couples and children who had no national identity papers. The very strict supervision by the Thai officials exposed several dozen illegal immigrants. They were taken away (but on the Thai side) to await transit permits and for their situation to be legalised. Migot walked back and forth to the middle of the bridge, trying to move people forwards.

Marie succeeded in infiltrating herself. She ran along to catch up with me. The Malay saw her. He was standing in the middle of the square with his new boss, observing the movement of the crowd. Behind them were some members of a women's commando unit and a dozen men from the garrison. I hissed at her between my teeth not to let herself be seen, but it was too late. A guard came and alerted the customs officers on the bridge. They eagerly turned around to identify her.

At the entry point the flood of refugees was held back to avoid a bottleneck at the final checkpoint. Laporte stepped forward with his wife and daughter. The Khmer hesitated over their identity, because their names had been added and there was no document. Dyrac assured them that the Laportes were indeed a married couple, drawing attention to the fact that the handwritten addendum appeared on both the lists. The matter was sent for arbitration to Nhem's replacement, who, under the influence of the Malay — who was antagonistic towards the French — spent a long time making up his mind. But the insistence of the consul and his assistant persuaded him to let them through.

Laporte, who was exhausted and looked distraught, stepped up onto the embankment and, with his family, passed the Khmer control point. At the other end of the bridge, the Thais were checking everybody individually. The Frenchman was invited to come forward on his own. His wife was frightened, wanted to follow him, and upset the entire procedure. The Khmer Rouge made her go back. Overcome by the situation, Laporte, like an automaton, also retraced his steps, but Migot summoned him back again. A Thai NCO, who was supervising operations, came up to help him and to examine his passport.

"Are you married? She is your wife?" he asked in English.

Confronted by this officer, Laporte did not know what to reply.

"Are you married?" the officer repeated, all of a sudden looking at him in the eye to see if he was telling the truth.

I was three yards away. The expression on the face of the ORTF announcer was anguished, and he was in a cold sweat.

"Answer him, for fuck's sake!" I shouted, holding my breath.

"I can't bloody well say we're married!" he burst out, turning to Migot and me. "I just can't! No!"

The officer interpreted the expression on his face and sent the queue jumper back.

"You!" he exclaimed in a loud voice, pointing at her with his finger. "No!"

On the Cambodian side, the guards reacted quickly. They cleared the entrance to the bridge, just as they had been ordered to do when the first incident occurred. The panic-stricken wife clutched at her husband with a trembling hand. A squad of fierce female orderlies ran up. I can see them still: some thirty years old, others fifteen, all with straight hair, cut in the Chinese style. Clinging to her man, she cried as she implored him; her outstretched arms pushed and pulled at his belt, trying to rouse him into action. He barely stirred, adopting an enquiring look as if to exonerate himself. The women soldiers beat this girl, who was trying to escape her fate, on her back with the barrels of their rifles. But they had to twist her fingers one by one to make her let go. Then her whole body was wracked with sobbing, as if her heart had broken. They took her away.

Laporte's daughter let out a loud howl as she rushed to follow her mother, and the quavering of her little voice was like the moan of a funeral lament. Unconcerned, the line of refugees re-formed, blotting out for ever the sound of the child's wails, whose devastating echoes still resound within me after many years.

On the bridge, our eyes wide with fury, we turned to the officers in all their finery to try to make them do something. They barely looked in our direction; our appeals met with no response. Crushed by his inconsistency, Laporte crossed to the Thai side of the border.

Marie called out to me. Two guards were trying to move her away from the entrance to the bridge. Once again I went to find Nhem's successor and walked straight up to him.

"Comrade!" I said to him with some force. "Our evacuation is all but done. I ask that it should end on a gesture of compassion. She is the daughter of a Frenchman. Authorise her to leave!"

My request made the Malay roar with anger, so exasperated was he at my insistence.

"*At oy té!*" replied the leader to whom I had addressed myself.

And with a wave of his hand that pacified his deputy's rage, he sent his wild Amazons to seize the adolescent girl, who was refusing to move from the gangway.

The girl was taken away and she passed by me, shoved along by the women; she looked at me, and her eyes, hollow with fear, bored two black holes into my brain that have never stopped deepening.

I returned to the bridge, not daring to focus my trembling gaze on that other shore, whose banks, treeless and sunburnt, nonetheless appeared to me as cool as a forest glade where walkers can take their rest. I longed for a new life, free of all violence. The last of the refugees were moving forward. My turn was approaching. I warned the Thais that I was bringing a car in.

The Khmers Rouges did not want to let me through. I leapt out of the vehicle in a fury and ran up the sloped path to where the two Communist leaders were standing, my regard still full of deadly hatred.

"When are you going to stop making a mockery of the orders of the vice-president of the command of the northern front of the city of Phnom Penh responsible for foreigners?" I yelled. "This business of the Land-Rover has been discussed and resolved. It must be allowed across the border! President Nhem was clear on this point!"

In the face of my bluff, the Malay once more did his best to assert his authority, but this time his senior officer would no longer listen to him, wanting to show he could make his own decisions.

Today I can't help thinking that if it had occurred to me to take the car over first before trying to rescue Marie, she might have reached the other side of the bridge.


I crossed over without looking back. Dusk fell over the land of the Khmers. Where the light had been swallowed away, a thickening darkness filled its space.

Falling upon a world abandoned to dark and terrifying powers, the primitive mob unleashed the hoard of dead in the storm we left behind. Their mechanical progress stamped and stamped the blood-drenched soil, pushing down the victims piled underfoot, for centuries past, to the deepest part of the earth.

Like a wandering soul that is freed — for the second time — by the judge of the dead, I emerged from the Cambodian hell by crossing the bridge of transmigration. I was expelled, like, the newborn, in the torments of an unspeakable pain. The vision of my own corpse rises up from these loathsome scenes. My voyage to the other side brought me to the centre of a precious isle. I entered the land of rose-apple trees to be reborn into a new existence.

But on this earth, there is no place of permanent refuge.

# Epilogue

*The foothills of the Cardamomes, January 2000*

The rather uncommunicative villager who has agreed to take me to the Anlong Veng camp is my age and can remember seeing a bearded fellow with a "long nose" shackled beneath the bamboo trees in 1971. I do my best to follow close behind him along a track heading west from Phum Thmar kok (ten kilometres south of Omleang), which turns into a concealed path, between sparse bushes, that only he can detect. I learn from him that the prison camp Douch controlled from 1971 to 1973, known to the Khmer Rouge as M. 13 (Bureau 13), was called Anlong Veng because it stood close to where a stream formed a long reach (*anlong*). In disuse for the past twenty-seven years, the grim site has reverted to forest, and nobody apart from him and a few other survivors could have led me there.

Ever since May 1999, when I learned of Douch's arrest, I have felt an urgent need to go back in time, to revisit the other side of the gate of my life, which has never been closed.

In the depths of his prison, my one-time persecutor awaits trial for crimes against humanity. He can brood over that period of his youth when murder, pillage and lies were not only permitted but commendable. Setting off with a flower in his rifle and a heart filled with hope, he had thrown himself into a primitive world filled with horror. Here, the dangers of war were slight in comparison to the dangers of revolution; in the most demanding confrontations, the warrior never stopped being wary of his neighbour. He was a child venturing among wolves: to survive, he had drunk their milk, and learned to howl like them, and let instinct take over. Terror, from that moment, became all-powerful. It seduced him by putting on the face of morality and order.

The old torturer has not forgotten me. Behind his bars, he replied with the utmost care to the questions I managed to put to him through intermediaries. To describe the site of the forest camp, for instance, he drew a precise sketch which enabled me to find the village of Thmar kok.

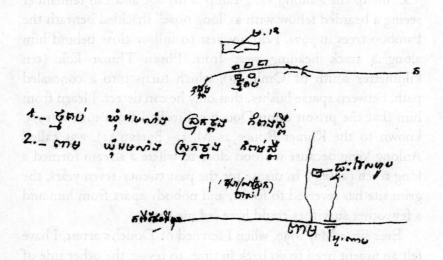

Beneath the burning sun, walking quickly behind my guide, I make my way among silvery bushes and large, glossy leaves like strange illuminated pages in the dust. I soon start to see indications that we are approaching the place of my ordeal. It is as if, from the depths of life, I am rising to the surface.

But further on, surveying the remnants of the forest before us, I can no longer find my bearings. The big trees have disappeared; those witnesses that do remain are dying where they stand, already ringed by the charcoal burner's axe. On each side, as far as the eye can see, only a skinny copse, branches drooping with the heat, sparingly claims my attention. Everything, down to the ground we are treading, now seems to me alien and unknown.

Most disconcerting of all is the disorder in my memories. Beneath the blindfold that Douch put over my eyes, I had been able to examine every detail of the path. My eye had fastened on to the tiniest details, and I can remember some of the minute shrubs, not unlike mimosa, that grew in dense tufts among the dead leaves. Now I cannot recognise a thing. The landscape is nothing but deceptive appearances shimmering beneath the sky, like dead vistas seen in dreams. I seem to recognise some places with certainty (such as the stream, where I had tripped as we clambered out the other side), but everything after that, like the islands that have now appeared in the middle of the Mekong, is a new area of perplexing topography: old fallow rice fields, cart tracks, burnt terrain.

I cannot describe the effect on me of this strange walk in the vanished undergrowth. My thoughts, escaping from the hold of words, drift over dark shadows, meandering into indescribable regions like when the mind is gripped by a nightmare. Language can no longer bind my unfolding thoughts. All I have is a mobile mosaic, where the syllables fly around one another like lugubrious birds, and my dark reverie frays in the vague contours of a grave dug straight into the white dust.

In spite of the confidence of the sturdy fellow in front of me, I tread the stony ground warily, as if groping through a maze. In places, my feet sink into dusty holes, throwing up clouds of ashes. Ahead of us, a bird of prey rises silently out of a thicket and ascends into the still air. A fly, bronze-corseted and humming like a cello, stirs the air beside my dripping temples.

After an hour, we make our way through a cluster of grey brambles, to find some knotty and shrivelled bamboos marking the end of a path. We force our way through the unfriendly undergrowth. My guide turns to me and purses his lips at the ground.

Stooping beneath drapes of thorns, I step forward at once, cautiously, as if entering a chapel. The ground is covered with a thick layer of branches and leaves. The dry dust cracks as I step on it, and I see, sunk into the dust against an enormous anthill, three large charred stones. Further off, the bottom of a small mildewed pillar can be seen protruding from the carpet of twigs. And in front of me I notice the great trunk of the *chhlik* tree: its solitary frame is now thirty metres tall, whereas I had never seen it as anything other than a column whose summit was lost beyond the canopy.

"Where is the stream?" I shout without turning around.

The peasant sets off in front of me. As I hurry to join him, he holds out his hand, showing me where to look. I can feel a clawing in my heart: at our feet the clear waters flow over mossy pebbles. At this time of the year, they seem less deep and limpid, but the shimmering reflection of the stream's banks can still be seen in the water's grey-green mirror.

Now I am on the dug-out bank where I went every evening. In order not to slip, I find footholds on the bare roots, and feel I am finding old marks. A dreamlike awareness descends on me, and I become sensitive to a multitude of things at once. Behind my back extends the withered clearing, covered with elephant grass, which at its furthest point gives way to a thorn hedge. On this burning, shadeless dryness, the old field of oppression stretches out in all its ever-present infamy, for now I can see the shelters: their lines are clearly marked out on the ground, right

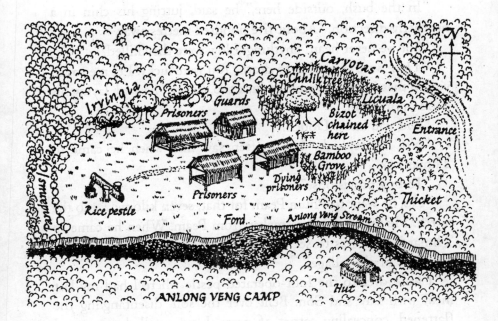

ANLONG VENG CAMP

over to the mound the guards had cut away vertically, for drying their laundry, as dictated by the ideologues of the Angkar.

We sit beside the stream and catch our breath. My mind surrenders to the thoughts assailing me from all sides. From deep in the scrub, I hear the distant call of an oriole.

My guide tells me with a laugh that I am the only prisoner who can make such a pilgrimage, for no-one else escaped from this camp alive.*

"Where were they executed?" I ask him.

*Of the approximately thirty Westerners arrested by the Khmers Rouges before 1975, I was apparently the only one released. Two others, Reverend J. Clavaud and his son, Olivier, along with the son of Dr Baudelet, were fortunate enough simply to be detained: the first two at the village of Chumreah Pen (Takeo), from 18 November 1970 until 3 January 1971, and the latter in a village in the site of Angkor, during June 1972.

"In the bush, outside here," he said, jutting his chin in a northerly direction. "About five hundred metres away."

"But we never heard anything. How were they killed?"

"They were cudgelled to death. You were lucky. Let me touch you so that I can have a bit of luck too, *lok euy!*" he said, laying his hand on my arm.

"Did you know Douch?"

"No," he replied, "but I often saw him when he came to Thmar kok."

"To buy provisions?"

"No, he went to Phum Peam for that, seven kilometres to the north. He married a dressmaker from Peam. When he came to Thmar kok, it was to see Ta Mok, who lived in a house on the outskirts of the village."

I walk over to the foot-operated pestle where I had my last meal with Lay and Son. Bent over the soil, disentangling the flattened, concealing carpet of grass, I can smell the scattered blossoms, borne on the dry breeze, and I seem to see my friends' footprints on the fallow land.

As I run my hands over this unchanged earth, I also recall the ambergris smell of my friends the hens, which would waft over to me every morning when they jumped down from the branches.

Then all my former companions, skulls smashed in, rise invisibly. Barely recognisable, they crowd around me as I set forth on the path they took to the place of horrors. Before dying, all these phantoms strode resolutely past me, trying to dispel their fear; their expressions sunk in the morbid gaze of a man who has lost all hope, yet makes a last attempt to save face and drive away despair. And in my heart, like flying scraps hanging from a thousand pupils pushed out of their orbits by the beatings, their empty remains start to jump and dance. On the way back, I can still see their souls slipping away like whitefish among the blades of grass as the breezes cover them with the smell of dust.

We are soon once more at Thmar kok, a dismal jumble of dilapidated cabins constructed of black partitions and mouldy thatched roofs. This is where the families of the former Khmers Rouges who had joined the village militias – all of whose sons were sent to the front – live as wretchedly as they did during the time of the loathsome regime. Before I leave their hamlet, the inhabitants laughingly show me Ta Mok's house.

On his map, Douch showed me how to find the spot where my farewell dinner took place. I set off for Phum Peam. The site is surrounded by sugar palms, which I have no memory of. After Anlong Veng was abandoned, the Khmer Rouge leaders erected their banqueting room there, immediately next door to a detention and interrogation base built in the aftermath. The whole place was destroyed in 1979 by the invading Vietnamese troops.

I retrace my steps, taking the long, dusty white track, the same road I took thirty years earlier, having eaten my fill, returning to Oudong next to Douch in the 404. Bureau 13 was so close that when the wind blew I used to be able to hear from my shelter the rare trucks that came by. Long after the noise of the engine died away, I would keep listening.

On my way back, I cross an area of plots of land of uniform size planted with sugar palms – in images such as this, the beauty of this country affects me almost painfully – their endless, floating, domelike shapes standing out like silhouettes. From this distance, the water, the air and the earth sparkle like the fount of life itself. I shudder at the impetuosity which made me ready to attempt an escape through such large expanses of open land.

With hindsight, some of the other information Douch sent me from his military prison also sends shivers down my spine. My links with the former torturer are distant and infrequent, conducted through intermediaries who prevent me from appealing to his memory as much as I want to. But he has often referred in his brief messages to the secret circumstances of my liberation.

The report he wrote on me, after ten weeks of questioning, had been duly passed to Sok Thuok, alias Von Veth, his immediate superior, who was then GRNUK's vice-minister of the interior and president of the special region. A copy was also sent to Ta Mok, himself a member of the military high command and of the party's Central Committee.

Some strange relationships were formed in the forest. The two men lived in different worlds; each had joined the partisans without previous training, as if setting off on an adventure. They had nothing in common: the former was a militant Communist from the fifties, passionate about ideals and justice; the latter was simply skilled in the use of force. A man of instinctive action, Ta Mok believed that doubts were resolved by swift decisions. In this respect – in that he despised theory – he was less equivocal than Von Veth. Von Veth's weakness arose from his belief that power was expressed primarily through ideas, and he was already getting bogged down in his duplicitous theories.

The document, which had been carefully composed, was based on a series of precise propositions. It cleared me of the accusation made against me, that I was a spy for the CIA. But Ta Mok rejected the conclusions of the report outright and directed (in about mid-December) that I be executed immediately. His reaction appeared to be based in particular upon an oral instruction given by the Angkar in 1971 that prisoners were no longer to be freed; in other words, once a dossier had been compiled, each prisoner was to be executed.

Von Veth had not supported me right away, originally thinking, like Ta Mok, that I belonged to the CIA.

"Look, comrade!" he said to Douch when he saw my first confession. "There's no such thing . . . no *barang* comes to

Cambodia to study Buddhism and Khmer pottery. He's a CIA agent!"

But during the course of my statements and explanations, the head of Bureau 13 succeeded in assembling a dossier which convinced the old revolutionary. In order to counter Ta Mok's stubborn intransigence, Von Veth, without saying anything and because of some deep-seated fair-mindedness that he still possessed, made up his mind to delay my execution and to call upon the arbitration of Saloth Sar (who would assume the name of Pol Pot in 1975), then deputy head of the military high command.

Upon discovering that my execution had been postponed against his instructions, Ta Mok grew all the more resentful because the decision had been left to one of his superiors. As bad luck would have it, Saloth Sar's response took a long time to arrive. Consumed with impatience and anger, the impenitent butcher ordered my death a second time. Von Veth turned a deaf ear and covered up for Douch's silence. Believing it was his duty to await the verdict from on high, he delayed carrying out the sentence.

I can remember Douch's comings and goings (probably to Phum Thmar kok) around this time. My impetuous outbursts were beginning to overwhelm him, and he didn't know what to say to keep me quiet. From his expression, I could tell (without understanding) that he was seeing things more clearly than before, but his eyes told me that he was never free of anxiety. Beneath the playful tone he affected to calm me, there was a profound worry which drove me mad.

Finally, in view of the detailed report Douch gave of our relationship, the future Pol Pot confirmed the verdict: release the Frenchman.

Ta Mok was quickly informed and summoned Douch in a fury, without disclosing to him any of the instructions he had received. His eyes were aflame. He urgently wanted to convince him (using reason) of my guilt, then persuade him (using threats) to hand me over to the guards entrusted with the task. After my death, he could swear that my letter of pardon had reached him too late.

Douch stood firm, and Von Veth came to the rescue. During a tour in the south, the president of the special region came to Phum Thmar kok, to the shack built on stilts that Ta Mok and his sentries occupied, to discuss current matters. The main local chiefs had been summoned to meet him on the way. He suddenly noticed Douch, who was waiting there beneath the shack.

"Well! What's the young comrade doing here?" he asked good-naturedly.

"I have been summoned by Comrade Mok – for the umpteenth time. I suppose it's something to do with the Frenchman again."

When the meeting was over, Ta Mok took Von Veth to a nearby house and had Douch join them. He launched into him immediately.

"This bloody Frenchman is from the CIA! I refuse to collaborate with a spy working for the Americans! Those at the top want to free him. But here on the ground we see things more clearly. There can be no question of his release!"

Douch had decided to keep quiet. The taciturn old Communist intervened immediately.

"This bloody Frenchman is *not* from the CIA!" he replied simply.

Ta Mok did not dare expose himself any further by persisting, and so I was released. But his opponent's stubbornness incited within him an interminable rage that would abate only with the death of my liberator. Seven years later, he himself arrested Von Veth and sent him to Tuol Sleng jail. Douch was responsible for the prison. An unfortunate turn of events forced him to have his former protector executed.

Douch immediately suggested attaching a certain emphasis to my release in order to forestall Ta Mok. He planned to arrange a farewell dinner and to chaperone me throughout. The preparation of the meal was entrusted to his mentor among the partisans, the executive head of the south-west regional office, Chay Kim Hour, alias Hok, like him a former maths teacher. He was the devil of a man who sat among the others and watched me eat, the man whose questions I had answered, trembling, never knowing the terrible secrets that this banquet concealed. Hok, too, would later be arrested by Ta Mok and taken to Tuol Sleng.

Douch also revealed something else. I hardly dare relate it: to do so provokes a sensation I cannot get rid of — it makes me feel morally and physically sick. In trepidation, I asked him what had become of Lay and Son. Had they been enlisted to fight (as I had expected)? Were they dead? Did Douch know? His reply, written in French at the bottom of my letter, was a shock which, in my thoughtlessness, I had not imagined possible:

*"After Von Veth released Bizot, he gave me orders to kill Lay and Son."*

Their execution, he states in Khmer on the back of the paper, had taken place at the end of the second month following my release. Having contravened Ta Mok's orders so resolutely to save me — no doubt at great risk to his own life — it was out of the question, he maintained, to try to protect Lay and Son as well.

I return to the market at Oudong and the following day set off along the track to Vat O, towards the pagoda where I had originally been captured, which I think of so often. Little remains of the old buildings; the monks, all very young, no longer know anything. I decide to pursue my quest three kilometres further on, at Phum Tuol Sophi, taking the road along which — my two companions already tied up — the Khmer Rouge militia had dragged me.

I retain a very precise picture of the empty lean-to shop where

I had been made to sit while waiting for an officer to arrive. Built at ground level adjoining the road, it used to stand beneath a large kapok tree a few metres from a trail leading due north. Now, recognising nothing, I spot a few peasants at the corner of a wooden house whose ground floor is used as a shop. They listen to me somewhat uncomprehendingly, then a little man of about forty, dressed in black, joins us and questions me excitedly. "The Frenchman who was taken prisoner at Vat O? The one who liked margosa flowers?"

In less than a minute, a crowd has gathered. Not only do people remember, but even the youngest ones know the story. The day of my arrest, a few days after my enforced departure towards Omleang, a large contingent of government troops had set out to recapture me. I remember that Douch mentioned this manoeuvre – which I knew nothing about – when we were in the Peugeot 404, and said that it had exacerbated the case against me. It had been responsible for two deaths and caused the Khmer Rouge column occupying the village to scatter. For fear of aerial reprisals, the inhabitants of Tuol Sophi had had to hide in the bush for over a week.

The man I am speaking to appears to know me well. His name is An. He is lively and friendly, but dark eyes are all that stand out from his dull and haggard face. He was fifteen at the time. Although I have no memory of him, he was fascinated by my arrest, and observed me from his aunt's disused shop, for the whole time I was held there.

"The person who arrested you lives very close," he tells me. "It's Duong!" he calls out for the others to hear. "When you arrived by car, with the two Khmers, a lookout from the monastery saw you and told a group of seven militia men. Duong's the one who was in charge of them."

They bring Duong along. The man was twenty-one when I was arrested. I take his callused hands in mine and we look at each other for a long time, laughing. Standing before me is the man who was the cause of it all, the man who decided to detain me and take me to his leader. Time etches people from our past deep in our memories, and even if they have been an instrument of our unhappiness, they eventually arouse a sort of affection within us. This is what I experience as I meet him. He is stocky, with a coarse face marked with sparse but deep lines; a white resin tooth attached to a gold dental plate has been inserted between his incisors and tapers to a point in the middle of his gum. Mistaking my emotion for resentment, the poor wretch immediately does his best to minimise his responsibility, laying the blame on Ta Teng, the officer who frisked me and who is now dead.

"Then," An continues, pointing to the crossroads, "you set off along this track on your own with two guards and arrived in the village, where you feasted on margosa shoots."

As he speaks, everything comes back to me. When we arrived, after walking quickly for several kilometres along a twisting road, dusk was falling. From some distance, I realised that everywhere people were anxious. The fields were empty; we did not encounter a single soul. Some soldiers then emerged from the thickets and led me to a small house where a village woman had been asked quickly to give me something to eat. The woman hadn't been told, and kept apologising for the little she was able to offer. I was already deeply worried, but her kindness and the compassion in the way she looked at me made me feel worse. Terribly apologetically, she brought me some fish soup and, to go with the rice, some young *sdao* shoots, which I loved because of their bitter taste. I gulped down my meal hurriedly but still took care to crunch the last bite of the delicious stems and their minute white bell-shaped flowers. My appetite for margosa shoots immediately became legendary. It was this detail that was reported by the guards on their return to Tuol Sophi.

"What's become of the superior at Vat O?" I enquire of the people gathered around us.

"Ta Hieng?" asks everybody in unison. "He's over eighty and now running the Vat Vieng Chas at Oudong."

I ask to be taken there without delay, and An offers to be my guide. As soon as we arrive in the courtyard of the great pagoda (rebuilt by Prime Minister Hun Sen), the monks take us into an open, high-ceilinged room with a large gilded statue of a Buddha. The venerable old man is dozing next to a bamboo partition. Beside him, a teapot and several cups rest on an upturned tea chest. The cement beneath his feet is covered with a piece of dusty matting, a few printed books, and a stemmed dish containing a box and some candles. We sit down. The silent old man facing us automatically brings to my mind an upsetting, wordless scene.

After leaving Hélène with one of Son's uncles in Phum O Slat, we set off for Vat O. As we drove along the red track a sadness came over us, for there were already many signs of decline: the bleak landscape, the destroyed bridges . . . An old local man, who knew everyone in the area, had come along to put us at our ease. There was not a cloud in the sky; birds sang in every bush. Unseen insects emitted quick, automatic stridulating sounds. The calm of the day lulled us into thinking that everything was as it had always been. Danger is like a wind that blows, disappears and returns again.

When we went in with Lay and Son to pay our respects to the superior of Vat O, he had instantly frozen into a silence that none of us had known how to interpret. His restless eyes were looking elsewhere; he was not listening to us. I even whispered to Lay how surprised I was at this apparent lack of politeness. When I turned around, I noticed an armed man dressed in black sneaking away furtively and running behind the hedges.

Ta Hieng suddenly rises from his bed, squinting in the daylight. The monks have deliberately woken him by talking rather loudly. When I see him more closely, a sort of fear grips me, for his uncovered body looks so withered that it is difficult to believe that there is still life within him. I immediately explain who I am. The old monk admits that he doesn't remember anything. I listen to his answer smilingly, finding it amazing but somehow comical that he should remember nothing of that grim meeting.

Refusing to believe that the old man could really have forgotten, An tells the story again, mentioning that I had also come to interview two *arak* singers, specialists in meditation rituals. The old man suddenly looks at me. A gentle glow comes over his soft wax face; his wrinkles come to life in a start of bewilderment. He has to be told several times who I am, the "Frenchman of the margosa shoots", and in his misty eyes, shining with a glaucous transparency, we see a glint of mounting surprise and happiness.

"Ah! *Gnom euy!* That's thirty years ago. I've been waiting for this moment without ever believing it would come. I thought you were dead. When you walked in that day, my blood ran cold. You were speaking, and I didn't dare say a word. *Pouttho!* Let me at last give you the blessing you came for, to your great misfortune."

"Well, hurry up then, Grandfather!" I say to him. I have to tighten my throat to control my voice. "And please don't stop. Because I, too, have been waiting for this moment for thirty years."

Crossing the gardens of the monastery, I leave Ta Hieng without noticing that the sky has changed. With wonder, I see the ground, cluttered with flower beds and pruned bushes, bathed in a strange light. The sun has now disappeared, but, behind us, its rays have tinged one edge of the clouds a vibrant shade of purple. On the other side of the clouds, as if made by untidy brush strokes, black stratifications smear the azure canopy. Like ink stains on blotting paper, they alter suddenly, in a process of erosion that covers the landscape with a mist of fine matter. When the blaze is almost extinguished, the moon rises, the thinnest of golden crescents. It looks like the half-closed eyelid of a Buddha of Sukhothay.

In 1988, I returned to Cambodia. Like every visitor, I went to see the former high school at Tuol Sleng that the Khmers Rouges had transformed into a macabre waiting room: tens of thousands of prisoners were systematically numbered, photographed and questioned before being sent to their deaths.

The ground-floor rooms, where the interrogations took place, were furnished with an iron bedstead, upon which the victim was laid. If you bent over them and listened very carefully, you could hear the continuous drizzle of blood flowing from the tortured faces: their photographs covered the walls. Faces, split open at the mouth, pierced with a pain that had left no visible trace, not even rust or wear on the iron. I pondered the significance of this piece of ironwork: in places I thought I could detect the mark of suffering on it – the gasp of agony, the ravings of terror – when suddenly the cry of man itself struck me as distant, derisory, prehistoric and so pointless that it was hard to distinguish it from the stutterings of life, the screams of the newborn.

On the bare metal bed-base – where shreds of material still hung from the mesh, with some tarnished handcuffs that had scratched the framework and some bent rivets – the same ghosts arose that had come from the gate, so loathsome that I turned pale with terror. I had to hold my breath in order to brace myself against this vision; I could feel my tears welling up uncontrollably.

The groups of buildings had been converted into a "Museum of Genocide". The cells, which were covered in thick dust, were just as they had been left by the guards on the afternoon of 7 January 1979, when they had fled with the arrival of the Vietnamese. Pell-mell upon the yellow-and-white-tiled floor were scattered a chain, a plastic bottle (for urine), a munitions box (for the faeces mingled with blood), a short metal bit with two stirrups, a desk and a chair (for the interrogator), a cotton floorcloth, some electric wires, a few instruments ranging from rattan rods to pliers, all as they were when pushed out of the way by the last of the mutilated bodies, dragged out over a floor spattered with black blood.

In one of the central rooms, a display had been set up by those who wanted to turn this place into a symbol. It featured the bathtub specially adapted for immersion; the sloping wooden partition used for suffocation; the cage full of spiders, centipedes, snakes and scorpions; the hooks; the bludgeons; the whips; the stained knives.

On the walls, among the tortured faces of a hundred or more martyrs, they had hung group photographs of a few of the torturers with their assistants. In one corner, in a prominent position, was an enlarged portrait of their master.

I had the greatest difficulty in recognising Douch. Not that the picture was bad: the laughing eyes, the bared teeth, the half-open lips, everything was true to life, even the big ears that I had forgotten. Above all, the picture showed the indiscernible bitterness that was always with him, as if all happiness were already lost to him for ever. But I could not bring myself to identify the man I had known, who so loved justice, with the principal torturer of this vile gaol, responsible for these atrocities. What monstrous metamorphosis had he undergone? I was plunged into torment; the stench of swamp and animal's den turned my stomach. Into my mind came the smell of the beast who had haunted them here.

There are experiences that make us reappraise everything. This pilgrimage into the sparse and remote bush, and the visit to Tuol Sleng the day after, is one such experience. Framed by barbed wire and sheet metal, I penetrate the scene in fear and trembling, to find the macabre march setting off again under the bamboos, and thumping against my brain. My eyes are opened. The glaring pupils of my companions are fixed on Douch. Those of the tortured from the high school join them, and they all begin to dance.

From the forest of Omleang to Phnom Penh prison, my wretched friend has not undergone any transformation. Nothing has changed. He did ask, in April 1975, to be transferred to the industrial sector. But he was refused; and like the good pupil that he is, he unfailingly continued the same work in the familiar atmosphere of clinking chains and fleshless faces. His security objective, which he carried out without pleasure but always with rigour, was to purge the country of the enemies the trucks tipped out for him every morning, using the same means: the stick, the spade and the butcher's knife.

For me, on the other hand, everything has changed. Upon returning from captivity, I gradually rediscovered a "normal life". This explains why, when confronted with the instruments at Tuol Sleng, I felt brutally unable to equate the vision of its loathsome executioner with the image of my liberator. In my mind, he was for ever the young revolutionary.

Back then, when I was chained up in the dust, the cries of my fellow prisoners awaiting their turn tended to drift away into the distance. Death was so close that we grew used to its fetid breath and its hideous countenance. It was so familiar to us that no-one in the camp could sustain the same degree of revulsion at its ubiquitous presence. Like them, like Douch, like man on earth, I had secretly tamed terror.

I am purged of my ghosts. I have emptied my memory. I close *The Gate* behind me. Puppets, hung clustered on a rail, dangle in the twilight, an offering to the wolves. I turn back one last time; on the other side of the grille, Douch has joined them.

# Acknowledgements

*The Gate* is a book that has been buried within me for thirty years. I owe this exhumation to the encouragement and support of several friends: Claude Allègre, Olivier de Bernon, Jean Boulbet, Josseline de Clausade, Jean Dyrac, Benoît Gysembergh, Boris Hoffman, Monique and Jan Migot, Jean-Cleade Pomonti, Nate Thayer and Léon Vandermeersch. I would like to express my deep gratitude to them.

Joseph West first came to work with me to evaluate problematic words and turns of phrase in the English translation. Then, in a re-reading of the text, he smoothed out obstacles of language, style and meaning, addressing each one meticulously. He too has my most sincere gratitude.

I have had the benefit of reading numerous books about the Khmer Rouge, from Ponchaud to Vickery, from Haing Ngor to Szymusiak, and in particular *Rivers of Time* by Jon Swain (Heinemann, 1995), which more than any other work combines poetry with a precise, rigorous description of the facts.

I would especially like to thank Jane and David Cornwell for their affection, advice and constant support.

This book would not have seen the light of day without the presence of my wife, Catherine. Although I did not have to invent any of the events, characters, feelings, conversations, or landscapes that I describe here, I had to make them come alive through writing and imagination and in so doing create an optical instrument whose effects on the reader eluded me. I have written *The Gate* from her viewpoint: it is she who has lived through it and related it to what she knew I had seen, felt or believed. She has put her heart into it alongside my own.